Restoring
Sanity
in the
Western
Church

Restoring
Sanity
in the
Western
Church

Maurice D. Perry

KINGDOM RESPONSE PUBLISHING
Murfreesboro, TN

© 2013 by Maurice D. Perry

Printed in the United States of America. All rights reserved. No part of this book may be reproduced, stored in a retrieval system, or transmitted in any form or by any means – electronic, mechanical, photocopy, recording, or otherwise – except for brief quotations for the purpose of review or comment, without the prior permission of the author.

Unless otherwise indicated, Scripture quotations are from the HOLY BIBLE, KJV Gift & Award Bible, Revised. Copyright © 2002 by Zondervan. All rights reserved.

Scripture quotations marked (ESV) are from the English Standard Version. Copyright © 2001 by Crossway Bibles. Scripture quotations marked (CEV) are from the Contemporary English Version. Copyright © 1995 by American Bible Society. Scripture quotations marked (MSG) are from the The Message Bible. Copyright © 1993, 1994, 1995, 1996, 2000, 2001, 2002 by Eugene H. Peterson. Scripture quotations marked (AMP) are from the Amplified Bible. Copyright © 1954, 1958, 1962, 1964, 1965, 1987 by The Lockman Foundation.

Italics, underlining, or bold print in Scripture quotations indicate emphasis added.

RESTORING SANITY IN THE WESTERN CHURCH

Maurice D. Perry
www.mauricedperry.com

ISBN   978-0-615-98212-0
1. Religion   2. Spirituality

Published by Kingdom's Response Publishing
www.kingdomsresponse.com/publishing

*This book is dedicated to four
great women in my life – my wife, Ericka, and my daughters,
Zuriel, Nyla, and Amena.
I love you all so much! You are my motivation!
Thank you for your unconditional love, support, patience and
inspiration! I could not have completed this journey without you!*

Table of Contents

Acknowledgements
Forward
Introduction — 1

Part One	**The First Century Church**	
1	Unified and On One Accord	9
2	Power Evangelism and Exponential Growth	29

Part Two	**The 21st Century Insane Western Church**	
3	Dueling Paradigms	47
4	The Cross	55
5	The Kingdom	63
6	The End of the World	71
7	The Apple of God's Eye	79
8	Ascension Gifts, Spiritual Gifts and Cessationalism	91
9	Predestination or Free Will?	109
10	Prosperity and Poverty	117
11	War and Peace	131
12	The Political Divide	145

Part Three	**Root Cause of the Insane Western Church**	
13	Biblical Illiteracy	155
14	Dispensationalism	171
15	The Rapture Theory	181
16	Misinterpreting 'Antichrist', 'Man of Sin' and the 'Beast'	189
17	Misinterpreting 'New Heaven' and 'New Earth'	203

Part Four	**Results of Church Insanity**		
	18	Hope Deferred, Laziness, Apathy and Fear	219
	19	Identity Crisis	233
	20	Unbridled Denominationalism and Witchcraft	243
	21	Exodus From the Western Church	251
Part Five	**The Remedy**		
	22	Sound Doctrine	261
	23	An Optimistic Church	275
		End Notes	285
		Scripture Index	291

Acknowledgements

I wouldn't be telling you the truth if I told you that writing this book was a piece of cake, or a very easy thing to do. To the contrary, it was one of the most difficult and meticulously time consuming things I've endured in my life. For that, I owe a debt of gratitude to the four greatest women in my life – my wife, Ericka, and my three daughters, Zuriel, Nyla, and Amena. I love you all dearly, and I thank you for your unconditional love, support and patience with me.

It would be inappropriate of me to not thank my parents, Bobby and Myrtis Perry. They have supported me in more ways than one could possibly imagine. I am eternally grateful for them, and I am proud of being able to say that I am their son. I'd also like to thank my two younger twin brothers, Marvin and Melvin. You two have been my 'checks and balance' while writing this book. There were plenty of times that I would call you guys to get feedback and it was good to hear another perspective on certain topics – even if I didn't necessarily agree with everything you guys had to say! That's the dynamic of siblings, I guess! None the less, iron definitely sharpens iron, and I am blessed to have you two as my brothers.

I'd also like to extend a thank you to Apostle John Eckhardt and the entire Crusaders Church family. It was the most interesting time when Apostle Eckhardt began to teach and preach from a fulfilled eschatological perspective. Simultaneously, I began to transition in my understanding of eschatology as well on my own. Perfect timing! It was a process that I'm glad that I was able to go through while at Crusaders Church in Chicago. But more importantly, one of the things that I truly appreciated was your sincere plea for people to begin writing. That is when the 'light bulb' went off in my head and a leap resonated in my spirit. I immediately knew that it was what I was called to do because I had been ignoring that prompting for many years prior to my time at Crusaders. And to my Crusaders family, though we are apart physically, I am still with you in spirit! To Sis. Darlene Cothron, Bro. Timothy Lacey, Sis. Monica Lacey, Sis. Marie Hobson, Sis. Renice Holman, and every other brother and sister that my wife and I co-labored within the Evangelism Department, we love you dearly! Though we do not get the chance to speak as often as we'd like, you guys are constantly on our minds and our time ministering in the streets of Chicago definitely made an imprint on the writing of this book.

Two other people that I would like to thank are Apostle Axel Sippach and Dr. Cindye Coates. It was about two years ago that I received an email from Apostle Sippach, encouraging me to begin writing a book (further confirmation). That has always stuck with me and is a reason for me taking on this endeavor. And to my sister in the faith, Dr. Coates, you are a southern ball of joy! Thank you for your encouragement, sense of humor, and being a warrior in the faith. You are an example of how to plow through opposition and religious mindsets in order to establish the kingdom in truth and in love. I appreciate you both tremendously.

Last, but definitely not least, I thank my Lord and Savior, Jesus Christ, for empowering me to persevere and finish this project. Paul said "I can do all things through Christ which strengtheneth me" (Philippians 4:13). I can truly testify to that because it was only by the grace of God that I was able to complete this book. There were many times over the course of the past year that I thought about giving up. But God wanted me to learn how to be a finisher. Thank you Lord, for instilling a finisher's anointing in me so that I could complete the task that you have given me. All glory and honor belongs to you!

Forward

I fully believe connecting with Maurice Perry was of divine design. We met a few years ago in a worldview discussion group on Facebook. I could tell immediately that he had the mind of an architect so I was not surprised when I learned that he had a degree in architecture!

Clearly, he is skilled in breaking ideas apart and building them back in a way they function best. Like many in his generation, he is a mosaic thinker. This means that he is able to piece things together and find patterns and threads to make up the big picture. He has a purely less cluttered and logical approach to things as well. How very refreshing.

Those who read this book will be able to better articulate what we all have felt for quite some time. We all know something is just not right. However, finding a credible resource who could construct a solution without some political agenda would be like finding gold. Well, consider this book that gold - seriously.

Maurice has taken his trained eye and precious time to boldly identify the cracks in the foundation that we call the modern western church. Some are obvious, and some are hidden and less obvious. The information gained will serve the reader well and provide the tools needed to begin to reform and reconstruct the shaky structure that currently exists.

We, who have been sent to shine the light of Christ in the modern church era, have all been given a very honorable task to rethink what is not working and make the shift in our mindsets to what can and will work. We are called to be legacy-builders and repairers of the foundations to their original intent. This book will surely give a blue print to make this happen.

- Dr. Cindye Coates
The Porch, Atlanta, Georgia
Speaker, Goodwill Ambassador
Author of "Matthew 24 Fulfilled"

Introduction

The modern western church has a serious issue on its hands. Generations 'Y' and 'Z' are becoming increasingly disenchanted and uninterested in being affiliated with the church of today. What has happened? How has this come about? What are the contributing factors to the departing from the institutional / fundamental church? Even more alarming, what has caused many young folks to lose respect for the church, and in some cases, flock to other belief systems, such as Islam, Hinduism, Kabbalah, New Age, or even Atheism (yes, Atheism is a belief system. To believe in "nothing" is still believing in something – SELF)?

Now, let me preface this book by stating that when I say "western church", I am speaking specifically about the American church. So, throughout this book, the two terms may be used interchangeably. I cannot speak for the universal church; for I know that there are some very exciting things that are happening in other parts of the world. The church is growing exponentially in China. Christianity is spreading in India and Africa. Even under extreme persecution, in some cases, the church is being established (or re-established) in the Middle East. These are definitely things to be jubilant about and even the more prayerful in regards to the kingdom of God being advanced and established on every square inch of this planet and in every generation. However, as the church continues to blossom and progress infinitely in other lands, the church in America has come to a virtual standstill in regards to growth and impact.

There are a number of factors that have contributed to the lack of impact that the church has had over the past few decades in America. One of the major "turn-offs", in the eyes of the younger generation, is the disparity between their perception of the early church (the first century church that they read about in the New Testament) and the modern western church. The American church (I am speaking in generalities) of today functions in a manner that is absolutely foreign to what a young reader of the Bible would comprehend as being 'authentic Christianity', or an authentic Christian church. According to the Merriam-Webster Dictionary definition of the word 'authentic', it is defined as "conforming to an original so as to reproduce essential features" and to be "made or done the same way as an original". So, when a new convert, or one that is seeking Truth, realizes the difference between the American church and the early church that they are reading about, confusion arises, spiritual stagnation develops, and ultimately, that individual never progresses into who he or she is called to be. Because the church (Body of Christ) is the summation of its parts (people), if the people are confused and stagnated, the church will exemplify confusion and stagnation as well.

Why did I use the word 'sanity' in the title of this book? First, it will be absolutely helpful to understand what 'sanity' means. 'Sanity' is the quality or condition of being sane, or sound in the mind and fully rational. The opposite of 'sanity' is 'insanity', which means a derangement of the mind. Some of the synonyms for 'insanity' paint an even more vivid definition – lunacy, craziness, aberration, extreme foolishness and senselessness. A church (or person) that exhibits insanity most likely is inhibited by states of schizophrenia and double-mindedness. In these types of cases, a person's comprehension of the written Word does not compliment what his or her eyes perceive (the current state of the church). James' famed quote "A double-minded man is unstable in all his ways" (James 1:8) couldn't be truer than it is now in the American church. With multiple interpretations on a myriad of theological subject matter, it's not hard to understand why the church in America has been rendered ineffective to some degree.

The objective of this book is to recognize the difference between the western church today and the "template" – the early church. A bulk of this book will be dedicated to identifying some, not all, of the contributing factors that are dividing the church. Furthermore, I will talk about the results and impact that a divided church has on not only the individual, but the entire Body of Christ. Of course, it would be absolutely irresponsible of me to 'nit-pick' and point out faults without having a tangible and applicable solution to the problems.

However, I must also warn you, the reader, that much of what you will read may not be easily digested. Some parts may trigger anger, rage, resentment, offense, hatred, rebellion, callousness and closed-mindedness. You may be compelled to slander me, label me as a heretic and want to 'burn me at the stake' (hopefully it doesn't get to that point!) These things are the natural reaction to something that challenges preconceived notions, belief-systems, patterns of thought, ideology, theology, one's entire paradigm and worldview, or biblical worldview. For this, I do not apologize, whatsoever. My obligation as a Truth-seeker is to share truth in the most simplistic manner possible, no matter whom it may offend or rub the wrong way. I am in no way trying to sound uncompassionate or un-loving. The opposite is the case! Shall we choose to remain silent if we see a 'member of our team' doing something that can, and will, jeopardize the overall mission of the team? In the case of the church, God forbid!

You may accept everything that is written in this book. Or, you may reject it. You may totally agree with certain parts, and reject others. That is fine, because as I've stated, much of what will be read will be a 'hard pill to swallow'. But my hope and prayer is for this book to be a tool that sparks further investigation and searching through the scriptures to see if what I have written in this book is of God or not. Ultimately, I long for the day when petty differences of opinion and theological squabbling can be put aside for the common cause of glorifying the name of Jesus.

Father, I pray for the eyes of the reader to be enlightened, and for the supernatural grace to tear down previous unbiblical paradigms that have been constructed in the heart and mind of man. I pray for every thought and preconceived notion that is a total contradiction and hindrance to Your eternal kingdom being built and advanced in the earth to be cast down and destroyed. God, I pray for simplistic clarity of Your Word, and what Your Word says about Your eternal kingdom! Let Your Light (Word) contrast and expose all false doctrine, false teaching and false believing so that nothing but The Truth remains. Let the western church, the American church, understand its true, eternal identity in the earth, and let it function in the manner that You have pre-destined it to function. And as always, may all the glory and honor belong only to you! In Jesus' name, Amen.

PART ONE

THE FIRST CENTURY CHURCH

Chapter One:
Unified and On One Accord

And he saith unto them, Follow me, and I will make you fishers of men.
                              Matthew 4:19

Before we can truly assess the state of the western church, we must first examine what will be the litmus test for the church today – the First Century Church. Beginning with a devoted band of twelve, the early church blossomed to numbers that were increasing so dramatically, various Roman emperors were concerned about the state of the Roman Empire! The message of freedom and liberty in Christ was infectious and unstoppable. Hence, today, Christianity remains the largest religion by far, and will continue to be so. But, why was the early church so successful in spreading the good news and seeing multitudes come into the church?

Following Jesus

Throughout the gospels, a common theme or phrase could be seen on multiple occasions – Jesus saying "Follow Me." 'Following Jesus' is the essence of Christianity. One of the first things that Jesus uttered to his potential disciples (Peter and Andrew) was "Follow me, and I will make you fishers of men". What a powerful recorded statement of Jesus. It summarizes the dual purpose of the Christian:

1. Follow Jesus – be a pupil / disciple
2. Fish for men – make pupils / disciples

Here are some other passages with the phrase "follow me":

Matthew 8:22 (Luke 9:59 is similar)
But Jesus said unto him, **Follow me**; and let the dead bury their dead.

Matthew 9:9
And as Jesus passed forth from thence, he saw a man, named Matthew, sitting at the receipt of custom: and he saith unto him, **Follow me**. And he arose, and followed him.

Matthew 16:24 (Mark 8:34 and Luke 9:23 are similar)
Then said Jesus unto his disciples, If any man will come after me, let him deny himself, and take up his cross, and ***follow me***.

Matthew 19:21 (Mark 10:21 and Luke 18:22 are similar)
Jesus said unto him, If thou wilt be perfect, go and sell that thou hast, and give to the poor, and thou shalt have treasure in heaven: and come and ***follow me***.

Mark 2:14 (Luke 5:27 is similar)
And as he passed by, he saw Levi the son of Alphaeus sitting at the receipt of custom, and said unto him, **Follow me**. And he arose and followed him.

John 1:43
The day following Jesus would go forth into Galilee, and findeth Philip, and saith unto him, **Follow me**.

John 10:27
My sheep hear my voice, and I know them, and they ***follow me***:

John 12:26
If any man serve me, let him ***follow me***; and where I am, there shall also my servant be: if any man serve me, him will my Father honour.

The Greek translation for the word 'follow' is '*deute*', which means come hither, come here, come; and the interjection, come!, come now![1] But I believe the Merriam-Webster definition of the word 'follow' is even more beneficial:

- to go, proceed, or come after

- to engage in as a calling or way of life: pursue
- to walk or proceed along <*follow* a path>
- to be or act in accordance with
- to accept as authority: obey
- to pursue in an effort to overtake
- to seek to attain
- to copy after: imitate
- to watch steadily
- to keep the mind on
- to attend closely to : keep abreast of
- to understand the sense or logic of [2]

When taking a look at the time that the disciples spent with Jesus, it is beyond apparent that many of the definitions for 'follow' were fulfilled in some way, shape or form. The disciples did proceed, or come after Jesus. Being a disciple was a calling, or way of life. The disciples did accept Jesus as authority, and they did obey Him. The disciples did seek to attain that which Jesus spoke about. The disciples did imitate the life of Jesus by 'taking up their crosses'. The disciples did watch Jesus steadily. The disciples were always mindful of Jesus. They attended closely to every word uttered by Jesus. Last, but not least, the disciples did understand what Jesus was saying and teaching, and were able to apply those teachings to their lives and ministry.

For the disciples, following Jesus was three years of training and apprenticeship. Not only were they witnesses of Jesus' ministry (preaching, teaching, and working miracles), they also were activated and released to minister as well.

Luke 9:1-6
1 Then he called his twelve disciples together, and gave them power and authority over all devils, and to cure diseases.
2 And he sent them to preach the kingdom of God, and to heal the sick.
3 And he said unto them, Take nothing for your journey, neither staves, nor scrip, neither bread, neither money; neither have two coats apiece.
4 And whatsoever house ye enter into, there abide, and thence depart.

5 And whosoever will not receive you, when ye go out of that city, shake off the very dust from your feet for a testimony against them.
6 And they departed, and went through the towns, preaching the gospel, and healing every where.

In the next chapter, Luke 10, we see Jesus addressing the seventy that he appointed to do the same work that he called the twelve disciples to do:

Luke 10:1-9
1 After these things the Lord appointed other seventy also, and sent them two and two before his face into every city and place, whither he himself would come.
2 Therefore said he unto them, The harvest truly is great, but the labourers are few: pray ye therefore the Lord of the harvest, that he would send forth labourers into his harvest.
3 Go your ways: behold, I send you forth as lambs among wolves.
4 Carry neither purse, nor scrip, nor shoes: and salute no man by the way.
5 And into whatsoever house ye enter, first say, Peace be to this house.
6 And if the son of peace be there, your peace shall rest upon it: if not, it shall turn to you again.
7 And in the same house remain, eating and drinking such things as they give: for the labourer is worthy of his hire. Go not from house to house.
8 And into whatsoever city ye enter, and they receive you, eat such things as are set before you:
9 And heal the sick that are therein, and say unto them, The kingdom of God is come nigh unto you.

Healing the sick and preaching the kingdom is what the disciples (including all followers of Jesus at that point) saw Jesus do throughout his earthly ministry. Likewise, the disciples were trained and equipped to do the same – heal the sick and preach / teach about the kingdom that was at hand. Later on in verse 17, we see that the seventy returns jubilantly because of their success in ministry:

Luke 10:17
17 And the seventy returned again with joy, saying, Lord, even the devils are subject unto us through thy name.

Jesus' Final Days and Consultation

Just before Jesus was apprehended to eventually be crucified, he spent an adequate amount of time revealing to the disciples the things that would take place in their generation. This is a very significant point to be made because the entirety of the rest of this book hinges upon this truth – Jesus speaking of things that His disciples would see in their lifetime. I will go more into detail about this subject matter later on.

The Olivet Discourse (Matthew 24, Mark 13 and Luke 21) is popularly known as Jesus' message concerning the 'last days', or 'the end of the world.' It was a rather lengthy warning that was given to the disciples so that they could know when they were in fact in the last days. Now, I know that this seems rather foreign and unfamiliar to most, but the fact of the matter is that the disciples, as well as all of the first century saints were living in the last days. How is that possible? Again, this will be something that will be hammered out in much detail later. But it is absolutely necessary to understand completely that the words that Jesus uttered in this passage were addressed to a first century audience – His disciples. Hence, the warnings within it were specifically for the disciples living in that generation. What were the warnings?

1. **There would be false Christs** (Matthew 24:4-5, 23-26; Mark 13:5-6, 21-22; Luke 21:8)
2. **There would be wars and conflicts between nations** (Matthew 24:6-7; Mark 13:7-8; Luke 21:9-10)
3. **They would be persecuted and killed** (Matthew 24:9, Mark 13:9, 13; Luke 21:12,16-17)
4. **There would be tribulation** (Matthew 24:21-22; Mark 13:19, Luke 21:23)
5. **To watch and pray** (Matthew 24:42, Mark 13:33, Luke 21:36)

Such warnings and seemingly pessimistic outlooks on the

disciples' future, let alone anyone's future, could definitely do one of three things –

1. "Paralyze" the disciples to the point of being ineffective
2. Make their hearts turn cold and fall into a state of disbelief and rejection of Jesus, and fall back into the established religious tradition
3. Galvanize, and become a strong community of believers who would stand the test of time and prevail.

Of course, the latter is what actually occurred, which has allowed the Church to continue to grow exponentially and have great influence in the history of humanity to this very day. However, if it were not for Holy Spirit, things may have been much different!

The Upper Room Experience

The things that Jesus shared with the disciples regarding the end could have definitely left them feeling abandoned and lost. Jesus picked up on those perceived emotions in John 16 by stating the following:

John 16:6
6 But because I have said these things unto you, sorrow hath filled your heart.

But those somber feelings of being left out in the cold, so to speak, were tempered by the Promised One – The Comforter, Holy Spirit.

John 16:7-16
7 Nevertheless I tell you the truth; It is expedient for you that I go away: for if I go not away, the Comforter will not come unto you; but if I depart, I will send him unto you.

8 And when he is come, he will reprove the world of sin, and of righteousness, and of judgment:
9 Of sin, because they believe not on me;
10 Of righteousness, because I go to my Father, and ye see me no more;
11 Of judgment, because the prince of this world is judged.
12 I have yet many things to say unto you, but ye cannot bear them now.
13 Howbeit when he, the Spirit of truth, is come, he will guide you into all truth: for he shall not speak of himself; but whatsoever he shall hear, that shall he speak: and he will shew you things to come.
14 He shall glorify me: for he shall receive of mine, and shall shew it unto you.
15 All things that the Father hath are mine: therefore said I, that he shall take of mine, and shall shew it unto you.
16 A little while, and ye shall not see me: and again, a little while, and ye shall see me, because I go to the Father.

A few very significant points that Jesus made-

- It was imperative that Jesus 'leaves the scene' so that The Comforter could come
- The Comforter would be vital to the disciples' (saints') continued ministry
- The Comforter (Spirit of Truth / Holy Spirit) would reveal nuggets of truth to the saints
- Holy Spirit would come to bring glory to Jesus and to the Father

In Acts 1, Jesus gives some final instructions to his chosen apostles in regards to what to do in the coming days. He tells them to stay inside of Jerusalem and wait for the "Promise of the Father (Acts 1:4). The last recorded words of Jesus before His ascension out of their sight were specifically about what would happen after the Holy Ghost comes:

Acts 1:8
8 But ye shall receive power, after that the Holy Ghost is come upon you: and ye shall be witnesses unto me both in Jerusalem, and in all Judaea, and in Samaria, and unto the uttermost part of the earth.

Of course, Acts 2 records the events that transpired on the day of Pentecost. The apostles, as well as a number of others were waiting in the upper room. Many believe that it was the 120 people mentioned in Acts 1:15. Whether or not this number is accurate, it doesn't diminish the fact that something tremendous took place in which was an immediate catalyst to ministry in the early church. Because it was a 'high time' in Jerusalem, there were many Jews from 'every nation' within the city. The Spirit of God fell in the place that the saints had gathered and they were immediately filled with the Holy Ghost, and speaking in other tongues. This left folks in the room absolutely befuddled:

Acts 2:5-13
5 And there were dwelling at Jerusalem Jews, devout men, out of every nation under heaven.
6 Now when this was noised abroad, the multitude came together, and were confounded, because that every man heard them speak in his own language.
7 And they were all amazed and marvelled, saying one to another, Behold, are not all these which speak Galilaeans?
8 And how hear we every man in our own tongue, wherein we were born?
9 Parthians, and Medes, and Elamites, and the dwellers in Mesopotamia, and in Judaea, and Cappadocia, in Pontus, and Asia,
10 Phrygia, and Pamphylia, in Egypt, and in the parts of Libya about Cyrene, and strangers of Rome, Jews and proselytes,
11 Cretes and Arabians, we do hear them speak in our tongues the wonderful works of God.
12 And they were all amazed, and were in doubt, saying one to another, What meaneth this?
13 Others mocking said, These men are full of new wine.

Peter then responded to the questions and apprehension that many had by stating emphatically that the people were not drunk because it was too early in the day for that to be the case! He continued by stating something that has been generally overlooked by most today – that is, what these men were witnessing was in fact the beginning of the fulfillment of what Joel had prophesied (Joel 2:28-32):

Acts 2:16-21
*16 But **this is that** which was spoken by the prophet Joel;*
17 And it shall come to pass in the last days, saith God, I will pour out of my Spirit upon all flesh: and your sons and your daughters shall prophesy, and your young men shall see visions, and your old men shall dream dreams:
18 And on my servants and on my handmaidens I will pour out in those days of my Spirit; and they shall prophesy:
19 And I will shew wonders in heaven above, and signs in the earth beneath; blood, and fire, and vapour of smoke:
20 The sun shall be turned into darkness, and the moon into blood, before the great and notable day of the Lord come:
21 And it shall come to pass, that whosoever shall call on the name of the Lord shall be saved.

Joel 2:28-32
28 And it shall come to pass afterward, that I will pour out my spirit upon all flesh; and your sons and your daughters shall prophesy, your old men shall dream dreams, your young men shall see visions:
29 And also upon the servants and upon the handmaids in those days will I pour out my spirit.
30 And I will shew wonders in the heavens and in the earth, blood, and fire, and pillars of smoke.
31 The sun shall be turned into darkness, and the moon into blood, before the great and terrible day of the Lord come.
32 And it shall come to pass, that whosoever shall call on the name of the Lord shall be delivered: for in mount Zion and in Jerusalem shall be deliverance, as the Lord hath said, and in the remnant whom the Lord shall call.

There are two things to take note of:

1. Peter inevitably states that they were living in the 'last days'
2. Peter states that signs, wonders, miracles, prophetic utterances, revelatory encounters and judgment would be evident at that time

After Peter brings to remembrance the things that Joel spoke, he immediately dives into preaching the gospel of Jesus Christ, and poignantly speaking from a historical standpoint as to how Jesus was the fulfillment of what King David had prophesied (Acts 2:25-35). Peter caps his statement with the following:

Acts 2:36
36 Therefore let all the house of Israel know assuredly, that God hath made the same Jesus, whom ye have crucified, both Lord and Christ.

In the very next verse, we see people asking what they must do. Peter responds by telling them that they must repent, be baptized in the name of Jesus for the remission of their sins, and then they would also receive the gift of the Holy Ghost. And this is exactly what happened! That very day, as a response to what the people had witnessed, coupled with the preaching and exhortation of Peter, about 3,000 people had been saved and joined the believers:

Acts 2:41
41 Then they that gladly received his word were baptized: and the same day there were added unto them about three thousand souls.

Close-Knit Community of Believers

Because of the warnings that Jesus had given the disciples, the believers immediately became a spiritual family that communed with each other regularly. After Jesus ascended, the 11 disciples gathered with others, including women, Mary, Jesus' mother, and His brothers. Acts 1:14 says they all came together in one accord in prayer and supplication. At that time, they voted on who would become the 12th apostle – Matthias (Acts 1:26).

The notion of being on one accord was a common theme throughout the first few chapters of Acts. After Pentecost, we see that what had begun in Acts 1 (the gathering together on one accord) continued:

Acts 2:42-47
*42 And **they continued stedfastly in the apostles' doctrine and fellowship,***

Unified and On One Accord | 19

and in breaking of bread, and in prayers.
43 And fear came upon every soul: and many wonders and signs were done by the apostles.
*44 And **all that believed were together, and had all things common;***
*45 And **sold their possessions and goods, and parted them to all men, as every man had need.***
*46 And **they, continuing daily with one accord in the temple, and breaking bread from house to house**, did eat their meat with gladness and singleness of heart,*
47 Praising God, and having favour with all the people. And the Lord added to the church daily such as should be saved.

Not only were they gathering, physically, but all of their belongings 'gathered' as well! No one possessed anything for themselves, but all resources went towards meeting the needs of others within that community of believers. Another passage that demonstrates this theme is found in Acts 4:

Acts 4:32-35
*32 And **the multitude of them that believed were of one heart and of one soul**: neither said any of them that ought of the things which he possessed was his own; but **they had all things common**.*
33 And with great power gave the apostles witness of the resurrection of the Lord Jesus: and great grace was upon them all.
34 Neither was there any among them that lacked: for as many as were possessors of lands or houses sold them, and brought the prices of the things that were sold,
*35 And laid them down at the apostles' feet: and **distribution was made unto every man according as he had need**.*

They truly became one, as Jesus had prayed in John 17:

John 17:11, 20-23
*11 And now I am no more in the world, but these are in the world, and I come to thee. Holy Father, keep through thine own name those whom thou hast given me, **that they may be one**, as we are.*

20 Neither pray I for these alone, but for them also which shall believe on me through their word;
*21 That **they all may be one**; as thou, Father, art in me, and I in thee, that **they also may be one in us**: that the world may believe that thou hast sent*

me.
*22 And the glory which thou gavest me I have given them; that **they may be one, even as we are one:***
*23 I in them, and thou in me, **that they may be made perfect in one;** and that the world may know that thou hast sent me, and hast loved them, as thou hast loved me.*

Jesus knew what the saints would be up against in the days to come. Therefore, His passionate plea for the saints to become one was imperative. This wasn't just for the sake of the saints in general, but it was also for the protection of the carriers of the gospel of Jesus Christ. The opposition that existed against Jesus at the hands of the unbelieving Jews would definitely intensify in the coming days. Thus, another portion of Jesus' prayer addresses this:

John 17:14-18
*14 I have given them thy word; and **the world hath hated them**, because they are not of the world, even as I am not of the world.*
*15 **I pray not that thou shouldest take them out of the world, but that thou shouldest keep them from the evil.***
16 They are not of the world, even as I am not of the world.
17 Sanctify them through thy truth: thy word is truth.
18 As thou hast sent me into the world, even so have I also sent them into the world.

Being together and on one accord was a basic survival strategy. In a day and age where persecution of the saints was beginning to increase, being a close-knit family was critical. But there were even greater benefits of this closeness – the 'world' was watching and becoming intrigued with their love and compassion for one another. Because of this, many were drawn to the community of believers and became believers themselves!

Acts 2:46-47
46 And they, continuing daily with one accord in the temple, and breaking bread from house to house, did eat their meat with gladness and singleness of heart,
*47 Praising God, and **having favour with all the people**. And **the Lord***

added to the church daily such as should be saved.

Encouraging One Another

Throughout the New Testament, we see numerous examples in which the first century saints were told or reminded to encourage one another. Prophecy was the vehicle by which encouragement was rendered. Peter's reciting of the prophecy of Joel 2 highlights this very thing:

Acts 2:17
*17 And it shall come to pass in the last days, saith God, I will pour out of my Spirit upon all flesh: and **your sons and your daughters shall prophesy**, and your young men shall see visions, and your old men shall dream dreams:*

Paul encouraged the saints to prophesy.

Romans 12:6
*Having then gifts differing according to the grace that is given to us, whether prophecy, **let us prophesy according to the proportion of faith**;*

1 Corinthians 14:1
*Follow after charity, and desire spiritual gifts, **but rather that ye may prophesy**.*

1 Corinthians 14:22
*Wherefore tongues are for a sign, not to them that believe, but to them that believe not: but **prophesying serveth not for them that believe not, but for them which believe**.*

1 Corinthians 14:31
*For ye may all **prophesy one by one, that all may learn, and all may be comforted**.*

1 Corinthians 14:39
*Wherefore, brethren, **covet to prophesy**, and forbid not to speak with tongues.*

1 Thessalonians 5:20
Despise not prophesyings.

In 1 Corinthians 14:3, Paul states that the person that prophesies edifies, exhorts, and comforts other men. To 'edify' means to build or establish. To 'exhort' means to urge strongly, or to make urgent appeals. To 'comfort' means to give strength and hope to something, or to ease the grief or trouble of something. Believers in the early church needed every single drop of prophesying to one another to get them through those times of trouble and persecution. When everything appeared dark or in despair, it was the continuous speaking words of life and encouragement to one another that kept them pressing on and prevailing, despite what the situation looked like around them. In a letter to the church of Thessalonica, Paul exhorts the readers to 'watch and be sober', but also tells them that God was on their side. In doing so, Paul summarized the gospel of Jesus Christ as a subtle reminder of the promises of God and His eternal plan of salvation. Whether they lived or died, God would not be slack on His promise.

1 Thessalonians 5:9-11
9 For God hath not appointed us to wrath, but to obtain salvation by our Lord Jesus Christ,
10 Who died for us, that, whether we wake or sleep, we should live together with him.
*11 Wherefore **comfort yourselves together, and edify one another, even as also ye do**.*

This passage brings to mind another passage in Revelation 19, where John hears a voice from the throne uttering the following:

Revelation 19:10
*... I am thy fellowservant, and of thy brethren that have the testimony of Jesus: worship God: for **the testimony of Jesus is the spirit of prophecy**.*

Revelation 19:10 (AMP)
...For the substance (essence) of the truth revealed by Jesus is the spirit of all prophecy [the vital breath, the inspiration of all inspired preaching and interpretation of the divine will and purpose, including both mine and yours].

I love the Amplified Bible's wording of this verse – 'the vital breath of God'. The word 'vital' means 'necessary to the maintenance of life', and 'of the utmost importance'. Prophesying was necessary for the maintenance of life for the first century saints. Prophesying was of the utmost importance to the sanity of the early church, as well as its overall effectiveness.

A 'Gifted' Church

As I've briefly discussed already, it was necessary for Jesus to go away to the Father so that the Comforter, Holy Spirit, would come. These words of Jesus were recorded in John 16. However, something very intriguing was said by Jesus in John 14. In John 14:6, Jesus tells the disciples "I am the way, the truth, and the life. No one can come to the Father except through me." Phillip then asks a question that seems to leave Jesus rather perturbed.

John 14:8-11
8 Philip saith unto him, Lord, show us the Father, and it sufficeth us.
9 Jesus saith unto him, Have I been so long time with you, and yet hast thou not known me, Philip? he that hath seen me hath seen the Father; and how sayest thou then, Show us the Father?
10 Believest thou not that I am in the Father, and the Father in me? the words that I speak unto you I speak not of myself: but the Father that dwelleth in me, he doeth the works.
11 Believe me that I am in the Father, and the Father in me: or else believe me for the very works' sake.

Jesus inevitably tells Philip that the works that he saw Jesus perform should be self explanatory. The works, according to Jesus, were not of His own doing, but of the Father. But take a look at what Jesus says next:

John 14:12-13
12 Verily, verily, I say unto you, **He that believeth on me, the works that I do shall he do also; and greater works than these shall he do;** *because I go unto my Father.*

13 And whatsoever ye shall ask in my name, that will I do, that the Father may be glorified in the Son.

Jesus says that those that believe in Him would do the same works as He did, and greater works! But really, what could be greater than raising the dead? The Greek word for the phrase "greater than" is *'meizon'*, which means greater, larger, elder, or stronger. I believe that in this case, Jesus was referring to the larger quantity of works that would be done by not only the disciples, but by all believers throughout eternity. Verse 12 is capped by the phrase "...because I go unto the Father."

In 1 Corinthians 12, we see Paul explaining spiritual gifts. He begins by telling the Corinthian reader that he doesn't want them to be ignorant about spiritual gifts and who they are from. 1 Cor. 12:4-6 defines the Source clearly:

1 Corinthians 12:4-6
*4 Now there are diversities of gifts, but **the same Spirit**.*
*5 And there are differences of administrations, but **the same Lord**.*
*6 And there are diversities of operations, but it is **the same God which worketh all in all**.*

Spirit, Lord, God – the source of all of the gifts, along with the administering and operating of them. In verse 7, Paul says that the manifestation of the gifts of the Spirit is for man's benefit. The English Standard Version translation reads as follows:

1 Corinthians 12:7 (ESV)
*7 To each is given the manifestation of the Spirit for the **common good**.*

The gifts were for the common good of the people – the people that had all things common – the early church. They benefited the saints, but were also expressions of God's power in ministry. The nine spiritual gifts are-

1. Spirit of Wisdom (v. 8)
2. Word of Knowledge (v. 8)

3. Faith (v. 9)
4. Healing (v. 9)
5. Miracles (v. 10)
6. Prophecy (v. 10)
7. Spiritual Discernment (v. 10)
8. Different Tongues (v. 10)
9. Interpretation of Tongues (v. 10)

In Ephesians 4, we read of another set of gifts that were given to the church. In verse 1, Paul exhorts the church at Ephesus to walk worthy of the vocation in which they are called. The word 'vocation' means a divine calling, but it also means a particular occupation and a special function of an individual or group.3 These gifts are sometimes referred to as 'ascension gifts' because of what Paul states in Ephesians 4:8:

Ephesians 4:8
8 Wherefore he saith, **When he ascended up on high, he led captivity captive, and gave gifts unto men.**

The gifts given unto men are five distinct functions within the church (Ephesians 4:11):

1. **Apostle** – Sent one, messenger
2. **Prophet** – Conveyer of the oracles of God
3. **Evangelist** – Bringer of good tidings
4. **Pastor** – A shepherd; one who cares for a group or people
5. **Teacher** - An instructor; expounder of the things of God

The divine purpose of these gifts was to assist in the development of the church. A properly functioning first century church would have all five of these administrations working together in tandem. Not one was more important than the other, for they were all necessary for the growth of the church, as well as the spiritual maturation of each individual that comprises the church. Paul speaks of this purpose in the following verses:

Ephesians 4:12-16
*12 For the **perfecting of the saints, for the work of the ministry, for the edifying of the body of Christ:***
*13 **Till we all come in the unity of the faith, and of the knowledge of the Son of God**, unto a perfect man, unto the measure of the stature of the fulness of Christ:*
14 That we henceforth be no more children, tossed to and fro, and carried about with every wind of doctrine, by the sleight of men, and cunning craftiness, whereby they lie in wait to deceive;
15 But speaking the truth in love, may grow up into him in all things, which is the head, even Christ:
16 From whom the whole body fitly joined together and compacted by that which every joint supplieth, according to the effectual working in the measure of every part, maketh increase of the body unto the edifying of itself in love.

According to Paul, there was a three-pronged purpose:

1. **To perfect the saints** (maturation of the believer, individually)
2. **For the work of the ministry** (the preaching of the gospel to people and in regions that had not received the good news)
3. **To edify (build) the body of Christ (The Church)**

Unity and love was the end result of a church that was functioning properly. When spiritual gifts were flowing, and the ascension gifts were working properly, the fruit that was yielded was a people full of love and compassion for each other, as well as for the lost, brokenhearted and down-trodden. In Luke 4:18-19, Jesus reads a passage in Isaiah (Isaiah 61:1-2) in which was speaking of Himself and the ministry that was given to Him.

Luke 4:18-19
18 The Spirit of the Lord is upon me, because he hath anointed me to

preach the gospel to the poor; he hath sent me to heal the brokenhearted, to preach deliverance to the captives, and recovering of sight to the blind, to set at liberty them that are bruised,
19 To preach the acceptable year of the Lord.

This passage was absolutely applicable to the early church (body of Christ) as well. The Spirit of the Lord was indeed upon the early church. It was anointed to preach the gospel. It was sent to heal the brokenhearted and preach deliverance to the captives. It was sent to open eyes that were spiritually blind and to bring freedom and liberty to those that were bruised and spiritually abused. Lastly, the early church definitely preached the acceptable year of the Lord!

Chapter Two:
Power Evangelism and Exponential Growth

³And I was with you in weakness, and in fear, and in much trembling.⁴ And my speech and my preaching was not with enticing words of man's wisdom, but in demonstration of the Spirit and of power:⁵ That your faith should not stand in the wisdom of men, but in the power of God.

1 Corinthians 2:3-5

Before the resurrection, before the cross, before the miracles, signs and wonders, before the 'band of twelve', before being tempted by the devil (Matthew 4), there was Jesus, the child, Jesus, the adolescent, and Jesus, the student. We often forget about Jesus in the days of His youth when He was drawn to the temple to be amongst the greatest religious minds of that time. In Luke 2:40-52, we read about Jesus staying behind in Jerusalem without the knowledge or approval of His parents, Joseph and Mary. When they returned to Jerusalem to search for Jesus (not unlike any pre-teen adolescent who wants to march to the beat of their own drum!), they find him in the temple listening to the doctors (most likely, the rabbis and religious leaders) intently and asking them questions. His ability to dialog with those learned, seasoned men left them astonished and bewildered.

Luke 2:47
47 And all that heard him were astonished at his understanding and answers.

Because of his interactions and dialog with the scholars of

that time, Luke writes that he increased in knowledge and wisdom and he gained favor with God and man.

Luke 2:40, 52
40 And the child grew, and waxed strong in spirit, filled with wisdom: and the grace of God was upon him.

52 And Jesus increased in wisdom and stature, and in favour with God and man.

Traditionally, Jewish rabbis believe that the greatest or highest form of worship is to study God's word (or Law, in their case). I believe there is a ton of truth in this statement, and it should be a foundational thought in every Christian's mind and heart. Nothing should have more significance in our lives than the Word of God. For spiritual growth, we need spiritual food. I believe Jesus 'waxed strong in spirit' and was 'filled with wisdom' because he did exactly what the word of the Lord instructed Joshua to do:

Joshua 1:8
8 This book of the law shall not depart out of thy mouth; but thou shalt meditate therein day and night, that thou mayest observe to do according to all that is written therein: for then thou shalt make thy way prosperous, and then thou shalt have good success.

Here are a few observations from this passage:

1. Joshua was indirectly told to continuously recite scripture (book of the law shall not depart out of thy mouth). There is a greater level of understanding when God's Word is spoken from our mouths. Words shape our destiny
2. The Word should be constantly rolling around and 'chewed on' in our mind, both day and night
3. When we understand what is written, then DO what is written
4. The benefits of DOING what is written leads to the

blessed life (our way is made prosperous, and we have good success in whatever we do)

Now, just imagine Jesus from the time that he was twelve years old in that temple, basking in a sea of deep theological discussions, to the time when He began his earthly ministry at the age of 30. That's 18 years worth of reciting scripture, meditating on scripture, and DOING what was in scripture. Beyond Him being God in the flesh, there's no wonder why His ministry was so successful! Who would have thought back then, that this same Jesus would, in a matter of three years, put together a 'band of twelve', impart to them what had been imparted to Him throughout all of those years of studying and communing with God, and that they would be the catalyst in taking the message of the kingdom to every tribe and tongue, in every land, and in every generation? It all began with a lifestyle of studying and becoming skilled with the scriptures.

Searching the Scriptures

The apostle Paul was well-versed in the Books of the Law and Prophets (Old Testament), as was the custom for most Jewish boys and men. Though he had once been a chief culprit in the imprisonment and persecution of Christians prior to his encounter with Jesus, he was learned and very astute. His ability to go in and out of different circles of people and speak to them at their level of understanding and comprehension is probably why he was chosen to be the mouth-piece for nearly half of the New Testament! In Paul's second letter to Timothy, he stressed the need for studying scripture (of course, the only scripture that they had then was the Old Testament – Law, songs, and Prophets).

2 Timothy 2:15
Study to shew thyself approved unto God, a workman that needeth not to be ashamed, rightly dividing the word of truth.

2 Timothy 2:15 (AMP)
Study and *be eager* and *do your utmost to present yourself to God* **approved** *(tested by trial), a workman who has no cause to be ashamed, correctly analyzing and accurately dividing [rightly handling and skillfully teaching] the Word of Truth.*

Interestingly, Paul's first instruction mirrors that of which Joshua received of the Lord in Joshua 1:8 – Study first! After studying, THEN do! Can you see the pattern? Studying scripture was a necessity.

Perhaps one of my favorite passages in scripture is found in Acts 17:10-12. A pretty short passage, but full of wisdom and insight as to how to approach scripture, the Bereans are said to be nobler than all of the other people in Thessalonica because of the manner in which they engaged Paul.

Acts 17:10-12
10 And the brethren immediately sent away Paul and Silas by night unto Berea: who coming thither went into the synagogue of the Jews.
11 These were more noble than those in Thessalonica, in that they received the word with all readiness of mind, and searched the scriptures daily, whether those things were so.
12 Therefore many of them believed; also of honourable women which were Greeks, and of men, not a few.

'Noble' is the Greek word *eugenēs,* which means 'to be well born', or of a family lineage that is well off and prosperous. They were educated, and most likely, aristocratic. But despite their nobility and probable comfortable lifestyles, there was something on the inside of them that was eager for Truth. Acts 17:11 says that they searched the scripture daily to see if what Paul was preaching and teaching in the synagogue was true. They evidently understood exactly what Paul was conveying in regards to the gospel of Jesus Christ, and many believed and became Christians.

Preached With Boldness

Something that the disciples witnessed during their three years of following Jesus was the manner in which he conveyed his messages to all of his audiences, especially the Pharisees, Sadducees, and scribes. Because of Jesus' mastery of the Mosaic Law and prophets (especially regarding Himself being the fulfillment of that which was spoken in times past), there was a unique confidence that exuded from Jesus' presence. This confidence, or boldness, accompanied by the gospel of the kingdom, is what drew men unto Him, and had many scratching their heads as to who this Jesus of Nazareth really was – including His disciples!

Matthew 21:10
And when he was come into Jerusalem, all the city was moved, saying, **Who is this?**

Luke 5:21
And the scribes and the Pharisees began to reason, saying, **Who is this** *which speaketh blasphemies? Who can forgive sins, but God alone?*

Luke 7:49
And they that sat at meat with him began to say within themselves, **Who is this** *that forgiveth sins also?*

Luke 9:9
And Herod said, John have I beheaded: but **who is this,** *of whom I hear such things? And he desired to see him.*

John 12:34
The people answered him, We have heard out of the law that Christ abideth for ever: and how sayest thou, The Son of man must be lifted up? **who is this Son of man?**

Matthew 8:27 *(Mark 4:41 and Luke 8:25 are similar)*
But the men marvelled, saying, **What manner of man is this,** *that even the winds and the sea obey him!*

Similarly, the disciples began to move, preach and teach

with the same level of boldness and confidence that they had seen Jesus speak and move with. It was practically inevitable that following Jesus for three years was going to be a highly intensive training and impartation of knowledge and mastery of the Mosaic Law and prophets as well. Knowing what had been written, and it pointing to Jesus as being the One that Israel was waiting for, the disciples carried with them the same weight of authority and regality that drew men to Jesus.

Acts 4:13
*13 Now **when they saw the boldness of Peter and John**, and perceived that they were unlearned and ignorant men, **they marvelled; and they took knowledge of them, that they had been with Jesus.***

The 'spiritual DNA' of Jesus was on Peter and John. The people knew from the manner in which they spoke and walked with authority and boldness that Peter and John had in fact been with the Jesus that they were speaking about! In Acts 4, we read about Peter and John being questioned by the religious leaders as to how they were performing the mighty acts. Acts 4:8 is the key to their being able to preach with boldness:

Acts 4:8
*8 Then Peter, **filled with the Holy Ghost**, said unto them...*

Ultimately, it is the Holy Ghost, the Comforter, who empowered the disciples, as well as the saints in the first century, to speak and move with boldness, despite the ridicule and persecution that would surely come. Jesus told His disciples that they wouldn't need to worry about what to say when they would be imprisoned, for the Comforter would fill their mouths and give them the words to say.

Luke 21:12-15
12 But before all these, they shall lay their hands on you, and persecute you, delivering you up to the synagogues, and into prisons, being brought before kings and rulers for my name's sake.
13 And it shall turn to you for a testimony.

14 Settle it therefore in your hearts, not to meditate before what ye shall answer:
*15 For **I will give you a mouth and wisdom**, which all your adversaries shall not be able to gainsay nor resist.*

John 14:26
*26 But **the Comforter, which is the Holy Ghost**, whom the Father will send in my name, he **shall teach you all things, and bring all things to your remembrance**, whatsoever I have said unto you.*

Paul, likewise, being skilled with the scriptures, but also having the face-to-face encounter with Jesus on the road to Damascus, preached and taught with a level of boldness and authority that captivated audiences.

2 Corinthians 7:4
***Great is my boldness of speech toward you**, great is my glorying of you: I am filled with comfort, I am exceeding joyful in all our tribulation.*

Philippians 1:20
*According to my earnest expectation and my hope, that in nothing I shall be ashamed, **but that with all boldness**, as always, so now also Christ shall be magnified in my body, whether it be by life, or by death.*

Paul also taught that the saints were to walk in the same boldness of faith:

Ephesians 3:11-13
11 According to the eternal purpose which he purposed in Christ Jesus our Lord:
*12 In whom **we have boldness and access with confidence by the faith of him**.*
13 Wherefore I desire that ye faint not at my tribulations for you, which is your glory.

Hebrews 10:18-19
18 Now where remission of these is, there is no more offering for sin.
*19 **Having therefore, brethren, boldness to enter** into the holiest by the blood of Jesus,*

Reigning in Suffering

I truly believe that something that fueled the early church's success in preaching the gospel and seeing multitudes accept Jesus Christ as Lord and Savior was the ability for the saints to endure the travail, persecution and tribulation that was meant to discourage and terrorize the church. From the stoning of Stephen, to the eventual murder of all of the disciples, with the exception of John, the number of new converts didn't waiver. Yes, there were some that evidently fell back in line with the Judaic Old Covenant system, mostly out of fear. But the growth of the church became as aggressive as a snowball rolling down a hill, gaining momentum with each yard that it plummets. The reason for this is quite simple – the early church understood the reality of eternity, and did not stay attached to earthly possessions, and thus, didn't worry about the cares of life. They took to heart the teachings of Jesus-

Matthew 6:31-34
31 Therefore take no thought, saying, What shall we eat? or, What shall we drink? or, Wherewithal shall we be clothed?
32 (For after all these things do the Gentiles seek:) for your heavenly Father knoweth that ye have need of all these things.
33 But seek ye first the kingdom of God, and his righteousness; and all these things shall be added unto you.
34 Take therefore no thought for the morrow: for the morrow shall take thought for the things of itself. Sufficient unto the day is the evil thereof.

Matthew 10:39 (Matthew 16:25, Mark 8:35, Luke 9:24 are similar)
He that findeth his life shall lose it: and he that loseth his life for my sake shall find it.

Paul also wrote quite often about how the afflictions and suffering that was taking place at that time was temporary, and paled in comparison to the glory that was to be revealed:

Romans 8:18
For I reckon that the sufferings of this present time are not worthy to be compared with the glory which shall be revealed in us.

2 Corinthians 1:5-7
5 For as the sufferings of Christ abound in us, so our consolation also aboundeth by Christ.
6 And whether we be afflicted, it is for your consolation and salvation, which is effectual in the enduring of the same sufferings which we also suffer: or whether we be comforted, it is for your consolation and salvation.
7 And our hope of you is stedfast, knowing, that as ye are partakers of the sufferings, so shall ye be also of the consolation.

Peter reiterates this point:

1 Peter 4:13
But rejoice, inasmuch as ye are partakers of Christ's sufferings; that, when his glory shall be revealed, ye may be glad also with exceeding joy.

It was in the suffering for the sake of the gospel that the early church felt even the more yoked to Jesus and the mission set out for them. They took Jesus' phrase "Take up your cross and follow me" literally. Jesus had set the precedent for the disciples and the early church. He had prepared them for what was to come and encouraged them that they would meet again. Holy Spirit, the Comforter, also played a critical role in bringing a spirit of peace – peace that definitely passed all understanding! It had to be absolutely mind-boggling to the unbelieving Jews and also to the gentile nations that a people would be so overwhelmingly sold out for Jesus and the gospel of the kingdom!

Power Flowing From Compassion

The disciples were eye-witnesses of the key to moving in power – that is, compassion. They saw Jesus do many miracles – so many that John writes that there wouldn't be enough time to document them all:

John 21:25
25 And there are also many other things which Jesus did, the which, if they should be written every one, I suppose that even the world itself could not contain the books that should be written. Amen.

But something that is very noticeable when reading through parts of the gospels where miracles and healings took place, a common phrase is found – Jesus was moved with compassion.

Matthew 14:14
*And Jesus went forth, and saw a great multitude, and **was moved with compassion toward them**, and he healed their sick.*

Matthew 15:32 *(Mark 8:2 is similar)*
*Then Jesus called his disciples unto him, and said, **I have compassion on the multitude**, because they continue with me now three days, and have nothing to eat: and I will not send them away fasting, lest they faint in the way.*

Matthew 20:34
*So **Jesus had compassion on them**, and touched their eyes: and immediately their eyes received sight, and they followed him.*

Mark 1:41
*And **Jesus, moved with compassion**, put forth his hand, and touched him, and saith unto him, I will; be thou clean.*

Mark 5:19
*Howbeit Jesus suffered him not, but saith unto him, Go home to thy friends, and tell them how great things the Lord hath done for thee, and hath **had compassion on thee**.*

Mark 9:20-27
20 And they brought him unto him: and when he saw him, straightway the spirit tare him; and he fell on the ground, and wallowed foaming.
21 And he asked his father, How long is it ago since this came unto him? And he said, Of a child.
*22 And ofttimes it hath cast him into the fire, and into the waters, to destroy him: but if thou canst do any thing, **have compassion on us, and help us**.*
23 Jesus said unto him, If thou canst believe, all things are possible to him that believeth.
24 And straightway the father of the child cried out, and said with tears, Lord, I believe; help thou mine unbelief.
25 When Jesus saw that the people came running together, he rebuked the foul spirit, saying unto him, Thou dumb and deaf spirit, I charge thee, come out of him, and enter no more into him.
26 And the spirit cried, and rent him sore, and came out of him: and he was as one dead; insomuch that many said, He is dead.

27 But Jesus took him by the hand, and lifted him up; and he arose.

Luke 7:12-15
12 Now when he came nigh to the gate of the city, behold, there was a dead man carried out, the only son of his mother, and she was a widow: and much people of the city was with her.
*13 And when the Lord saw her, he **had compassion on her**, and said unto her, Weep not.*
14 And he came and touched the bier: and they that bare him stood still. And he said, Young man, I say unto thee, Arise.
15 And he that was dead sat up, and began to speak. And he delivered him to his mother.

Jesus even had compassion for the people that he taught!

Mark 6:34
*And Jesus, when he came out, saw much people, and was **moved with compassion toward them**, because they were as sheep not having a shepherd: and he began to teach them many things.*

What a great pattern for ministry that the disciples were able to witness and then put into action themselves. Jesus told his disciples to do the same things that He did. He wanted the disciples to replicate Him as they went forth in ministry. This is exactly what happened. Not only did the disciples have compassion on the people, just as they had witnessed Jesus doing, but they also taught the saints to have compassion for one another. Peter and John both mention this very thing in their epistles:

1 Peter 3:8-9
*8 Finally, be ye all of one mind, **having compassion one of another**, love as brethren, be pitiful, be courteous:*
9 Not rendering evil for evil, or railing for railing: but contrariwise blessing; knowing that ye are thereunto called, that ye should inherit a blessing.

1 John 3:16-17
16 Hereby perceive we the love of God, because he laid down his life for us: and we ought to lay down our lives for the brethren.

17 But whoso hath this world's good, and seeth his brother have need, and shutteth up his bowels of compassion from him, how dwelleth the love of God in him?

Compassion is defined as 'the sympathetic consciousness of others' distress together with a desire to alleviate it'.[1] Compassion is the mental and psychological 'stepping into another's shoes to feel their pain and anguish which triggers something on the inside (the pulling on the 'heart-strings') to make one proactive and take initiative to do something about that situation, rather than have pity on that individual. This is the essence of ministry. Compassion is the foundation of ministry. There's no power without compassion. I believe that the early church understood this dynamic completely and it was what assisted in the church's exponential growth. The people saw the first century believers who preached and taught about a supernatural God, a supernatural Savior, and a supernatural Holy Spirit, move in the same power and authority in which Jesus moved in, and this verified their witness.

World Turned Upside Down

The carnal mind would find it unfathomable that one Man, Jesus, could gather a non-religious group of twelve individuals and within a span of 40 years (one generation), they absolutely turn the world upside down, figuratively! But this is exactly what took place. Men and women responded to the preached word and the power which confirmed the word. I can imagine the throngs of people that were asking "What must we do to be saved?" We see this type of scene played out after Pentecost. But in a day and age when there were no cell phones, internet, televisions, and radios, the news went as viral as viral can get! Not only were the enemies of the gospel (unbelieving Jews) becoming increasingly irritated at the inability to stop the church from growing and expanding, but the Roman Empire began to feel the pressure as well. The emperors during this time period, who the people claimed to be like gods, and who also demanded worship, saw the blossoming church as a threat to the empire. A people that would not bow their knee to any man, let alone, any god, were thought of as a nuisance and rebellious. So, the Christians began to feel persecution from not only the unbelieving Jews, but also the Roman Empire.

Acts 17:5-8
5 But the Jews which believed not, moved with envy, took unto them certain lewd fellows of the baser sort, and gathered a company, and set all the city on an uproar, and assaulted the house of Jason, and sought to bring them out to the people.
6 And when they found them not, they drew Jason and certain brethren unto the rulers of the city, crying, These that have turned the world upside down are come hither also;
7 Whom Jason hath received: and these all do contrary to the decrees of Caesar, saying that there is another king, one Jesus.
8 And they troubled the people and the rulers of the city, when they heard these things.

The unbelieving Jews tried to instigate and prod Caesar to do its own bidding, which was to put a halt to the growth of the church. Despite the church being the target, it didn't stop them, and the gates of hell surely didn't prevail against them!

CONCLUSION

- The early church was a close-knit community
- The early church was a strict follower of Jesus
- The early church was empowered by Holy Spirit to do everything that Jesus did
- The saints strengthened and encouraged each other
- The early church had structure
- The early church moved in signs, wonders and miracles
- The early church was on a mission to make disciples of men
- The early church was skilled with the scriptures
- First century saints moved with boldness

- The early church was not afraid of persecution
- The early church grew exponentially
- The early church turned the world upside-down

PART TWO

THE 21ST CENTURY INSANE WESTERN CHURCH

Chapter Three:
Dueling Paradigms

A double minded man is unstable in all his ways.

James 1:8

In Part I, the early church, its function and impact on the world was the focal point. I believe that it is essential that we have a general understanding of what the 1st century saints went through, how the church operated, and how the church related to the known world. Only then will we be able to fully diagnose the status of the modern western church. Does the church today resemble, in any way, shape, or form, the church of the 1st century? Does the oneness and unity that was so evident throughout the New Testament exist in our churches today? Can we honestly say that the western church is having the same influence and impact on society and the culture today, as did the early church?

My immediate answer is, emphatically, "NO!" It's not a difficult question to respond to either, considering the various bullet points in the conclusion of the previous chapter which summarized the early church. Where did we 'fall off the wagon' in regard to our lack of resemblance to the early church? Well, I believe that the crux of the matter specifically deals with our lack of understanding of scripture and its proper contextual parameters. However, I will speak on that in more detail in Part III.

So, what makes the western church insane? What could make a Christian seem to be insane? As I've already mentioned in the introduction, 'sanity' is the quality or condition of being sane, or sound in the mind and fully rational. The opposite of 'sanity' is 'insanity', which means a derangement of the mind. I've come to the conclusion that the western church, as it is today, suffers from a severe case of insanity. I know you're probably thinking, "What on God's green and blue earth is this dude talking about?" Trust me. I'm going somewhere with this! Over the next eight chapters, I will discuss various theological subject matter that exemplifies exactly what I'm trying to convey – the western church suffers from, supports, and exports a schizophrenic – double-minded brand of 'Christianity' that is absolutely foreign to that in which we read and learn about in our Bibles (Let me make it clear that this is not necessarily talking about every single church in the western hemisphere – specifically in America. But in regards to the brand of mainstream Christianity that we find on our favorite Christian television stations, or our favorite online ministries… if the shoe fits…).

What is a Paradigm?

Before moving any further, I believe that it is necessary that I talk about the term 'paradigm', for it is the existence of conflicting paradigms within the western church that cultivates 'church insanity'. 'Paradigm' is defined as follows:

1. Example, pattern; especially : an outstandingly clear or typical example or archetype
2. An example of a conjugation or declension showing a word in all its inflectional forms
3. **A philosophical and theoretical framework of a scientific school or discipline within which theories, laws, and generalizations and the experiments performed in support of them are formulated; broadly: a philosophical or theoretical framework of any kind**[1]

The third definition of 'paradigm' is what I want to focus on. A paradigm is basically a frame of thought. Theologically speaking, a paradigm is created by the summation of every bit of information that we receive in regards to God. How we interpret, teach and preach the scriptures is molded and determined by the paradigm that we use. That paradigm acts as a filter for our discernment and perception. Typically, paradigms are rigid and uninviting to anything that attempts to challenge those paradigms (frames of thought).

So what happens when two paradigms collide? What is the outcome when two differing frames of thought attempt to co-exist? Well, as James so eloquently put it, "A double minded man is unstable in all his ways" (James 1:8). Since paradigms are generated by perception, and perception utilizes the mind's thought process, we can assume that two different paradigms not only create friction, but instability. So is the case when there are two or more dueling paradigms within the church.

In Galatians 2:11-21, we read about Paul's confrontation with Peter. It was in regards to how he acted differently when the 'men of the circumcision' (Hebrew Christians from Jerusalem) were in their presence. These men still felt that it was necessary to carry out the rituals and customs of the old covenant (works of the law), which included not eating with the gentiles. Though Peter had already received the revelation that God was no respecter of persons, and that the gospel of Jesus Christ was being accepted amongst the gentiles as well, he still became timid and did not declare the truth for the 'Jerusalem bunch'. The thing that I believe really got Paul upset was not what Peter had done, but what the other Hebrew believers, including Barnabas, Paul's 'right-hand man' in ministering to the gentiles, began to do.

Galatians 2:11-21
*11 But when Peter was come to Antioch, **I withstood him to the face, because he was to be blamed.***
12 For before that certain came from James, he did eat with the Gentiles: but when they were come, he withdrew and separated himself, fearing

them which were of the circumcision.
13 And the other Jews dissembled likewise with him; insomuch that Barnabas also was carried away with their dissimulation.
14 But when I saw that they walked not uprightly according to the truth of the gospel, I said unto Peter before them all, If thou, being a Jew, livest after the manner of Gentiles, and not as do the Jews, why compellest thou the Gentiles to live as do the Jews?
15 We who are Jews by nature, and not sinners of the Gentiles,
16 Knowing that a man is not justified by the works of the law, but by the faith of Jesus Christ, even we have believed in Jesus Christ, that we might be justified by the faith of Christ, and not by the works of the law: for by the works of the law shall no flesh be justified.
17 But if, while we seek to be justified by Christ, we ourselves also are found sinners, is therefore Christ the minister of sin? God forbid.
18 For if I build again the things which I destroyed, I make myself a transgressor.
19 For I through the law am dead to the law, that I might live unto God.
20 I am crucified with Christ: nevertheless I live; yet not I, but Christ liveth in me: and the life which I now live in the flesh I live by the faith of the Son of God, who loved me, and gave himself for me.
21 I do not frustrate the grace of God: for if righteousness come by the law, then Christ is dead in vain.

This is a vivid illustration of the two major dueling paradigms of the 1st century – The New Covenant (justification by faith in Jesus Christ) versus The Old Covenant (works of the law). Though Peter had come out of the clutches of the law, there was still some 'residue' of religiosity that he had to deal with! Should it be any surprise, now that I think of it, that it would take Peter some time to fully adjust? I mean, he is the same guy that Jesus said would deny Him (Jesus) three times! Something that is also interesting is recalling the discussion that Jesus had with Peter:

Luke 22:31-33
31 And the Lord said, Simon, Simon, behold, Satan hath desired to have you, that he may sift you as wheat:
*32 But I have prayed for thee, that thy faith fail not: and **when thou art converted, strengthen thy brethren**.*

I believe that this confrontation between Paul and Peter was the final step in the process of Peter's conversion. I could only imagine that the shame and sorrow that he felt after the cock crowed, signifying Peter's three denials of Jesus, is the same shame and sorrow that he may have felt after being rebuked by Paul in the midst of his peers!

Proverbs 27:5
Open rebuke is better than secret love.

Believe it or not, open rebuke was a critical tool that was used (and still should be used) in order to make sure that the 1st century church was on one accord, unified and without strife. Knowing Israel's own history of flip-flopping, in regards to its hot and cold relationship with God (Old Testament), it's easy to understand why Jesus stressed that His followers should not have any division amongst them.

Matthew 12:25 *(Luke 11:17 is similar)*
25 And Jesus knew their thoughts, and said unto them, ***Every kingdom divided against itself is brought to desolation; and every city or house divided against itself shall not stand:***

Mark 3:24-25
24 And if a kingdom be divided against itself, that kingdom cannot stand.
25 And if a house be divided against itself, that house cannot stand.

Two dueling paradigms within the church create a divided house. How can there possibly be One Lord, One Faith, One Baptism, and then differing opinions and frames of thought on a myriad of subject matter within the church? Not only did Jesus exhort His followers to not allow any division to come in the midst of them, but we find throughout much of scripture references being made to having a sound mind and being stable. To be 'sound' is to be free from flaw, defect, or decay; free from error, fallacy, or misapprehension; to exhibit or be based on thorough knowledge and experience; logically valid and having true premises; showing good judgment or sense.[2] To be 'stable' is to be firmly established; not changing or fluctuating; stead in purpose: firm in resolution; not subject to insecurity or emotional illness: sane, rational.₃

We serve a sound and stable-minded God-

1 Corinthians 14:33
*33 For **God is not the author of confusion**, but of peace, as in all churches of the saints.*

In other words, God is not the creator or source of conflicting viewpoints and paradigms. There aren't dual truths. God is not a double-minded God. Jesus isn't a double-minded Messiah. He only did what He saw the Father do (John 5:19). There aren't any contingency plans with the will of God. Let God be true, and every man a liar (Romans 3:4).

2 Peter 3:16
*16 As also in all his epistles, speaking in them of these things; in which are some things hard to be understood, which **they that are unlearned and unstable wrest, as they do also the other scriptures, unto their own destruction.***

This is a very interesting verse because at its core, Peter is saying that an unlearned or unstable mind will have difficulty understanding the mysteries of God. Peter makes reference to the letter that Paul had previously written to the church at Galatia. Apparently, there were some things within it that some of the people couldn't understand. But Peter doesn't stop with Paul's letters, as he says that the unlearned and unstable struggle with other scriptures as well – namely, the Old Testament (law and prophets). This isn't anything new because taking a look back at the gospels, we find on numerous occasions where Jesus is talking with the scribes and Pharisees about scripture, and yet, they could not comprehend Jesus' fulfillment of various passages. Their ignorance of scripture that pointed to Jesus as being Messiah is what eventually led to their desolation and destruction – something that Peter associates with being unlearned and unstable.

James 4:8
8 Draw nigh to God, and he will draw nigh to you. Cleanse your hands, ye sinners; and **purify your hearts, ye double minded.**

Being double-minded is a heart issue. Yes, from the abundance of the heart, the mouth speaks (Matthew 12:34). But what is inside of the heart of man is shaped or tainted by the flesh. The flesh consists of mind, body, will and emotions. The flesh is susceptible to outside influence in which can corrupt the heart. A double-minded man has a corrupted heart. A corrupt heart can only be healed when, by the grace of God, man's eye becomes single (solely focused on the light that comes from God, and not the darkness of the world) (Matthew 6:22, Luke 11:34).

2 Timothy 1:7
7 For God hath not given us the spirit of fear; but of power, and of love, and of **a sound mind.**

In Paul's second letter to Timothy, Paul exhorted Timothy to not be ashamed or fearful of that which he was called to be. Timothy saw the persecution that Paul was experiencing. Paul wanted to make sure that Timothy wouldn't shrink back and become immobilized by fear and anxiety – something that would have definitely hindered Timothy's effectiveness to minister and carry the mantle of Paul's apostleship onward.

Philippians 4:7
7 And **the peace of God,** *which passeth all understanding,* **shall keep your hearts and minds** *through Christ Jesus.*

This is yet another reference to the heart and mind being closely related to each other. But it is only the peace of God that sustains and fortifies the heart and mind. The phrase 'the peace' in this passage is the Greek word *eirēnē*, which is defined as being in a state of national tranquility – exempt from the rage and havoc of war; security, safety, prosperity, and felicity. The definition that I love the most is 'the tranquil state of a soul assured of its salvation through Christ, and so fearing nothing from God and content with its earthly lot, of whatsoever sort that is'.4 It is the knowing without a shadow of a doubt that Jesus, being the once and for all atonement (Hebrews 9:26-28), is what assures us of our right-standing with God – we are made righteous because of what He did, and not because of what we do.

Titus 2:6
*6 Young men likewise exhort to **be sober minded**.*

'To be sober minded' is the Greek word *sōphroneō*, which is to have a sound mind, or be right in the mind.5 It also refers to exhibiting self-control, whether in a man's thoughts, or in the restricting of a man's passions and fleshly desires.

There are plenty of other verses that deal with the mind and Christian thinking. A phrase that is commonly used regarding our thoughts is "our thoughts determine our actions, and our actions determine our outcome". In other words, who we are individually, and collectively as the church, is determined by our thinking.

Proverbs 23:7
For as he thinketh in his heart, so is he: *Eat and drink, saith he to thee; but his heart is not with thee.*

In the following chapters, I will talk about different theological subject matter in which there are multiple viewpoints that are obviously contradictory. While reading, please keep in mind that for the most part, there can only be one truth. As previously mentioned, God is not the author of confusion, and there are no multiple-track programs regarding the kingdom of God. There is no contradiction with the mind of God. We do not serve a double-minded, schizophrenic God.

Chapter Four:
The Cross

Wherefore seeing we also are compassed about with so great a cloud of witnesses, let us lay aside every weight, and the sin which doth so easily beset us, and let us run with patience the race that is set before us, Looking unto Jesus the author and finisher of our faith; who for the joy that was set before him endured the cross, despising the shame, and is set down at the right hand of the throne of God.

Hebrews 12:1-2

"At the cross, at the cross, where I first saw the light and the burdens of my heart rolled away. It was there, there by faith, I received my sight. And now, I am happy all the day." These lyrics were forever emblazoned into my mind as a youngster. The song would be sung when "the doors of the church were open" – for those that were raised Baptist, you definitely know what I'm talking about! For those that weren't, it simply meant an invitation to Christ! But the simple lyrics of that song define the foundation of Christianity. For it is definitely at the cross where all of our Christian journeys begin. "No cross, no crown" – yet another cliché that I heard quite often in the days of my youth. The list of songs and phrases can go on and on regarding the significance of the cross. But the questions that I would like to present are what exactly happened at the cross, and what was the result of the work of the cross? Since Christ's crucifixion is a paramount part of our faith, it is necessary to fully understand the spiritual implication of the gory, yet, beautiful cross. It is beneficial to start with taking a look at passages in the Old Testament that foreshadowed this world changing event.

Prophetic Foreshadowing of Christ Crucified

From the Pentateuch (first five books of the bible) to the latter books of the minor prophets, we find numerous prophetic declarations regarding the torment that Jesus would undergo – not only on the cross, but the hours leading up to the crucifixion. One of the earliest foreshadows of Jesus and the cross is found in Numbers 21:6-9.

Numbers 21:6-9
6 And the Lord sent fiery serpents among the people, and they bit the people; and much people of Israel died.
7 Therefore the people came to Moses, and said, We have sinned, for we have spoken against the Lord, and against thee; pray unto the Lord, that he take away the serpents from us. And Moses prayed for the people.
8 And the Lord said unto Moses, **Make thee a fiery serpent, and set it upon a pole: and it shall come to pass, that every one that is bitten, when he looketh upon it, shall live.**
9 And Moses made a serpent of brass, and put it upon a pole, and it came to pass, that if a serpent had bitten any man, when he beheld the serpent of brass, he lived.

In John 3, we read about Nicodemus, a Pharisee, and ruler of the Jews (v. 1), coming to Jesus at night to enquire about the miracles that Jesus was performing. Astonishingly, after Jesus explains to him about the necessity of being born again, he brings to Nicodemus's remembrance what Moses was instructed to do in Numbers 21:8:

John 3:14-15
14 **And as Moses lifted up the serpent in the wilderness, even so must the Son of man be lifted up:**
15 That whosoever believeth in him should not perish, but **have eternal life.**

Jesus undoubtedly compares himself to the fiery serpent that was set upon the pole in Numbers 21:8. The serpent represents the sin nature. Jesus, on the cross, engulfed the sins of the world into himself. He became the sin nature. Just as the Israelites were healed of their serpent bites (which were due to sinfulness and rebellion against God) when they looked upon that brass serpent on a pole, so is the case with whosoever looks upon and believes Jesus! But the latter is much greater! The healing is salvation and eternal life!

Psalm 22 is full of prophetic foreshadowing of the cross and events leading up to it. In verse 1, David writes "My God, my God, why hast thou forsaken me?" Jesus utters these exact words while he was on the cross.

Matthew 27:46 (Mark 15:34 is similar)
And about the ninth hour Jesus cried with a loud voice, saying, Eli, Eli, lama sabachthani? that is to say, **My God, my God, why hast thou forsaken me?**

In Psalm 22:16, David makes reference to the piercing of his hands and feet (this did not happen literally to David!). Roman crucifixion was just that – the piercing of the hands and feet by way of nails. Keep in mind that during David's day, crucifixion would not have been a form of execution. The Roman Empire didn't come to power until hundreds of years later.

Psalm 22:16
16 For dogs have compassed me: the assembly of the wicked have inclosed me: **they pierced my hands and my feet.**

Zechariah making reference to wounds in the hands –

Zechariah 13:6
6 And one shall say unto him, **What are these wounds in thine hands?** *Then he shall answer, Those with which I was wounded in the house of my friends.*

Probably the most familiar passage that deals with the crucifixion of Jesus is found in Isaiah 53. Verses 5 through 8 give a vivid depiction of the suffering of Christ.

Isaiah 53:5-8
5 But **he was wounded for our transgressions, he was bruised for our**

*iniquities: the chastisement of our peace was upon him; and **with his stripes we are healed**.*
*6 All we like sheep have gone astray; we have turned every one to his own way; and **the Lord hath laid on him the iniquity of us all**.*
*7 **He was oppressed, and he was afflicted**, yet he opened not his mouth: **he is brought as a lamb to the slaughter, and as a sheep before her shearers is dumb**, so he openeth not his mouth.*
*8 He was taken from prison and from judgment: and who shall declare his generation? for **he was cut off out of the land of the living: for the transgression of my people was he stricken**.*

Jesus did this for the world. He did this for all ages. But most importantly, He did it to fulfill the will of the Father. Jesus, who was fully God and fully man, experienced the excruciating pain of having the weight of the sins of the world upon his shoulders. The sins, transgressions and iniquity of all times were weighing down on him to the point that we read from Luke's perspective (a physician) about Jesus sweating blood while praying in the Garden of Gethsemane.

Luke 22:44
*44 And being in an agony he prayed more earnestly: and **his sweat was as it were great drops of blood falling down to the ground**.*

I can't fathom anything being more intense and agonizing than this. And yet, meanwhile, the Father was pleased with what was taking place because it was HIS will, HIS plan, in order to reconcile HIS people back unto Himself. The blood of bulls and goats was no longer acceptable. It was the once and for all sacrifice of his only begotten Son that created the way in which men and women could be reunited with the Father and be in right standing.

Isaiah 53:10-12
*10 Yet **it pleased the Lord to bruise him**; he hath put him to grief: when thou shalt make his soul an offering for sin, he shall see his seed, he shall prolong his days, and the pleasure of the Lord shall prosper in his hand.*
*11 **He shall see of the travail of his soul, and shall be satisfied**: by his knowledge shall my righteous servant justify many; for he shall bear their iniquities.*

12 Therefore will I divide him a portion with the great, and he shall divide the spoil with the strong; because he hath poured out his soul unto death: and he was numbered with the transgressors; and he bare the sin of many, and made intercession for the transgressors.

Jesus was obedient to the Father from the time that he told His earthly parents (Mary and Joseph) that He must be about His Father's business (Luke 2:49), all the way to His last breath. The words before His last breath were "It is finished."

Finished Work, or Not?

What did Jesus mean when he uttered "It is finished" (John 19:30)? What was finished? What came to an end? I believe the answer lies in what Jesus told his disciples – it was not His will, but the will of the Father who sent Him that Jesus had finished (John 5:30). The 'assignment' that the Father had set forth for His Son to accomplish had come to a close. It was the horrid end of the 'assignment' (crucifixion) that Jesus had prayed to the Father about at Gethsemane, asking for another way to accomplish the Father's will. Yet, Jesus immediately followed the inquisition with saying that it was the will of the Father that is the last word.

Matthew 26:39, 42, 44
39 And he went a little farther, and fell on his face, and prayed,
saying, ***O my Father, if it be possible, let this cup pass from me: nevertheless not as I will, but as thou wilt.***

42 He went away again the second time, and prayed, saying, ***O my Father, if this cup may not pass away from me, except I drink it, thy will be done.***

44 And he left them, and went away again, and prayed the third time, ***saying the same words.***

The will of the Father hinged upon Jesus completing the task of dying on the cross for the sins of the world. The finished work also entailed the fulfilling of everything that was prophesied about Jesus – from the womb (of Mary) to the tomb. It was the fulfilling of the prophetic decrees about Messiah, coupled with the miracles that assisted in the growing number of Christ followers during Jesus' earthly ministry. Something that seems to be overlooked is that the high priest, Caiaphas, also prophesied about Jesus' death, and the significance of it for the people!

John 11:49-53
49 And one of them, named Caiaphas, being the high priest that same year, said unto them, **Ye know nothing at all,**
50 **Nor consider that it is expedient for us, that one man should die for the people, and that the whole nation perish not.**
51 And this spake he not of himself: but being high priest that year, **he prophesied that Jesus should die for that nation;**
52 **And not for that nation only, but that also he should gather together in one the children of God that were scattered abroad.**
53 Then from that day forth they took counsel together for to put him to death.

So, the death of Jesus was the completing of the task that God had for Him, and it was also the fulfilling of a lot of Old Testament prophetic decrees regarding Messiah. The question is, however, if Jesus' death was the finished work, then why do so many Christians today seek further action from Jesus to 'finish what has already been finished'? Wouldn't the necessity of a '2nd coming' (as assumed by most Christians in the western church) make the work of the cross of non-effect? If Jesus defeated death, hell and the grave at the cross and with His subsequent resurrection, and we believe that we are made alive in Christ (1 Corinthians 15:22), then what is the reason for a '2nd coming'? Death and the grave were the enemies.

1 Corinthians 15:55-57
55 O death, where is thy sting? O grave, where is thy victory?
56 The sting of death is sin; and the strength of sin is the law.
57 But thanks be to God, which giveth us the victory through our Lord Jesus Christ.

These enemies (death and the grave) were conquered. We have victory because of what Jesus did. If we have the victory, why do we subconsciously belittle the work of the cross with our believing that Satan is taking over the world and that there is no hope outside of a physical return of Jesus to restore things back to order? Either we fully accept that believing in the work of the cross and the resurrection yields eternal life and victory in Christ, or we create another scenario in which makes Jesus' statement, "It is finished", nonsensical and an untruth.

Chapter Five:
The Kingdom

Of the increase of his government and peace there shall be no end, upon the throne of David, and upon his kingdom, to order it, and to establish it with judgment and with justice from henceforth even for ever. The zeal of the Lord of hosts will perform this.

Isaiah 9:7

"Repent ye: for the kingdom of heaven is at hand." These were the words of John the Baptist. Matthew 3:2 is the first place in the New Testament that the word 'kingdom' is used. In totality, the terms 'kingdom', 'kingdom of God', or 'kingdom of heaven' are used 154 times throughout the New Testament. Suffice it to say, the term 'kingdom' is absolutely significant. It is imperative that we truly understand what the kingdom is, when it was, or is established, and how long the kingdom (of God) lasts.

I'll get back to John's quote in a bit. I think it will be beneficial to identify the various viewpoints on the kingdom of God and 'lay them out on the table':

Viewpoint #1: "The Kingdom of God is now, but not yet."

The subscribers of this viewpoint believe that the kingdom of God did come spiritually in the first century during Jesus' earthly ministry. However, they believe that the fullness of the kingdom has not come yet. They see the fullness of the kingdom of God as a future physical kingdom, not just spiritual. They believe that in the future, every literal, physical kingdom will come under the rule / subjugation of a literal, physical kingdom of God in which Jesus will sit on a literal, physical throne in a literal place called New Jerusalem.

Viewpoint #2: "The Kingdom has not come because of the current state of the world."

Those that hold this viewpoint do not believe that the kingdom of God is currently here in any way, shape or form due to what is perceived to be an ever-increasingly evil world that we live in. They believe that the kingdom of God will come in the future with a physical return of Jesus and the creation of a new heaven and new earth (Isaiah 65:17, 66:22, 2 Peter 3:13, Revelation 21:1).

Viewpoint #3: "The kingdom came in its fullness in the 1st century"

The people that believe that the kingdom of God came in the 1st century believe that Jesus brought the kingdom, and there was nothing partial about it. They believe that Jesus did not teach or preach about a partial kingdom. They also believe that the kingdom of God is spiritual, and not a literal, physical place or thing.

Daniel's Visions of the Kingdom of God

In Daniel 2, we read about the dream of Babylonian king, Nebuchadnezzar. He summoned all of the magicians, astrologers and sorcerers in the land to not just interpret his dream, but to show the king exactly what he dreamed! Death was the reward for an incorrect interpretation. Talk about pressure! Unfortunately for them, they couldn't show the king his dream and a decree went forth to kill all of the 'wise men'. After a time of seeking God for the secret of the king's dream (v. 18), Daniel received the secret (v. 19), and then asked to be

The Kingdom | 65

taken to the king to interpret his dream.
Daniel 2:31-45
31 Thou, O king, sawest, and behold a great image. This great image, whose brightness was excellent, stood before thee; and the form thereof was terrible.
32 This image's head was of fine gold, his breast and his arms of silver, his belly and his thighs of brass,
33 His legs of iron, his feet part of iron and part of clay.
34 Thou sawest till that a stone was cut out without hands, which smote the image upon his feet that were of iron and clay, and brake them to pieces.
35 Then was the iron, the clay, the brass, the silver, and the gold, broken to pieces together, and became like the chaff of the summer threshingfloors; and the wind carried them away, that no place was found for them: and the stone that smote the image became a great mountain, and filled the whole earth.
36 This is the dream; and we will tell the interpretation thereof before the king.
37 Thou, O king, art a king of kings: for the God of heaven hath given thee a kingdom, power, and strength, and glory.
38 And wheresoever the children of men dwell, the beasts of the field and the fowls of the heaven hath he given into thine hand, and hath made thee ruler over them all. Thou art this head of gold.
39 And after thee shall arise another kingdom inferior to thee, and another third kingdom of brass, which shall bear rule over all the earth.
40 And the fourth kingdom shall be strong as iron: forasmuch as iron breaketh in pieces and subdueth all things: and as iron that breaketh all these, shall it break in pieces and bruise.
41 And whereas thou sawest the feet and toes, part of potters' clay, and part of iron, the kingdom shall be divided; but there shall be in it of the strength of the iron, forasmuch as thou sawest the iron mixed with miry clay.
42 And as the toes of the feet were part of iron, and part of clay, so the kingdom shall be partly strong, and partly broken.
43 And whereas thou sawest iron mixed with miry clay, they shall mingle themselves with the seed of men: but they shall not cleave one to another, even as iron is not mixed with clay.
44 And in the days of these kings shall the God of heaven set up a kingdom, which shall never be destroyed: and the kingdom shall not be left to other people, but it shall break in pieces and consume all these kingdoms, and it shall stand for ever.
45 Forasmuch as thou sawest that the stone was cut out of the mountain without hands, and that it brake in pieces the iron, the brass, the clay, the

silver, and the gold; the great God hath made known to the king what shall come to pass hereafter: and the dream is certain, and the interpretation thereof sure.

Here are a few noteworthy observations:

- There were four historical kingdoms
    1. Babylonian Empire (605-539 BC)[1]
    2. Median-Persian Empire (539-330 BC)[2]
    3. Grecian Empire (330 BC-188 BC)
    4. Roman Empire (188 BC-363 AD)[3]
- The 'feet' being part iron and part clay represent a mixed, or dual authority
- The God of heaven sets up a kingdom (The kingdom of God) in the days of the mixed-dual authority
- God's kingdom will stand forever – it will be everlasting

Before even taking into consideration the New Testament texts concerning the kingdom, we can see from this passage that a prophetic context was created for the arrival of the kingdom of God, which, by the way, was, and is, an everlasting kingdom. It arrived during the time of a 'mixed kingdom'. Historically speaking, Israel was allowed by the Roman Emperors to conduct its own affairs, especially in reference to the things involving the temple practices (rituals, feasts / high times, worship, etc.). There was a prefect (overseer) that was assigned by the Roman Empire to Judea (part of the Roman province, Iudaea). During Jesus' time, Pontius Pilate was the prefect. Caiaphas was the appointed chief priest of the temple. It was the literal co-mingling of Caiaphas and Pontius Pilate that led to the crucifixion of Jesus.

Jesus Preaches the Kingdom

John the Baptist said "The kingdom is at hand" in Matthew 3:2. In Matthew 4, we see Jesus tempted by the devil, being offered 'all the kingdoms of the world, and the glory of them' (v. 8). After rebuking the devil, we later read that Jesus began to preach the same thing that John was proclaiming.

Matthew 4:17
From that time Jesus began to preach, and to say, ***Repent: for the kingdom of heaven is at hand.***

What does the phrase 'at hand' mean? The Greek translation for this phrase is 'eggizō', which means to bring near, to join one thing to another; to draw or come near to, to approach.[4] In essence, Jesus (and John) was saying that the kingdom had been brought near, that it was approachable, within reach, and the opportunity to join it had been made available! Luke's interpretation sheds light to this then-present reality:

Luke 16:16
The law and the prophets were until John: ***since that time the kingdom of God is preached, and every man presseth into it.***

It was in Jesus' days that men and women began to press into the kingdom. In John 3, Jesus told Nicodemus that the only way to enter into the kingdom of God is by being born again:

John 3:5
Jesus answered, Verily, verily, I say unto thee, ***Except a man be born of water and of the Spirit, he cannot enter into the kingdom of God.***

Being born again is a spiritual matter. It was hard for the carnal, religious mind of Nicodemus to understand this. Thus, Jesus' frustration in v. 10! But this sheds light upon a significant point about the kingdom – it is by no means physical! The kingdom of God is spiritual and not seen by the naked eye. Jesus validates this point with his own words regarding the kingdom:

Luke 17:20-21
20 And when he was demanded of the Pharisees, when the kingdom of God should come, he answered them and said, **The kingdom of God cometh not with observation:**
21 Neither shall they say, Lo here! or, lo there! for, behold, **the kingdom of God is within you.**

Bombshell! The kingdom of God cannot be observed, according to Jesus! The Amplified Bible's wording makes this point even clearer:

Luke 17:20-21 (AMP)
20 Asked by the Pharisees when the kingdom of God would come, He replied to them by saying, **The kingdom of God does not come with signs to be observed or with visible display,**
21 Nor will people say, Look! Here [it is]! or, See, [it is] there! For behold, **the kingdom of God is within you [in your hearts] and among you [surrounding you].**

The subscribers of the "now, but not yet" theory about the kingdom will have a tough time trying to wiggle out of what Jesus emphatically states about the nature of the kingdom of God. It is an invisible, non-observable kingdom – it is spiritual. It is around us and in the heart of every believer!

There are many other verses within the gospels where Jesus speaks about the attributes of the kingdom and also the qualities and traits that would confirm if one is in the kingdom or not. The kingdom of God was, and is for the poor in spirit, or those that exhibit humility and are not proud (Matthew 5:3, Luke 6:20, 7:28). The kingdom is for those that undergo persecution for righteousness' sake – It is for those that speak truth to power and stand up for the powerless and confront injustice (Matthew 5:10). Seeking the kingdom first is the doorway to a prosperous life (Matthew 6:33, Luke 12:31). Jesus instructed others to preach that the kingdom was at hand (Matthew 10:7, Luke 9:2). Deliverance by means of casting out devils was a sign that the kingdom had come (Matt. 12:28,

Luke 11:20). There are mysteries of the kingdom of God and they are hidden from some (Matthew 13:11, Luke 8:10). The kingdom of God is given to people who produce fruit for it (Matthew 21:43). One must have child-like faith to enter the kingdom of God (Matthew 18:33, Mark 10:13-15, Luke 18:16-17). The kingdom of heaven starts small, but becomes infinitely larger (Matthew 13:31-33, Luke 13:18-21). The kingdom of God was, and is, accessible to anyone, and not just the religious folks (Matthew 21:31). Those that place their trust in their riches will find it very difficult to enter the kingdom of God (Mark 10:23-25, Luke 18:24-25). The kingdom age is an eternal age (Luke 1:33). One that dwells on the past is not fit for the kingdom (Luke 9:62). A person must be born again to see the kingdom (John 3:3-5). The kingdom of God is not of this world. It cannot be entered or possessed by natural means. (John 18:36).

The kingdom of God is an 'upside-down kingdom'. It is the exact opposite, in many cases, of what we perceive a natural, earthly kingdom to be. Throughout history, kingdoms have risen and fallen. Most of the time, this was due to militaristic conflict. In Jesus' day, the Jews were looking for a king that would usher in the eternal kingdom age that they had read about via the prophets of old. The lowly, humble and servant-like character of Jesus made it impossible for the Jewish zealots to believe that Jesus could possibly be the Messiah. They were only enamored with the thoughts and aspirations of becoming free and independent from the tentacles of the Roman Empire. They were looking for another David to lead Israel in revolt against Rome. Even the disciples inquired of Jesus about when the physical kingdom of Israel would be restored to its "glory days of prominence", as was the case when David was king:

Acts 1:6
When they therefore were come together, they asked of him, saying, **Lord, wilt thou at this time restore again the kingdom to Israel?**

Even after Jesus was with the disciples for nearly three years, after all the miracles, signs and wonders, after the extensive preaching and teaching about the kingdom of God, and even after Jesus' death, burial, resurrection, and being with them for forty days and speaking to them specifically about the kingdom of God (Acts 1:3), they still were somewhat clueless!

The kingdom of God was a mystery to many then, and it still is a mystery to many today. Preconceived, unbiblical notions of what the kingdom is, by what means it should come, and in what manner it should appear, has created confusion and disillusionment and has contributed to the on-going ignorance within the western church. Much of what shapes the modern day opinions of the kingdom of God is spear-headed by various end-time viewpoints.

Chapter Six:
The End of the World

For then must he often have suffered since the foundation of the world: but now once in the end of the world hath he appeared to put away sin by the sacrifice of himself.

Hebrews 9:26

The engine that fuels much of the confusion and double-mindedness that we see in the western church is directly related to various interpretations of end-time bible prophecy. The 'end of the world' is such a mysterious subject that Hollywood wastes no time jumping on the money-train! Movies, TV shows, books, teaching videos, conferences, workshops, Christian programming, and the list can go on and on and on – they all have been inundated with end-time subject matter from time to time. The 'end-time industry' is a 'cash cow'! Movies that have something remotely to do with the end of the world always seem to do well in the box office. People are simply drawn to and intrigued by the unknown. But, are the end-times really unknown? Is there no way to understand what the end-times are, when are the end-times, and how folks are affected by the end-times?

Eschatology is the study of last things (end times). There are three general eschatological viewpoints – Futurism, Historicism, and Preterism. Within these three viewpoints, you will find even more splintering and minute differences of opinion on various biblical texts and passages. Some are too flaky and controversial to cover within the confines of one book. But for the purpose of this chapter, focusing on the differences between the three major interpretations is what's necessary.

The Futurist

The terms 'futurism' or 'futurist' should give away the meaning of this end-time interpretation. Futurists subscribe to the belief that Jesus' 2nd coming and the "rapture" are future, and that virtually the entire book of Revelation is yet to be fulfilled (specifically, everything from chapter 4 onward). Futurists believe that the Olivet discourse (Matthew 24, Mark 13 and Luke 21) is also speaking of things that will occur in the future. Futurists use a literal approach to interpret scripture. Though they acknowledge the usage of apocalyptic, idiomatic language throughout Revelation, they still deem it necessary to read the letter with a literal interpretive mindset. Futurists believe that there is precedent for reading Revelation with a literal interpretation – the early church fathers. Because the futurist interpretation was a popular way to interpret Revelation in the 2nd-4th centuries, the conclusion drawn by the futurist is that futurism must be the correct eschatological viewpoint. To this day, futurism remains the most popular end-time viewpoint, especially in the western church. Dispensationalism is probably the most popular stream of futurism today. I will talk about Dispensationalism in more detail later on.

The Historicist

The 'historicist' believes the book of Revelation depicts the course of history from the time of the writing of the letter by John to the end of the age. Accordingly, the apocalyptic symbols that are found throughout Revelation are relative to historical events that primarily took place, or take place in Europe. Such events as the French Revolution and the Protestant Reformation are keystone in the historicist's eschatological interpretation. Some view the first three chapters of Revelation as John prophetically addressing seven different church periods in history. For example, many historicists take the viewpoint that we are now living in the Laodicean church period, which they believe is described in the following passage:

Revelation 3:14-19
14 And unto the angel of the church of the Laodiceans write; These things saith the Amen, the faithful and true witness, the beginning of the creation of God;
15 I know thy works, that thou art neither cold nor hot: I would thou wert cold or hot.
16 So then because thou art lukewarm, and neither cold nor hot, I will spue thee out of my mouth.
17 Because thou sayest, I am rich, and increased with goods, and have need of nothing; and knowest not that thou art wretched, and miserable, and poor, and blind, and naked:
18 I counsel thee to buy of me gold tried in the fire, that thou mayest be rich; and white raiment, that thou mayest be clothed, and that the shame of thy nakedness do not appear; and anoint thine eyes with eyesalve, that thou mayest see.
19 As many as I love, I rebuke and chasten: be zealous therefore, and repent.

By ascribing this passage to what the historicist believes is the seventh, and final church period, he or she is essentially saying that a prevailing characteristic within that church period would be 'lukewarmness' in the church.

Much of the historicist's interpretation of Revelation deals specifically with the Roman Empire, and more poignantly, the Roman Catholic Church. They interpret Revelation 4 through 10 as depicting the fall of the Roman Empire. In Revelation 13, the historicist makes a distinction between what they believe is the true church and the counterfeit church – the Roman Catholic Church. Consequently, the following chapters in Revelation, according to the historicist view point, depict God's judgment coming upon the Roman Catholic Church, and its eventual fall.

The Protestant Reformation was the fuel to the historicist's fire. It was during this time period of tension between prominent men in the 14th and 15th centuries and the Roman Catholic Church, that a lot of the shaping and molding of the historicist viewpoint took place. In essence, Rome was (or is) declared 'Babylon', the Roman Catholic Church was (or is) the beast system, and the Pope was (or is) 'The Antichrist'.

The Preterist

The 'preterist' believes that much, if not all, of bible prophecy concerning the 'end times' or 'last days' was fulfilled in the first century. The term 'preterism' derives from the Latin *praeter,* which means 'past', or 'beyond'. Other commonly used terms for preterism are 'fulfilled eschatology', 'covenant eschatology' and 'victorious eschatology'. Where futurists and preterists differ the most is in the interpretation of the Olivet Discourse and Revelation. Unlike the futurist, the preterist believes that 'the end of the world', which was made reference to by the disciples in Matthew 24:3, was in regards to the end of that current age, or dispensation (which is the meaning of 'aion', the Greek translation of 'world' in this verse).

Preterists believe that the first century audience fully understood that they were definitely living in the last days, or at the 'end of the world (age)'. Matthew 16:28 (also Luke 9:27) and 26:63-64 are critical supports for the context of what generation would see Jesus' second coming.

Matthew 16:28
28 Verily I say unto you, **There be some standing here, which shall not taste of death, till they see the Son of man coming in his kingdom.**

Matthew 26:63-64
63 But Jesus held his peace, And the high priest answered and said unto him, I adjure thee by the living God, that thou tell us whether thou be the Christ, the Son of God.
64 Jesus saith unto him, Thou hast said: nevertheless I say unto you, **Hereafter shall ye see the Son of man sitting on the right hand of power, and coming in the clouds of heaven.**

Preterists believe that the word 'generation' in Matthew 24:34 refers to the people that were alive at that time. They also believe that the Old Testament reference of the length of a generation (40 years - see Numbers 32:13 and Psalm 95:10) is applicable in determining the timeframe in which all the events that Jesus' prophesied about in the Olivet Discourse would take place. Assuming that Jesus was born in 4 B.C., it would place Jesus' death, burial and resurrection in the year 29 AD (the year of birth is debatable, and thus, would affect the 29 AD date). Utilizing the preterist argument that a generation is 40 years, this means that everything regarding the end times or last days would have to begin to happen between the years of 29 AD and 69 AD. The preterist believes that the 'great tribulation' of Matthew 24:21 was literally fulfilled in the days leading up to the eventual destruction of the temple in 70 AD by the Roman armies. Luke 21:20 is seen as the prophetic decree by Jesus regarding the Roman armies surrounding Jerusalem, which did happen in 66 AD.

Luke 21:20
*20 And **when ye shall see Jerusalem compassed with armies**, then know that the desolation thereof is nigh.*

Preterists believe that Revelation was not a letter written to a future generation far off, but to seven literal churches in Asia (Rev. 1:20) that existed during the first century to warn them of what was to come. Revelation 1:1-3 is seen as critical in interpreting the rest of the book because of its contextualization.

Revelation 1:1-3
*1 The Revelation of Jesus Christ, which God gave unto him, to shew unto his servants **things which must shortly come to pass**; and he sent and signified it by his angel unto his servant John:*
2 Who bare record of the word of God, and of the testimony of Jesus Christ, and of all things that he saw.
*3 Blessed is he that readeth, and they that hear the words of this prophecy, and keep those things which are written therein: for **the time is at hand**.*

In Revelation 22:6, we see a similar statement that further solidifies the preterist argument that the events foreshadowed within the letter were to take place within a relatively short period of time:

Revelation 22:6
6 And he said unto me, These sayings are faithful and true: and the Lord God of the holy prophets sent his angel to **shew unto his servants the things which must shortly be done.**

The preterist believes that his argument is even further supported by various statements made by the apostles in which seem to identify the first century as being 'the time of the end':

Peter saying that the outpouring of Holy Spirit on the day of Pentecost signified that they were living in the last days, as Joel had prophesied (Joel 2:28-32)-

Acts 2:15-21
15 For these are not drunken, as ye suppose, seeing it is but the third hour of the day.
16 But **this is that which was spoken by the prophet Joel;**
17 And **it shall come to pass in the last days**, saith God, I will pour out of my Spirit upon all flesh: and your sons and your daughters shall prophesy, and your young men shall see visions, and your old men shall dream dreams:
18 And on my servants and on my handmaidens I will pour out in those days of my Spirit; and they shall prophesy:
19 And I will shew wonders in heaven above, and signs in the earth beneath; blood, and fire, and vapour of smoke:
20 The sun shall be turned into darkness, and the moon into blood, before the great and notable day of the Lord come:
21 And it shall come to pass, that whosoever shall call on the name of the Lord shall be saved.

Jesus saying that the gospel must be preached in the entire world, then the end would come, and Paul stating that the gospel had been preached in all of the world and to every creature-

Matthew 24:14
*14 And **this gospel of the kingdom shall be preached in all the world** for a witness unto all nations; and **then shall the end come**.*

Romans 10:17-18
17 So then faith cometh by hearing, and hearing by the word of God.
*18 But I say, Have they not heard? Yes verily, **their sound went into all the earth, and their words unto the ends of the world**.*

Romans 16:26
*26 But now is made manifest, and by the scriptures of the prophets, according to the commandment of the everlasting God, **made known to all nations** for the obedience of faith:*

Colossians 1:5-6, 23
*5 For the hope which is laid up for you in heaven, whereof **ye heard before in the word of the truth of the gospel**;*
*6 Which is come unto you, **as it is in all the world**; and bringeth forth fruit, as it doth also in you, since the day ye heard of it, and knew the grace of God in truth:*

*23 If ye continue in the faith grounded and settled, and be not moved away from the hope of **the gospel, which ye have heard, and which was preached to every creature which is under heaven**; whereof I Paul am made a minister;*

John stating that because there were many antichrists present at the time he was writing his letters, it was a sign that they were living in the 'last time' (similar to last day, latter days, end of days, end of age / world)-

1 John 2:18
*18 Little children, **it is the last time**: and as ye have heard that antichrist shall come, even now are there many antichrists; whereby **we know that it is the last time**.*

The writer of Hebrews (who I personally believe is Paul) stating that Jesus appeared at the end of the world to put away sin-

Hebrews 9:26
26 For then must he often have suffered since the foundation of the world:

*but **now once in the end of the world hath he appeared to put away sin by the sacrifice of himself.***

The Dilemma?

Obviously, common sense would tell us that in the case of a declared 'end of the world', there can't be more than one 'end' that scripture is referring to. Either it refers to a coming 'end' in the future, or it has to be in the past. Both the futurist and historicist eschatological viewpoints perceive a coming cataclysmic end to the way things are now. They both look forward to a literal new heaven and earth where the wicked will be judged and cast into hell, or outer darkness. However, the problem that is presented with this view is that it must unapologetically deny that these letters had any meaning at all to the intended audience in the first century. Also, all of the writers of the verses pointing to a first century fulfillment would have to be discredited. Why would the writer of Hebrews waste his breath and say that Jesus appeared at the end of the world if it weren't true? Why would John say that antichrists being prevalent signified that they were living in the 'last time' if it wasn't the 'last time'? If the authors of these letters were that off course in regards to their understanding of "the end", then what else in scripture should be subjected to being labeled as off course and incorrect?

Chapter Seven:
The Apple of God's Eye

For the Lord's portion is his people; Jacob is the lot of his inheritance.
He found him in a desert land, and in the waste howling wilderness; he led
him about, he instructed him, he kept him as the apple of his eye.

Deuteronomy 32:9-10

There are varying viewpoints as to who the 'apple of God's eye' is today. Unfortunately, I have yet to see this subject debated or talked about in mainstream Christendom. I have my reasons for believing why this is the case, but I'll save them for another time! Nonetheless, it is imperative that we have an accurate depiction of who the 'apple of God's eye' is. Of course, the passage above is referring to Jacob, whose name was changed to Israel.

Genesis 32:28
28 And he said, Thy name shall be called no more Jacob, but Israel: for as a prince hast thou power with God and with men, and hast prevailed.

Genesis 32:28 (AMP)
28 And He said, Your name shall be called no more Jacob [supplanter], but Israel [contender with God]; for you have contended and have power with God and with men and have prevailed.

The apple of God's eye is Israel, but just who is Israel? The great majority of Christians in the American church believe that natural, secular Israel is the 'apple of God's eye'. They believe that we are to honor the modern day nation of Israel as being God's covenant people – the "chosen ones". However, there are a growing number of people that hold a different opinion. They believe that Israel is the "one new man", which consists of Jews and Gentiles that are made new in Christ. Paul addresses this issue in his letter to the church at Ephesus:

Ephesians 2:11-22
11 Wherefore remember, that ye being in time past Gentiles in the flesh, who are called Uncircumcision by that which is called the Circumcision in the flesh made by hands;
*12 That **at that time ye were without Christ, being aliens from the commonwealth of Israel, and strangers from the covenants of promise, having no hope, and without God in the world:***
13 But now in Christ Jesus ye who sometimes were far off are made nigh by the blood of Christ.
14 For he is our peace, who hath made both one, and hath broken down the middle wall of partition between us;
15 Having abolished in his flesh the enmity, even the law of commandments contained in ordinances; for to make in himself of twain one new man, so making peace;
16 And that he might reconcile both unto God in one body by the cross, having slain the enmity thereby:
17 And came and preached peace to you which were afar off, and to them that were nigh.
18 For through him we both have access by one Spirit unto the Father.
19 Now therefore ye are no more strangers and foreigners, but fellowcitizens with the saints, and of the household of God;
20 And are built upon the foundation of the apostles and prophets, Jesus Christ himself being the chief corner stone;
21 In whom all the building fitly framed together groweth unto an holy temple in the Lord:
22 In whom ye also are builded together for an habitation of God through the Spirit.

Here are a few key observations from what Paul stated:

- The commonwealth of Israel is the Body of Christ, or body of believers
- Being without Christ makes one a stranger of the covenantal promises of God
- There is no hope without Christ
- The blood of Christ brings one near to God

- God had dismantled the partition between Jew and Gentile
- Jew and Gentile come together as one new man in Christ
- Jew and Gentile are reconciled to God via the cross
- Gentiles become fellow citizens through Christ
- Gentiles become fellow citizens of the household of God

In support of what Paul says in Ephesians, Paul's letter to the Romans is littered with passages that further solidify who Israel is and who Israel isn't. Perhaps in the opinion of the Pharisees and Sadducees, the most incredulous remark that Paul made was in claiming that flesh and blood had nothing to do with determining who was and who wasn't a Jew.

Romans 2:28-29
*28 For **he is not a Jew, which is one outwardly;** neither is that circumcision, which is outward in the flesh:*
*29 But **he is a Jew, which is one inwardly; and circumcision is that of the heart, in the spirit, and not in the letter;** whose praise is not of men, but of God.*

Paul making reference to there being people of Israel who are not really Israel-

Romans 9:1-8
9 I say the truth in Christ, I lie not, my conscience also bearing me witness in the Holy Ghost,
2 That I have great heaviness and continual sorrow in my heart.
3 For I could wish that myself were accursed from Christ for my brethren, my kinsmen according to the flesh:
4 Who are Israelites; to whom pertaineth the adoption, and the glory, and the covenants, and the giving of the law, and the service of God, and the promises;
5 Whose are the fathers, and of whom as concerning the flesh Christ came, who is over all, God blessed for ever. Amen.
*6 Not as though the word of God hath taken none effect. **For they are not all Israel, which are of Israel:***
*7 **Neither, because they are the seed of Abraham, are they all children: but, In Isaac shall thy seed be called.***
*8 That is, **They which are the children of the flesh, these are not the children of God: but the children of the promise are counted for the seed.***

Paul drawing reference from Hosea and his prophetic decree that there would be a people who were not known as God's people in which at some point would be identified as God's people-

Hosea 2:23
*23 And I will sow her unto me in the earth; and **I will have mercy upon her that had not obtained mercy; and I will say to them which were not my people, Thou art my people; and they shall say, Thou art my God.***

Romans 9:25-26
*25 As he saith also in Osee, **I will call them my people, which were not my people; and her beloved, which was not beloved.***
*26 And **it shall come to pass, that in the place where it was said unto them, Ye are not my people; there shall they be called the children of the living God.***

Paul continues with mentioning that it is only by faith that we are made righteous, and not by the keeping of the law-

Romans 9:30-33
30 What shall we say then? That the Gentiles, which followed not after righteousness, have attained to righteousness, even the righteousness which is of faith.
31 But Israel, which followed after the law of righteousness, hath not attained to the law of righteousness.
*32 Wherefore? **Because they sought it not by faith, but as it were by the works of the law. For they stumbled at that stumblingstone;***
33 As it is written, Behold, I lay in Sion a stumblingstone and rock of offence: and whosoever believeth on him shall not be ashamed.

The unbelieving Jews stumbled at the stumbling stone, Jesus Christ. He was the rock of offence because everything that He did and taught seemed contrary to the religious folks of that day. They were offended by the miracles and the people calling Him Messiah. They were offended by His knowledge of the law and prophets and pointing out the fact that they both were pointing to Him. They were offended by His claim to being the only begotten Son of God. Interestingly, Jesus spoke about the doom that would come upon those that were in offence:

Matthew 18:7
*Woe unto the world because of offences! for it must needs be that offences come; but **woe to that man by whom the offence cometh!***

Luke 17:1
*Then said he unto the disciples, It is impossible but that offences will come: but **woe unto him, through whom they come!***

Paul understood very well what Jesus was saying in the verses above. He expressed his anxiety and being torn because of what he knew in regards to the latter end of the unbelieving Jews:

Romans 9:1-5
1 I say the truth in Christ, I lie not, my conscience also bearing me witness in the Holy Ghost,
*2 That **I have great heaviness and continual sorrow in my heart.***
*3 **For I could wish that myself were accursed from Christ for my brethren, my kinsmen according to the flesh:***
4 Who are Israelites; to whom pertaineth the adoption, and the glory, and the covenants, and the giving of the law, and the service of God, and the promises;
5 Whose are the fathers, and of whom as concerning the flesh Christ came, who is over all, God blessed for ever. Amen.

All Israel Will Be Saved

Most people in the western church believe that there is coming a day when all of the secular nation of Israel will eventually accept Jesus Christ as Lord and Savior, and thus, all of Israel (in the flesh) will be saved. They believe that secular Israel will be provoked to jealousy and return to the Lord:

Deuteronomy 32:21
*They have moved me to jealousy with that which is not God; they have provoked me to anger with their vanities: and **I will move them to jealousy with those which are not a people; I will provoke them to anger with a foolish nation.***

Paul recalls this passage in Romans 10:19:

Romans 10:19
But I say, Did not Israel know? First Moses saith, ***I will provoke you to jealousy by them that are no people, and by a foolish nation I will anger you.***

Paul begins Romans 10 with stating that his heart's desire and prayer is for Israel (first century Israel) to be saved. The problem, according to Paul, was that they did not know God (Romans 10:2) and were stubborn and sought righteousness via the law and not by faith in Jesus (Romans 10:4-11).

This brings us to Romans 11, a point of contention regarding the salvation of Israel. Paul makes the point early on in the chapter that God has not forsaken Israel because even he was an Israelite (Romans 11:1). He recalls the story of Elijah and his pleading with God regarding the wicked state of Israel. God told Elijah that He had reserved seven thousand men that had not bowed their knee to Baal (Romans 11:3-4). Paul then compares the current state of Israel to how God dealt with Israel in the past:

Romans 11:5
5 Even so then at this present time also ***there is a remnant according to the election of grace.***

Romans 11:5 (AMP)
5 So too at the present time there is a remnant (a small believing minority), selected (chosen) by grace (by God's unmerited favor and graciousness).

There was a remnant – a small believing minority, which would not bow their knee to unbelief. These Hebrew Christians, Paul being one of them, confessed with their mouths and believed in their hearts that Jesus Christ was Lord (Romans 10:9-10). Romans 11:5 mentions this remnant as being the election of grace. Jesus, in His Olivet Discourse, says that the time of tribulation would be shortened for the elect's sake:

Matthew 24:21-22
21 For then shall be great tribulation, such as was not since the beginning of the world to this time, no, nor ever shall be.
*22 And except those days should be shortened, there should no flesh be saved: but **for the elect's sake those days shall be shortened.***

This remnant (Hebrew Christians) coupled with the believing Gentiles constituted the Body of Christ, or the church. This was the Israel of God, as described by Paul in his letter to the Galatians:

Galatians 6:15-16
*15 For **in Christ Jesus neither circumcision availeth any thing, nor uncircumcision, but a new creature.***
*16 And **as many as walk according to this rule, peace be on them, and mercy, and upon the Israel of God.***

It is the Israel of God that is saved. Once again, the Israel of God consisted of Hebrew Christians and believing Gentiles. To this day, the Israel of God, which is the church, consists of all those that believe in Jesus. Nothing has changed. Nothing will change. The church is eternal. The Israel of God is eternal.

In his letter to the Ephesians, Paul ends a prayer with a statement about the everlasting nature of the church:

Ephesians 3:20-21
20 Now unto him that is able to do exceeding abundantly above all that we ask or think, according to the power that worketh in us,
*21 **Unto him be glory in the church by Christ Jesus throughout all ages, world without end.** Amen.*

Ephesians 3:21 (AMP)
*21 **To Him be glory in the church and in Christ Jesus throughout all generations forever and ever.** Amen (so be it).*

So far, I've established, contrary to popular opinion in the western church, that according to Paul, a true Jew is someone that is circumcised in the heart – someone that has faith in Jesus Christ. Also, according to Paul, natural / secular Israel is not the Israel of God. In Revelation, the Lord reveals to John on two different occasions in the letter that the gathering of unbelieving Jews was the synagogue of Satan:

Revelation 2:9
*9 I know thy works, and tribulation, and poverty, (but thou art rich) and **I know the blasphemy of them which say they are Jews, and are not, but are the synagogue of Satan.***

Revelation 3:9
*9 Behold, **I will make them of the synagogue of Satan, which say they are Jews, and are not, but do lie**; behold, I will make them to come and worship before thy feet, and to know that I have loved thee.*

Throughout Romans 11, Paul talks about how the unbelieving Jews were blinded, and were branches broken off of the tree (Israel of God). The believing gentiles are grafted into the tree (Israel of God) and become partakers in the blessings and favor of God which was designated for Israel:

Romans 11:17
*17 And if some of the branches be broken off, and **thou, being a wild olive tree, wert grafted in among them, and with them partakest of the root and fatness of the olive tree;***

A tree is always nourished at its roots. The "fatness of the olive tree" refers to the tree's yield – its fruit or benefits. But Paul gives a stern warning also, stating that just as the Gentiles were easily added to the tree because of their belief, they could just as easily be cut off because of unbelief as well:

Romans 11:20-21
*20 Well; because of unbelief they were broken off, and thou standest by faith. **Be not highminded, but fear:**
21 **For if God spared not the natural branches, take heed lest he also spare not thee.***

Paul goes on to say that the unbelieving Jews could be grafted back into the tree if they begin to have faith in Jesus:

Romans 11:23-24
*23 And they also, **if they abide not still in unbelief, shall be grafted in**: for God is able to graft them in again.*
24 For if thou wert cut out of the olive tree which is wild by nature, and wert grafted contrary to nature into a good olive tree: how much more shall these, which be the natural branches, be grafted into their own olive tree?

This brings us to probably the two verses in which the majority of the western church leans on for their support for a soteriology (study of salvation) and eschatology that is determined by the status of modern day Israel.

Romans 11:25-26
*25 For I would not, brethren, that ye should be ignorant of this mystery, lest ye should be wise in your own conceits; **that blindness in part is happened to Israel, until the fulness of the Gentiles be come in.***
*26 And so **all Israel shall be saved**: as it is written, There shall come out of Sion the Deliverer, and shall turn away ungodliness from Jacob:*

Many in the western church believe that since natural Israel is still blind to the reality of Jesus being Messiah, then that means that verse 26 has not been fulfilled. According to them, how is it possible for "all Israel to be saved" when all Israel (modern day nation of Israel) hasn't accepted Jesus as Lord and Savior? They also believe that the fulness of the gentiles have not come in, and therefore, all Israel isn't saved. We are essentially in a holding pattern, watching and praying for the modern day nation of Israel to come into the knowledge of Jesus Christ. This all would seem absolutely plausible, if it were not for the context of the entire letter to the Romans! To correctly interpret Romans 11:25-26, one cannot just ignore everything that Paul had just talked about in regards to who was a true Jew (Romans 2:28-29) and his mentioning that 'all that were in Israel were not Israel' (Romans 9:6). Salvation is a spiritual matter that is available to all, but the prerequisite is faith in Jesus. The Israel of God is saved. The Israel of God is the true Israel which consists of Jews and Gentiles that become a new creature in Christ. In essence, Jesus is Israel! Earlier in this chapter, the Amplified Bible defined Israel in Genesis 32:28 as 'contender with God'. The transliteration of 'Israel' in Hebrew is *Yisra'el*. The two root words of *Yisra'el* are as follows:

Sarah - contend, have power, contend with, persist, exert one's self, persevere

'El - god, god-like one, mighty one; mighty things in nature; strength, power

It was Jesus who contended with sin and death on the cross. It was Jesus who exhibited the power over sin, death, hell and the grave. It was Jesus who was, and is, and forevermore will be The Victorious One! It is at the powerful name of Jesus that demons tremble and men are saved! All Israel is saved because all Israel is He, the man, Christ Jesus! Israel is the Body of Christ! The Israel of God is the church!

Unfounded Loyalty

Some folks may be turning beet red right now because of what I just stated, but it's the truth. Many in the western church have misappropriated the blessings and cursing found in Genesis 12. If the believer is in Christ, then he or she is the seed of Abraham and are made joint heirs to the promises that were given to Abraham. A correct understanding must come in regards to the interpretation of Genesis 12:2-3:

Genesis 12:2-3
2 And ***I will make of thee a great nation, and I will bless thee***, *and make thy name great; and thou shalt be a blessing:*
3 And ***I will bless them that bless thee, and curse him that curseth thee:*** *and in thee shall all families of the earth be blessed.*

All Christians, and specifically, those in the western church, must realize that this passage is in reference to the family of faith – the church! It is because of Abraham's faith in God that he was justified and made righteous. Likewise, it is because of our faith in Jesus that makes us justified and righteous. The household of faith is privy to the benefits of the blessings of Abraham. So, in essence, when we read the above passage, it should be read from the standpoint of God blessing the nations / people groups that bless the church (Israel of God) and cursing the nations / people groups that curse the church (Israel of God).

Many will try to label this as "replacement theology", but that is a nonsensical suggestion. This is consistent theology, and a consistent understanding of God's relationship with the people that He calls His own (the apple of His eye). There was no replacement. Israel is the same Israel. Romans 11 illustrates just that – a tree that is the Israel of God, and always will be the Israel of God – some branches (unbelieving Jews) that were broken off of the tree – some wild branches (believing Gentiles) that were grafted into the tree – the unbelieving Jews can be grafted back into the tree if they become believers – the believing Gentiles can be cut off from the tree if they fall into unbelief. The root of the tree never changes. The fruit of the tree never changes either! Thus, John the Baptist addresses the fruitlessness of the multitude in Luke 3:

Luke 3:7-9
7 Then said he to the multitude that came forth to be baptized of him, O generation of vipers, who hath warned you to flee from the wrath to come?
8 Bring forth therefore fruits worthy of repentance, and begin not to say within yourselves, We have Abraham to our father: for I say unto you, That God is able of these stones to raise up children unto Abraham.
*9 And now also **the axe is laid unto the root of the trees: every tree therefore which bringeth not forth good fruit is hewn down, and cast into the fire.***

In Matthew 7, we see Jesus speaking about the ramifications of not bearing fruit:

Part Two: The 21st Century Insane Western Church

Matthew 7:15-20
15 Beware of false prophets, which come to you in sheep's clothing, but inwardly they are ravening wolves.
*16 **Ye shall know them by their fruits**. Do men gather grapes of thorns, or figs of thistles?*
17 Even so every good tree bringeth forth good fruit; but a corrupt tree bringeth forth evil fruit.
18 A good tree cannot bring forth evil fruit, neither can a corrupt tree bring forth good fruit.
*19 **Every tree that bringeth not forth good fruit is hewn down, and cast into the fire.***
*20 **Wherefore by their fruits ye shall know them.***

The Israel of God bears fruit in all seasons. The Israel of God and its fruit are for the blessing of the nations (Genesis 12:2). The Israel of God is the tree of life whose leaves are for the healing of the nations (Revelation 22:2). Now, is there any coincidence to God's people being called the "apple" of God's eye? I think not! It was always God's intent for a people to be called His own who would steward the earth and all that was, and is, within it. The fruit that the tree yields is for humanity.

Chapter Eight:
Ascension Gifts, Spiritual Gifts, and Cessationalism

Wherefore he saith, When he ascended up on high, he led captivity captive, and gave gifts unto men.

Ephesians 4:8

Every child eagerly waits for those special times of the year when gifts will be given to them for some reason or another. Whether it's a birthday, Christmas morning, a stellar report card, graduation, or whatever it may be, children's faces will be aglow and their hearts will be warm and fuzzy with gratitude and thanks (hopefully) after receiving the gifts. But it's not just the recipient of the gift that partakes in the jubilant satisfaction. The giver of the gift (a parent, family member, or whomever), cherishes the moment of seeing that child's face light up with excitement and admiration. We see throughout scripture the listed benefits of being a giver. The giver of gifts should be just as excited, or even more so than the recipient of the gifts!

Luke 6:38
Give, and it shall be given unto you; good measure, pressed down, and shaken together, and running over, shall men give into your bosom. For with the same measure that ye mete withal it shall be measured to you again.

Malachi 3:10
Bring ye all the tithes into the storehouse, that there may be meat in mine house, and prove me now herewith, saith the Lord of hosts, if I will not open you the windows of heaven, and pour you out a blessing, that there

shall not be room enough to receive it.

Paul encouraged the saints in Corinth to give with no strings attached or no conditions:

2 Corinthians 9:7
*Every man according as he purposeth in his heart, so **let him give; not grudgingly, or of necessity:** for God loveth a cheerful giver.*

If children are excited to receive gifts, and if parents are just as excited to give gifts, then how do you think our Heavenly Father feels about giving gifts? I mean, He is the ultimate Gift Giver, isn't He?

Matthew 7:11 (Luke 11:13 is similar)
*If ye then, being evil, know how to give good gifts unto your children, **how much more shall your Father which is in heaven give good things to them that ask him?***

We can see all throughout Genesis 1 the references to God giving something, whether it be light, plants, animals, the air that we breathe, or even man. God enjoyed creating everything and the phrase "it is good" was continuously used.

Genesis 1:29-31
*29 And God said, **Behold, I have given you every herb bearing seed, which is upon the face of all the earth, and every tree, in the which is the fruit of a tree yielding seed; to you it shall be for meat.***
*30 And **to every beast of the earth, and to every fowl of the air, and to every thing that creepeth upon the earth, wherein there is life, I have given every green herb for meat: and it was so.***
*31 And **God saw every thing that he had made, and, behold, it was very good.** And the evening and the morning were the sixth day.*

God was also pleased to give the greatest gift of all, Jesus, so that man could be saved and reconciled back unto Him. We have emotions because God has emotions. We're made in the image and likeness of Him (Genesis 1:26-27). Just as we give gifts to the people that we love, God gave the greatest gift to

Ascension Gifts, Spiritual Gifts, and Cessationism | 93

the people that He loves - the world.

John 3:16
*16 For **God so loved the world, that he gave his only begotten Son**, that whosoever believeth in him should not perish, but have everlasting life.*

God was pleased with His Son dying on the cross so that we may have eternal life through Him:

Isaiah 53:10-11 (AMP)
*10 Yet **it was the will of the Lord to bruise Him**; He has put Him to grief and made Him sick. When You and He make His life an offering for sin [and He has risen from the dead, in time to come], He shall see His [spiritual] offspring, He shall prolong His days, and **the will** and **pleasure of the Lord shall prosper in His hand**.*
*11 **He shall see [the fruit] of the travail of His soul and be satisfied**; by His knowledge of Himself [which He possesses and imparts to others] shall My [uncompromisingly] righteous One, My Servant, justify many and make many righteous (upright and in right standing with God), for He shall bear their iniquities and their guilt [with the consequences, says the Lord].*

I don't think there is any dispute as to what was just mentioned. Where the division comes is in regards to spiritual gifts and whether or not they are prevalent today. There are essentially three distinct viewpoints when it comes to spiritual gifts:

1. All spiritual gifts have ceased
2. All gifts are in the process of being restored
3. All gifts are fully operational in the church today

The Cessationist

The cessationist believes that all of the gifts of the Spirit (1 Corinthians 12:8-10) have ceased, or are no longer in operation. They believe that spiritual gifts were given to the early church for the sole purpose of establishing the church. Cessationists believe that the gifts passed away well before the canon of scripture was completed. There are two passages in scripture that are used as a crutch for their argument:

1 Corinthians 13:8-12
8 Charity never faileth: **but whether there be prophecies, they shall fail; whether there be tongues, they shall cease; whether there be knowledge, it shall vanish away.**
9 For we know in part, and we prophesy in part.
10 But **when that which is perfect is come, then that which is in part shall be done away.**
11 When I was a child, I spake as a child, I understood as a child, I thought as a child: but when I became a man, I put away childish things.
12 For now we see through a glass, darkly; but then face to face: now I know in part; but then shall I know even as also I am known.

Hebrews 2:3-4
3 How shall we escape, if we neglect so great salvation; which at the first began to be spoken by the Lord, and was confirmed unto us by them that heard him;
4 **God also bearing them witness, both with signs and wonders, and with divers miracles, and gifts of the Holy Ghost,** *according to his own will?*

The cessationist believes that the church was brought to maturity via the 1st century apostolic era. Since that is the case, in their opinion, they believe that the spiritual gifts can no longer be operational and are 'done away', according to 1 Corinthians 13:10. Many preterists believe that the vanishing away of spiritual gifts is directly tied to salvation, or the sign of salvation which they attribute to the destruction of the temple in 70 AD. Hence, the significance that they see in Hebrews 2:3-4 is critical to their interpretation. Signs and wonders, according to some preterists (not all) were to accompany and validate the gospel of salvation in the first century. When the work of salvation was complete and judgment came upon those that were responsible for killing the apostles and prophets (Matthew 23:34-38, Luke 11:49), this signified the end of the age, and to the cessationist preterist, the end of spiritual gifts as well.

The 'Latter-Day' Saint

With the term 'Latter Day', I am not referring to Mormonism. I am using this term to describe the believer that believes that the gifts of the Spirit are being restored to the church today. Their viewpoint hinges on Joel's prophetic decree in Joel 2, and Peter's reaffirming that position in Acts 2. The 'latter-day' saint's eschatological position is futurism. Thus, they believe that those two passages refer to events that are to take place in what they perceive as the last days in which they believe we are living in today. They believe that signs, wonders and miracles are a sign of the 'restoration of all things'. For there to be a restoration of something, they must also believe that there was a period of time when that something was non-active. Interestingly, the 'latter-day' saint's position on spiritual gifts rides on the back of the cessationist preterist's position.

Many Christians believe that spiritual gifts are alive, well, and thriving in the church today. Unlike the cessationist, or the 'latter-day' saint, they believe that the spiritual gifts never became dormant, and they don't need to be restored because they have always been active and necessary for the progress of the church throughout the ages. There are two different sets of gifts that are given to the church by God:

1. Ascension Gifts
2. Gifts of the Spirit

Ascension Gifts

In Ephesians 4, Paul makes mention of gifts that were given to the church by God at Jesus' ascension:

Ephesians 4:8-16
8 Wherefore he saith, **When he ascended up on high, he led captivity captive, and gave gifts unto men.**
9 (Now that he ascended, what is it but that he also descended first into the

lower parts of the earth?
10 He that descended is the same also that ascended up far above all heavens, that he might fill all things.)
*11 And **he gave some, apostles; and some, prophets; and some, evangelists; and some, pastors and teachers**;*
*12 **For the perfecting of the saints, for the work of the ministry, for the edifying of the body of Christ:***
*13 **Till we all come in the unity of the faith**, and of the knowledge of the Son of God, unto a perfect man, unto the measure of the stature of the fulness of Christ:*
*14 **That we henceforth be no more children, tossed to and fro, and carried about with every wind of doctrine**, by the sleight of men, and cunning craftiness, whereby they lie in wait to deceive;*
*15 But **speaking the truth in love**, may grow up into him in all things, which is the head, even Christ:*
*16 From whom the whole body fitly joined together and compacted by that which every joint supplieth, according to the effectual working in the measure of every part, **maketh increase of the body unto the edifying of itself in love.***

These ascension gifts were given to the church as structural support and organization of the body of Christ. Though there are different functions of each gift, they are all equally necessary in the growth and productivity of the church (corporately and communally). A general description of each is as follows:

Apostle – The sent one; graced with the ability to enter a region or territory and tear down, plant, rebuild and restore. Uncanny boldness to confront false doctrine and false teaching, and to bring rebuke and correction

Prophet – The seer; one that spends time in the presence of God and is gifted in the revealing of God's real-time plan for a region or people group; works closely with apostle to strategize and map out 'game plans' to impact the region

Evangelist – God's 'paratrooper and infantry division'; given assignments from God to go in and out of the enemy's camp to drop spiritual bombs of love; brings the gospel of Jesus Christ to the people where they're at and has the ability to blend in and associate to gain trust and be palatable to the unlearned or non-believer

Pastor – A shepherd to the flock; the caretaker and overseer of the church; addresses the spiritual, physical, psychological and emotional needs of the people; supernatural kindness and compassion are his or her portion

Teacher – Skilled laborer in ascertaining the Word of God; has a Berean spirit and will always search the scriptures to see if something is correct; will convey truths of scripture systematically; exemplifies patience and temperance when explaining a subject that may be hard to understand

A healthy, mature church must have all of these entities present and active. This is not to be dogmatic, insinuating that one must have the title of apostle, prophet, evangelist, pastor and teacher. An individual may very well be gifted in multiple areas. But the fact remains that these gifts are given to the church by God, and their primary purpose is found in Ephesians 4:12:

Ephesians 4:12
12 For the perfecting of the saints, for the work of the ministry, for the edifying of the body of Christ:

The 'perfecting of the saints' is the maturation of the believer. Growing in the knowledge of the Lord and becoming like Him is difficult when we're on an island. Part of the process of being perfected is being in relationships with other saints (the community of believers – the church) in which we are held accountable. Christian 'Lone Rangers' can find themselves drifting away from truth and isolated from Christian familial support. Just as the early church was a tight-knit community of believers, the church today, local, and then corporate, should be a tight-knit community as well. Becoming perfected or mature creates an atmosphere where strife and division cannot sneak in unaware. Perfecting is also in regards to our nature changing from that of a 'ravenous wolf' to that of 'sheep'. Instead of hatred, envy and jealousy (traits of our 'old man'), others will know that we are mature in the faith because of our love walk:

Ephesians 3:17
That Christ may dwell in your hearts by faith; that ye, **being rooted and grounded in love,**

John 13:35
By this shall all men know that ye are my disciples, if ye have love one to another.

John 17:23
I in them, and thou in me, **that they may be made perfect in one***; and that the world may know that thou hast sent me, and hast loved them, as thou hast loved me.*

    The 'work of the ministry' is just that – the work of the ministry! It's the preaching, the teaching, the evangelism / outreach, visiting the orphans, widows, the shut in, and the imprisoned. The work of the ministry is the declaration of who Jesus Christ is, not just in words, but in actions. The work of the ministry is the Lord's work. Jesus declared and confirmed that He was sent to do the following (reading the words of Isaiah about Himself):

Luke 4:18-19
18 The Spirit of the Lord is upon me, because he hath anointed me to **preach the gospel to the poor***; he hath sent me to* **heal the brokenhearted***, to* **preach deliverance to the captives***, and* **recovering of sight to the blind***, to* **set at liberty them that are bruised***,*
19 To **preach the acceptable year of the Lord***.*

    The church is the body of Christ in which continues to do the work that Jesus did. In John 14:12, Jesus mentions to the disciples that the believer would do even greater works than He did in the earth. Jesus wasn't talking about the believer moving in more tangible power than He did, but he was speaking in terms of the volume of work that would be done. Jesus knew the future of the church and its dynamic explosion and impact in the earth. This wasn't just an isolated foreshadowing either in which compartmentalizes the first century church from the rest of church history. Jesus' hope and prayer for the church to be one included the generations that would hear the gospel decades, years, and centuries down the line.

John 17:20-21
*20 Neither pray I for these alone, **but for them also which shall believe on me through their word;***
21 That they all may be one; as thou, Father, art in me, and I in thee, that they also may be one in us: that the world may believe that thou hast sent me.

Though we are nearly 2000 years removed from the apostolic era, we still believe on Jesus through the words of the apostles in the first century. Paul, who authored the letters that make up nearly two-thirds of the New Testament, has shaped and molded our Christian perspective. God took a man that was an enemy and terror to the saints, transformed his heart and made him the carrier of the gospel to the masses outside of Israel. If that isn't a miracle, I don't know what is! But that same transformation happens today in many believers' lives, leaving the 'old man' behind and walking in newness of life with a heart set ablaze and full of zeal for Jesus!

Gifts of the Spirit

Perhaps more 'controversial' than the ascension gifts are the gifts of the Spirit. Paul speaks in detail about these gifts in 1 Corinthians 12:

1 Corinthians 12:1-11
1 Now concerning spiritual gifts, brethren, I would not have you ignorant.

2 Ye know that ye were Gentiles, carried away unto these dumb idols, even as ye were led.
3 Wherefore I give you to understand, that no man speaking by the Spirit of God calleth Jesus accursed: and that no man can say that Jesus is the Lord, but by the Holy Ghost.
4 Now there are diversities of gifts, but the same Spirit.
5 And there are differences of administrations, but the same Lord.
6 And there are diversities of operations, but it is the same God which worketh all in all.
7 But the manifestation of the Spirit is given to every man to profit withal.
8 For **to one is given by the Spirit the word of wisdom; to another the word of knowledge by the same Spirit;**
9 **To another faith by the same Spirit; to another the gifts of healing by the same Spirit;**
10 To **another the working of miracles; to another prophecy; to another discerning of spirits; to another divers kinds of tongues; to another the interpretation of tongues:**
11 But all these worketh that one and the selfsame Spirit, dividing to every man severally as he will.

Paul begins this passage by stating that he did not want the reader to be ignorant concerning spiritual gifts. He sheds light on the truth of the significance of Holy Spirit - not just concerning spiritual gifts, but in regards to the knowledge of who the Holy One of Israel is. It is Holy Spirit who leads us into all truth. Paul boasts in the role of Holy Spirit to set the table for discussing the various workings of Holy Spirit in more detail. In verses 4 thru 6, Paul talks about there being different gifts, administrations and operations, but the source of them is one and the same – Holy Spirit, Jesus (Lord) and God – the Three-In-One Source. So, if God is the same and never changes, then we must conclude that Holy Spirit is the same and never changes as well. If God is the same yesterday, today and forever, then Holy Spirit is the same yesterday, today and forever.

In verse 7, Paul gives the reason for the gifts of the Spirit and their manifestations (public display of power). He says that they are given to every man to profit with. The Greek term for 'profit with' is *spympherō,* which means to bear or bring together, to collect or contribute in order to help, to be profitable and expedient.₁ In other words, the gifts are given to men to help bring men together; to gather resources to help carry out a mandate, or an agenda.

The nine gifts of the Spirit are as follows:

1. **Word of Wisdom** – The ability, by the Spirit of God, to give wise counsel based on experience; to know the right words to say and when to say them
2. **Word of Knowledge** – The ability, by the Spirit of God, to reveal hidden things in a man or woman's life and in their past history
3. **Faith** – The supernatural gift to believe the impossible; The Spirit of God assisting in the overriding of unbelief in one's heart
4. **Healing** – The ability, by the Spirit of God, to lay hands on the sick and expect healing
5. **Working of Miracles** – The ability, by the Spirit of God, to create a way out of no way; to be able to defy logic and the parameters of natural law and bring to fruition the substance of things hoped for and the evidence of things not seen (Hebrews 11:1)
6. **Prophecy** – By the Spirit of God, the foretelling of the mind, counsel and will of God for individuals, nations and people groups
7. **Discernment** – Heightened spiritual awareness and the ability to decipher and identify changes in a spiritual climate or atmosphere
8. **Tongues** – A Spirit-driven, heavenly language not for the natural ears of man, but for communication with God and the building up of the inner man (spirit-man)
9. **Interpretation of Tongues** – The ability, by the Spirit of God, to interpret unknown tongues, or a heavenly language

According to Paul, these gifts are distributed to men

according to how God sees fit. A number of these gifts are dependent on others, and thus, one may demonstrate multiple gifts of the Spirit. Yet, there may be some that are only capable of moving in one of the gifts. Again, it is to the discretion of God as to what gifts are opened for individuals. These individuals are part of a corporate body - the body of Christ. As Paul alludes to in verses 11 thru 27, the body of Christ is made up of many members with different abilities and gifts, but each member needs the other members in the body to fully function.

As mentioned earlier, Paul says that the gifts were for men to profit with. But the collective profiting is for the body of Christ – the church:

1 Corinthians 12:25-27
*25 That **there should be no schism in the body**; but that **the members should have the same care one for another**.*
26 And whether one member suffer, all the members suffer with it; or one member be honoured, all the members rejoice with it.
*27 Now **ye are the body of Christ, and members in particular**.*

This passage speaks to the unifying character of the early church and its focus on caring for one another and making sure that not one of the members of the body lacked in any way. Compassion being the hallmark of Jesus' ministry, the act of placing one's self in a brother or sister's shoes and feeling their pain was commonplace. The gifts of the Spirit were given to the church for this purpose. They were a necessity then, and they are definitely a necessity now. Not only are they for the benefit of the body – the church, but they are also for a sign to the unbeliever. The cohesion and caring for one another through the utilization of spiritual gifts in the church is what verifies the message of the gospel. Paul commented on the dynamic duo of word and power:

1 Corinthians 2:4
*And my speech and my preaching was not with enticing words of man's wisdom, but in **demonstration of the Spirit and of power**:*

1 Corinthians 4:20
*For **the kingdom of God is not in word, but in power.***

1 Thessalonians 1:5
*For **our gospel came not unto you in word only, but also in power, and in the Holy Ghost**, and in much assurance; as ye know what manner of men we were among you for your sake.*

Cessationalism is Anti-Kingdom

One of the most visible signs of the kingdom being present is the demonstration of supernatural power through Holy Spirit. From the days of Jesus' ministry, to the early church, to today, and forever more, the gifts of the Spirit will validate and signify the kingdom has come. Jesus said that it was the casting out of devils which lets the people know that the kingdom was present:

Luke 11:20
But if I with the finger of God cast out devils, no doubt the kingdom of God is come upon you.

The people were absolutely astonished and drawn in by not only His words, but the power accompanying His words:

Luke 4:32, 36
*32And they were astonished at his doctrine: for **his word was with power.***

*36And they were all amazed, and spake among themselves, saying, What a word is this! **for with authority and power he commandeth the unclean spirits, and they come out.***

To assume that the ascension gifts and gifts of the Spirit are no longer operational is the assertion that God no longer desires for His church to grow and prosper. The church did not cease to exist in the first century, or after the apostolic era. The church age, which is synonymous with the kingdom age, has no end:

Ephesians 3:21
*21 Unto him be glory in the church by Christ Jesus **throughout all ages, world without end. Amen.***

The cessationist finds himself at odds with Paul in regards to God not taking away gifts and callings for His people:

Romans 11:29
*29 For the **gifts and calling of God are without repentance**.*

James also addresses gifts, and how God doesn't change his mind when they are given:

James 1:17
Every good gift and every perfect gift is from above, and cometh down from the Father of lights, with whom is no variableness, neither shadow of turning.

One of the main 'crutches' that the cessationist uses is an interpretation that is terribly taken out of context. In regards to 1 Corinthians 13, the context is absolutely critical. The reader must first acknowledge what the 'book ends' of the chapter are:

1 Corinthians 13:1
*Though I speak with the tongues of men and of angels, and have not **charity**, I am become as sounding brass, or a tinkling cymbal.*

1 Corinthians 13:13
*And now abideth faith, hope, charity, these three; but **the greatest of these is charity**.*

The context of the chapter is charity (love). 1 Corinthians 13 is what is commonly called "the love chapter". What Paul is doing throughout the verses sandwiched in between the first and last verse of the chapter is comparing "temporal things" to something that is eternal, and that is love. God is love and He is eternal.

Take a look at the last verse of 1 Corinthians 12:

1 Corinthians 12:31
*31 But covet earnestly the best gifts: and **yet shew I unto you a more excellent way.***

What was 'the more excellent way'? It is love. Something that must also be considered is this - What logical reasoning would there be for Paul to say in 1 Corinthians 12:31, "covet earnestly the best gifts", and yet, in the following chapter, those gifts that he told the people to covet would cease at some point? Not only that, but take a look at the first verse of 1 Corinthians 14:

1 Corinthians 14:1
Follow after charity, and desire spiritual gifts, but rather that ye may prophesy.

When considering 1 Corinthians 12:31 and 1 Corinthians 14:1, it is absolutely apparent that Paul is using 1 Corinthians 13 as an 'aside' so that his audience would not be caught up in the over-emphasis of gifts, but to identify the primary purpose of the church - to demonstrate love. It is from this purpose, a posture of love, that they, and we, then begin to move in the gifts of the Spirit.

"That which is perfect" (1 Corinthians 13:10) is in reference to love, not a literal, physical coming of the Lord. This is the major misunderstanding of not only most preterists, but cessationists in general. When 'perfect love' is demonstrated in the church and comes to a region / territory, there is harmony and unity, no strife, no division, and everyone is walking in the ways of the Lord. This is the case, whether in the body (alive) or absent from the body (in the literal presence of the Lord eternally after physical death).

We see Jesus praying for this state of being in John 17:

John 17:23
*I in them, and thou in me, **that they may be made perfect in one;** and that the world may know that thou hast sent me, and hast loved them, as thou hast loved me.*

John speaking of 'perfect love'-

1 John 2:5
But whoso **keepeth his word, in him verily is the love of God perfected**: hereby know we that we are in him.

1 John 4:12
No man hath seen God at any time. **If we love one another**, God dwelleth in us, and **his love is perfected in us**.

1 John 4:18
There is no fear in love; but **perfect love casteth out fear**: because fear hath torment. He that feareth is not made perfect in love.

Paul's farewell address in his 2nd letter to the Corinthians as a reminder-

2 Corinthians 13:11
Finally, brethren, farewell. **Be perfect**, be of good comfort, **be of one mind, live in peace;** and **the God of love and peace shall be with you**.

To "be perfect" is to be mature in the things of God. The immaturity of the Corinthian church was absolutely evident at the beginning of Paul's first letter to the church.

1 Corinthians 1:10
Now **I beseech you**, brethren, by the name of our Lord Jesus Christ, **that ye all speak the same thing, and that there be no divisions among you; but that ye be perfectly joined together in the same mind and in the same judgment.**

Issues of pride (1 Corinthians 4:18, 5:2, 6-7), fornication (1 Corinthians 5:1, 6:18), vain disputes in public (1 Corinthians 6:1-8), improper mindsets regarding marriage (1 Corinthians 7), and misconduct in the church (1 Corinthians 11:18-34) were all extremely valid motives for what Paul wrote in chapter 13. The Corinthian church was an absolute mess! Unfortunately, many of our churches today fit the same description! They lack maturity because they have shunned the very things that were set up for the church to facilitate maturity.

A mature church will be known in a region for the love within that church (member for member) and for the love it has for the surrounding community and humanity as a whole. We must always take on the mind of God - 'God so loved the world'. We demonstrate God's love through our love / charity, compassion, the giving of ourselves and our daily sacrifice for the things that move God's heart.

So, in essence, a church that is operating in the fulness of this thing called LOVE will be at a point where gifts are unnecessary. Will this ever happen? Strangely, the answer is "Yes and No." Yes, when we die and are in the literal presence of the Lord forever (face to face - 1 Corinthians 13:12). No, because the church is eternal (Ephesians. 3:21) and the gospel must be preached from generation to generation, world (age) without end. There will always be work to do, and new people to 'be perfected' (come into the knowledge of God and His kingdom). Remember, the ascension gifts (Apostle, Prophet, Evangelist, Pastor and Teacher) are for the PERFECTING OF THE SAINTS (Ephesians 4:11-12). There is NO END to the church age. The church has been firmly established in the earth forever to be the representation of God's love in the earth - which is the message of the gospel.

The focus of 1 Corinthians 13 should not be, and IS NOT, gifts ceasing. Love is the Source from which all gifts of God flow. Besides, as mentioned earlier, God does not take away gifts:

Romans 11:29 *(AMP)*
For God's gifts and His call are irrevocable. [He never withdraws them when once they are given, and He does not change His mind about those to whom He gives His grace or to whom He sends His call.]

So the question is how can the cessationist come to the conclusion that gifts are not active in the church today? This seems absolutely contradictory of scripture and inconsistent with a church and kingdom that is eternal. How is it possible to have an eternal kingdom that increases in size and influence infinitely when the gifts that were given to the church to assist in church / kingdom growth and influence are no longer operational? To me, this seems rather double-minded and is, in essence, an anti-kingdom mindset that absolutely needs to be destroyed.

Chapter Nine:
Predestination or Free Will?

And the world passeth away, and the lust thereof: but he that doeth the will of God abideth for ever.

1 John 2:17

Perhaps one of the most divisive topics in all of Christian theological history is the debate between those that subscribe to a free-will view of scripture, and those that subscribe to a pre-destined, or, determined view of scripture (determinism). Without going into a lot of historical detail, this debate goes back all the way to the 5th century. Augustine 'laid the gauntlet' in favor of predestination by stating, essentially, that man could do nothing right, he is incapable of accepting salvation, and that God chooses who He brings to salvation. In the early 16th century, Martin Luther (1483–1546) summed up his position by stating that man, by nature, lacks the ability to do good. This, of course, falls in line with the sentiments of Augustine. Later, John Calvin (1509-1564) would pick up the mantle of the Protestant Reformation that Martin Luther had sparked with his *Ninety-Five Theses on the Power and Efficacy of Indulgences*, in which openly criticized the Roman Catholic church and the pope. John Wycliffe (1320-1384) and Jan Hus (1369-1415), spiritual predecessors of Martin Luther, first sought to reform the Roman Catholic Church.

In 1963, a booklet written by David N. Steele and Curtis C. Thomas, entitled *The Five Points of Calvinism Defined, Defended, Documented*, summarizes the five key elements and theological piers of Calvinism. The mnemonic "TULIP" is used to help remember the five points that follow:

1. **Total Depravity** – The belief that after the fall, man became a slave to sin; people are naturally inclined to reject God and His rule and be selfish; man is incapable of choosing to follow God due to his sinful nature
2. **Unconditional Election** – God chooses who He will save, not based on individual merit, or even faith of that individual, but based on His mercy alone; from eternity, God chose who He would and would not extend His mercy to – to them that received His mercy, salvation – to them that did not receive His mercy, wrath and judgment
3. **Limited Atonement** – The atonement of Jesus's death is solely for the elect; it is intended for some, but not all
4. **Irresistible Grace** – The assertion that the saving grace of God cannot be 'out-done', or revoked by any of the elect. When God intently saves someone, that person cannot lose their salvation; Holy Spirit causes the elect sinner to repent and believe freely in Jesus Christ
5. **Perseverance of the Saints** – The elect (saints – the ones that are set apart) will continue in the faith until the end; those that 'fall away' or become unbelievers either never had true faith and were not part of the elect, or they will return to the faith at some point in the future

Tensions began to ratchet up when a man by the name of Jacobus Arminius (1560-1609) challenged the position of Calvinism. Arminius began to serve as a professor of theology at the University of Leiden in 1603. While there, he penned many books that combated the standard Reformed theology. Arminius believed that predestination and unconditional election pigeon-holed God into being the creator of evil. Instead of unconditional election, he believed that election was based on the faith of the believer.

Similar to how followers of Calvin composed The Five Points of Calvinism, the followers of Arminius (Arminians, also called Remonstrants) composed what is known as *The Five Articles of Remonstrance*. These propositions were written in 1610, one year after the death of Jacobus Arminius. Below is a brief summary of the articles:

- **Article I** – God determined to save those out of the fallen, sinful race that believe in Jesus; the unbelieving shall be left in sin, under wrath, and alienated from Christ (John 3:36)
- **Article II** – No man, except for the believer, enjoys redemption and the forgiveness of sins that resulted from Jesus Christ, the Savior of the world, dying on the cross (John 3:16, 1 John 2:2)
- **Article III** – No man can save himself; it is necessary for every man to be born again and renewed in his mind so that he can rightly comprehend that which is good (John 15:5)
- **Article IV** – Without the grace of God, man cannot do anything good and cannot resist evil temptations; however, the grace of God is not irresistible, as scripture yields precedent to such, where men resisted the Holy Ghost (Acts 7)
- **Article V** – He that is in Christ is fully equipped and capable of crucifying the flesh and being victorious over the propensity to sin with the assistance of Holy Spirit; he cannot be plucked out of the hands of Christ (John 10:28); however, no conclusion has been made in regards to whether or not he is capable of falling away back into the cauldron of a wickedly dark world and the ultimate result of him turning away from the holy doctrine that he received

As you can see, the Calvinists and the Arminians make good points with scriptural support for both theological viewpoints. But it's quite apparent how much on the polar opposite ends of the spectrum both of these views are in regards to God's relationship to man and its affect on perceived soteriology (doctrine of salvation). To state it plainly, Calvinism teaches that God is sovereign and man is merely 'puppets on a string' and are used in God's universal orchestra of affairs. Consequently, man has no input or responsibility in regards to salvation because it is all the plan of God. Arminians, on the other hand, sees things from a different perspective, in that they believe that man's role is in responding to the message of the gospel with his faith in Christ.

Scriptural Support for Predestination and Free Will

Below is a list of just a few verses that either supports the claims of Predestination (Calvinists) or Free Will (Arminians). This is not an exhaustive list. I'm pretty sure that there are many more verses that can be added to support one, or both. But I believe that these few passages can paint a clearer picture for the non-theologians!

Passages supporting Predestination-

Jeremiah 1:5
Before I formed thee in the belly I knew thee; *and before thou camest forth out of the womb I sanctified thee, and I ordained thee a prophet unto the nations.*

John 15:16, 19
16 ***Ye have not chosen me, but I have chosen you****, and ordained you, that ye should go and bring forth fruit, and that your fruit should remain: that whatsoever ye shall ask of the Father in my name, he may give it you.*

*19 If ye were of the world, the world would love his own: but because ye are not of the world, but **I have chosen you out of the world**, therefore the world hateth you.*

Romans 8:28-30
28 And we know that all things work together for good to them that love God, to them who are the called according to his purpose.
29 ***For whom he did foreknow, he also did predestinate to be conformed***

to the image of his Son, that he might be the firstborn among many brethren.
30 **Moreover whom he did predestinate, them he also called:** and whom he called, them he also justified: and whom he justified, them he also glorified.

Ephesians 1:3-5, 9-11
3 Blessed be the God and Father of our Lord Jesus Christ, who hath blessed us with all spiritual blessings in heavenly places in Christ:
4 **According as he hath chosen us in him before the foundation of the world,** that we should be holy and without blame before him in love:
5 **Having predestinated us unto the adoption of children by Jesus Christ to himself, according to the good pleasure of his will,**

9 Having made known unto us the mystery of his will, according to his good pleasure which he hath purposed in himself:
10 That in the dispensation of the fulness of times he might gather together in one all things in Christ, both which are in heaven, and which are on earth; even in him:
11 **In whom also we have obtained an inheritance, being predestinated according to the purpose of him who worketh all things after the counsel of his own will:**

Passages supporting Free Will-

Joshua 24:15
15 And if it seem evil unto you to serve the Lord, **choose you this day whom ye will serve;** whether the gods which your fathers served that were on the other side of the flood, or the gods of the Amorites, in whose land ye dwell: but as for me and my house, we will serve the Lord.

Isaiah 7:15
15 Butter and honey shall he eat, **that he may know to refuse the evil, and choose the good.**

Isaiah 56:4
4 For thus saith the Lord unto the eunuchs that keep my sabbaths, and **choose the things that please me, and take hold of my covenant;**

John 3:15-16
15 That **whosoever believeth in him should not perish,** but have eternal life.
16 For God so loved the world, that he gave his only begotten Son, that **whosoever believeth in him should not perish,** but have everlasting life.

Revelation 3:5
5 He that overcometh, the same shall be clothed in white raiment; and I will not blot out his name out of the book of life, but I will confess his name before my Father, and before his angels.

The Quandary?

There are three major problems that arise due to the conflicting viewpoints of predestination and free-will:

1. Predestination can create apathetic Christians
2. Free-Will can create dogmatic and judgmental Christians
3. Predestination and Free-will causes a distinguishable schism in the Body of Christ

One that is a proponent of predestination, or determinism, can be susceptible to becoming detached from the reality of the state of the world with feelings of having no obligation to make the world a better place. In his mind, God is holy, God is sovereign, and God will do whatever God wants to do, with, or even without his involvement. The subscriber to predestination can feel as if there is nothing that he can do to change the course of history. Therefore, he chooses to not become involved in the different aspects of society because he doesn't feel a burden to do so. Furthermore, "God's 'irresistible grace' and the 'perseverance of the saints'" will, for some, become "legal license" to continue in ungodly behavior without feeling a need to change. The belief that there is nothing that a person that is saved can do to nullify his being 'saved' can be extremely problematic because it lends itself to belief systems and mindsets that are contrary to the ways of God, which are duly noted by the Arminians.

On the other hand, the proponent of free will can find himself overly focused on carrying out religious practices and in a place of uncertainty in regards to their identity in Christ. A 'works oriented' mindset can put unwarranted stress and anxiety on that individual to the point that he is unable to 'rest in the Lord'. It can lead to self-condemnation and the feeling of not being worthy of God's love and grace. Looking through the prism of free will can also lead to someone acting as the 'religious police'. He begins to point out every flaw that he sees in another, while not fully understanding the kingdom concept of 'planting, watering, and seeing God make the increase' (1 Corinthians 3:6-8). Just as the Pharisees were caught up in how they appeared on the 'outside', some that hold a free will perspective do their best to appear holy and righteous on the outside, but on the inside they are rotting and in a desert place because of the striving to be something without the assistance of Holy Spirit.

Perhaps most worrisome is the division within the body of Christ that has been created because of these two polarizing perspectives. Entire movements as well as denominations were off-shoots of both of these ideologies. While the predestination camp is generally found in churches that are Reformed or Presbyterian, the free-will camp is found in churches that are Pentecostal, Seventh-Day Adventist, Holiness and General Baptist. Unfortunately, this theological rift between the two camps has impeded the corporate unity that is necessary to spark sustained revival in the western church. It caters to the disjunction and dysfunction of the church in America and is one of the undergirding systemic issues that is preventing the church from being what God desires it to be.

Chapter Ten:
Prosperity and Poverty

A feast is made for laughter, and wine maketh merry: but money answereth all things.
                              Ecclesiastes 10:19

"The pastor shouldn't be driving that type of car!" "How is he living in the lap of luxury when his congregation is poor, with many on the verge of homelessness?" "That pastor is nothing but a pimp, and y'all are the tricks!" "I'll never go to that church because they are money-hungry." "I'm not paying for a pastor's private jet!" "Why are they passing the collection plate around for the 3rd time?" "All they ever preach about is money and giving!"

I just listed a few comments that you may hear or read from time to time when it comes to the subject matter of money and the church. More specifically, it is what's seemingly done with the money that is the concern to most of the people that make those types of comments. Are the comments over the top? Perhaps, yes. But the comments do raise a legitimate question about how money should be viewed in the church and what it should be used for.

Negative Connotations of Prosperity Preaching

It's almost like clockwork when mainstream media focuses in on a ministry, or a pastor, and the term "prosperity gospel", or "prosperity preacher" is used. Those terms are typically used for what are considered 'Mega-Churches', or the ministers of these churches. One particular stream within evangelical circles seems to be the brunt of the majority of prosperity gospel labeling – the Word of Faith movement. Without naming any ministries in particular (because that is not the focus of this book), the word of faith movement is distinct because it elects to preach primarily from the standpoint of the promises of God in scripture. The promises of favor, blessing, increase, enlarged territories and influence, as well as money are central to the core of the movement. The principle of sowing and reaping is taught 'ad nausem', according to some, to the point of being turned off and viewing the church or the pastor as having ulterior motives.

'Name it, Claim it' - a common 'mantra' that is used within the Word of Faith camp. I used the term 'mantra' on purpose because it best describes the ideology. The word mantra comes from Sanskrit and means "tool/instrument of thought". They are sounds, syllables, words or groups of words that are repeated with the goal of creating a positive transformation within the person.[1] The Word of Faith movement teaches that there is power in our words and we have the power to create what we desire with our words.

Romans 10:17
So then faith cometh by hearing, and hearing by the word of God.

Word of Faith pastors preach from the standpoint of our words having the power to shape every aspect of our lives, including our faith. Accordingly, it is by faith that miracles happen and blessing comes. Abraham was blessed because of his faithfulness. Hence, according to the Word of Faith camp, since we are the seed of Abraham through Christ Jesus, our faith should produce the same results of blessings and favor.

Where this movement gets a bit questionable is in regards to believing that one cannot truly be blessed until or unless they have 'something to show for it'. Wealth, good jobs, extravagant material things, no debt, a big house, big car and exquisite clothes should be the hallmark of someone that is truly blessed, according to pastors in the Word of Faith community. Being 'broke, busted and disgusted' is not a sign of a child of the King, according to them. Someone that is experiencing lack, poverty, debt, bad health condition and all types of negative things are looked upon as having done something sinful, which has given Satan a breach into that person's life to hinder them economically, mentally, spiritually and emotionally. I guess they must have skipped over the story of Job!

Many view prosperity preaching as being in love with money, which they express is the root of all evil.

1 Timothy 6:10
*10 For **the love of money is the root of all evil**: which while some coveted after, they have erred from the faith, and pierced themselves through with many sorrows.*

Critics of prosperity preaching say that it promotes a culture of greed and lust. They see the message of prosperity preaching as being contrary to what Jesus, as well as the apostles, taught in regards to not being focused on money and material things. The critics also see prosperity preaching as a form of abuse, manipulation and mind control. Constantly telling the congregation that they need to sow in order to be blessed financially, while members of that congregation have unpaid bills and are struggling to make ends meet, is seen as ungodly and teaching the people how not to operate in wisdom. Furthermore, critics often question the necessity of a pastor to have fine things when his congregation is visibly struggling from paycheck to paycheck. "Do you really need to ride around in that $100,000 car? Do you really need to live in that 9,500 sq. ft. home worth 2.5 million dollars?" These are absolutely legitimate questions that critics raise when they see a pastor that is living 'high on the hog', especially when that pastor has no other means of income (business, books, etc.). And meanwhile, the one that is supposed to 'shepherd' the people is seemingly oblivious to the financial hardship of his own sheep.

Something appears to be wrong with that picture. Would that have been the case in the 1st century church?

The Poverty Persona

For every Christian that is supportive of the overall message of the "prosperity gospel", there is another that supports the exact opposite of it. I call this mindset the 'poverty persona'. This type of Christian believes that we should not be consumed with the pursuit of wealth because it is the antithesis of what Jesus taught to his disciples, as well as the people that listened to Him.

Matthew 16:24
Then said Jesus unto his disciples, If any man will come after me, **let him deny himself***, and take up his cross, and follow me.*

They believe that the 'denying of self' is the denial of self-gratification that would come from wealth and prosperity. Seeking money and material things that bring 'comfort' are frowned upon and seen as a hindrance to being a Christian and preaching the gospel. In Matthew 19, we read of a young man having a dialog with Jesus in regards to the things that he needed to do to have eternal life. The response of Jesus is the foundation of those that have the poverty persona:

Matthew 19:16-24
16 And, behold, one came and said unto him, Good Master, what good thing shall I do, that I may have eternal life?
17 And he said unto him, Why callest thou me good? there is none good but one, that is, God: but if thou wilt enter into life, keep the commandments.
18 He saith unto him, Which? Jesus said, Thou shalt do no murder, Thou shalt not commit adultery, Thou shalt not steal, Thou shalt not bear false witness,
19 Honour thy father and thy mother: and, Thou shalt love thy neighbour as thyself.
20 The young man saith unto him, All these things have I kept from my youth up: what lack I yet?
21 Jesus said unto him, If thou wilt be perfect, go and sell that thou hast,

and give to the poor, and thou shalt have treasure in heaven: and come and follow me.
22 But when the young man heard that saying, he went away sorrowful: for he had great possessions.
23 Then said Jesus unto his disciples, Verily I say unto you, That a rich man shall hardly enter into the kingdom of heaven.
24 And again I say unto you, It is easier for a camel to go through the eye of a needle, than for a rich man to enter into the kingdom of God.

Well, I guess we're all guilty and absolutely incapable of entering into the kingdom of God and having eternal life! Of course, I say that jokingly because we know that there is nothing that we can do to earn eternal life since it has already been paid for by Jesus on the cross. But for the Christian with a poverty persona, this would have to be an unwarranted prerequisite. Unfortunately, this type of mentality is a 'works' mindset. When taken out of context of what Jesus was really trying to say, someone could end up with the idea that we in fact must give up everything that we have, and sell it to the poor. The principle of the message that Jesus was conveying was that with riches and materialistic things, man can become so comfortable with life that he feels no need to have a relationship with God. Selfishness, self-absorption and pride are key hindrances to one's understanding of God's desire for His people. The heart of God in man is always a heart to give, rather than to receive.

Other passages of scripture that support the 'poverty persona Christian' are as follows:

Matthew 6:19-20, 24, 31-34
*19 **Lay not up for yourselves treasures upon earth**, where moth and rust doth corrupt, and where thieves break through and steal:*
20 But lay up for yourselves treasures in heaven, where neither moth nor rust doth corrupt, and where thieves do not break through nor steal:

*24 No man can serve two masters: for either he will hate the one, and love the other; or else he will hold to the one, and despise the other. **Ye cannot serve God and mammon.***

31 Therefore take no thought, saying, What shall we eat? or, What shall we drink? or, Wherewithal shall we be clothed?
32 (For after all these things do the Gentiles seek:) for your heavenly Father knoweth that ye have need of all these things.
33 But seek ye first the kingdom of God, and his righteousness; and all these things shall be added unto you.
34 Take therefore no thought for the morrow: for the morrow shall take thought for the things of itself. Sufficient unto the day is the evil thereof.

1 Timothy 6:6-10, 17
*6 But **godliness with contentment is great gain**.*
7 For we brought nothing into this world, and it is certain we can carry nothing out.
8 And having food and raiment let us be therewith content.
*9 But they **that will be rich fall into temptation and a snare, and into many foolish and hurtful lusts, which drown men in destruction and perdition.***
*10 For the **love of money is the root of all evil: which while some coveted after, they have erred from the faith, and pierced themselves through with many sorrows.***

*17 **Charge them that are rich in this world, that they be not highminded, nor trust in uncertain riches**, but in the living God, who giveth us richly all things to enjoy;*

Just in these few verses, we are told-

- To not seek to make a huge sum of money in which we won't be able to take with us after we die
- To not try to serve God and trust in deceitful riches and possessions at the same time
- To not fret about what's going to happen tomorrow
- To be satisfied with living a devout, simplified life before God
- Being rich can lead to bad decision making, which then will lead to bad predicaments
- All evil is rooted in the love, or lust of money
- Chasing after riches and fame have caused people to fall away from the faith
- Being rich can lead to pride, conceit and arrogance

Well, 'case closed', it seems on seeking wealth and prosperity! Or is that really the case? How can God, who blessed Abraham mightily, want to have sons and daughters that live below the standards of even Abraham? Does it make sense for the King of Kings to have citizens of His kingdom that do not reflect the richness of the glory of the King? Wouldn't it be a bad reflection of the God that we serve and the God that we tell people lives on the inside of us if our lives are in financial disarray and ruins?

Positive Support for Prosperity and Money

I believe that it is essential for Christians, as well as non-Christians, to fully understand what prosperity truly is. Prosperity is defined as 'the condition of being successful or thriving; especially: economic well-being'.$_2$ To be prosperous is to be marked by success or economic well-being, and to enjoy vigorous and healthy growth.$_3$ It is the over-all well-being of an individual that is intact. There are no inhibitors of the mind, body, will and emotions. He that is prosperous has not only a healthy relationship with God, but a healthy relationship with his family, friends, co-workers, and all people that he comes in contact with. Another trait of someone that is prosperous is him lacking absolutely nothing in life. He has everything that he needs to live a happy life. It is the true meaning of being blessed.

In 3 John, we see John greeting Gaius with a blessing of prosperity:

3 John 1:1-2
1 The elder unto the wellbeloved Gaius, whom I love in the truth.
*2 Beloved, **I wish above all things that thou mayest prosper and be in health, even as thy soul prospereth.***

3 John 1:2 (Amplifed Bible)
2 Beloved, I pray that you may prosper in every way and [that your body] may keep well, even as [I know] your soul keeps well and prospers.

What's interesting with this blessing that John gives to Gaius is that he makes a statement that suggests that the prospering, or well-being of Gaius, including the health of his physical body, is contingent upon the prosperity, or well-being of his soul. John then speaks of the great things that he had heard of Gaius in regards to him walking in integrity and truth (v. 3), and being a faithful servant to not only the community of believers, but to those outside of that community as well (v. 5). This is what it looks like when the soul prospers. Integrity, truth, and faithfulness are fruits of a prospering soul. It's also what Jesus alludes to in Matthew 6, regarding 'laying up for yourselves treasures in heaven (Matthew 6:20). There is one passage in particular that speaks of the ailments in the body being related to sinful behavior:

Matthew 9:2 (Mark 2:5 is similar)
And, behold, they brought to him a man sick of the palsy, lying on a bed: and Jesus seeing their faith said unto the sick of the palsy; Son, be of good cheer; ***thy sins be forgiven thee.***

Apparently, according to Jesus, this man that suffered from palsy was inflicted because of sin in his life. The scribes that were present and witnessed this event were absolutely flabbergasted and appalled at the audacity of Jesus to say that this man's sins were forgiven. They deemed it a blasphemous statement. They certainly weren't prepared for it! But I think that no one there would have been prepared either because everybody was waiting on this man, Jesus, to heal this guy with palsy just as he had healed everyone else of their infirmities. However, I believe that Jesus was seeking to demonstrate that sickness and disease is in fact tied to sinful behavior. Perhaps the first order of business when seeking to lay hands on the sick and see them recover is to deal with issues of hidden sin in their lives, and then address the physical ailment. But I digress.

The love of money may be the root of all evil, but it doesn't negate the fact that money is a tool that is necessary to conduct business and even advance the kingdom. Various passages speak of the significance of money in the hands of God's people:

Ecclesiastes 10:19
*19 A feast is made for laughter, and wine maketh merry: but **money answereth all things**.*

Money is essential in our day-to-day operations. It 'answers all things'. We utilize currency to pay our bills, to put food on the table, to have a roof over our heads, to start a business, to lend, to help those in need, and to give to the church (kingdom of God) to assist in the advancing of the kingdom, world without end. The sweat of our brow (our labor) is translated into a monetary value in which we then use to sustain ourselves and our family. Unfortunately, many people today do not want to work (believe it or not), and want an easy way out. Consequently, this leads to a poverty-stricken lifestyle in most cases, and we know that scripture says the man that doesn't work, doesn't eat (2 Thessalonians 3:10). I recall developing relationships with the homeless in Chicago. Everyone had a story, but there was one common thread – many of them wanted to be there. They didn't want to be set free from a lifestyle of addiction, whether it be alcohol or drug-related. They didn't want to seek employment. More specifically, they didn't want to "live by anyone's rules". Thus, this is a lifestyle that they have chosen for themselves until they awaken out of their slumber. But it's the perfect case of a decision being made that affects an individual's well-being.

Proverbs 13:22
*22 **A good man leaveth an inheritance to his children's children**: and the wealth of the sinner is laid up for the just.*

Proverbs 13:22 (MSG)
22 A good life gets passed on to the grandchildren; ill-gotten wealth ends up with good people.

Two things come to mind with this passage. First, he that

considers himself to be a good man should leave his children and grandchildren in a better financial condition than he is in. I believe that this verse ties in well with what Paul wrote in his letter to Timothy:

1 Timothy 5:8
*But **if any provide not for his own, and specially for those of his own house, he hath denied the faith, and is worse than an infidel.***

Paul considers this issue to be so important that he states that it is a sign of denying the faith! Wow! How can that be? How can not providing for your family make one worse than the worst unbeliever? Perhaps, in regards to the relationship with children, we can find an answer to why Paul responded in such a manner. Remember that cute little song that you use to sing in Sunday School, or Children's Church? You know-

> *Jesus loves the little children,*
> *All the children of the world.*
> *Red and yellow, black and white,*
> *All are precious in His sight,*
> *Jesus loves the little children of the world.*

The Lord cares so much for the children, that mistreating them in any way, shape or form is sinful. It is recorded that Jesus rebuked even his disciples when it came to them forbidding the children to come to Jesus. So, that being said, a good man, a good Christian man, will care for his children and grandchildren in the same manner and with the same heart that Jesus cares for the children. This principle of caring for the future of children is what ultimately leads to generational wealth and prosperity. From one generation to another, a family can climb out of the depths of poverty by utilizing this simple principle – leave an inheritance for the children.

Another interesting principle that we find in Proverbs 13:22 is the mentioning of the deceitful riches of sinners inevitably ending up in the hands of the righteous people of God. There's always the question as to why the wicked seem to be swimming in financial security and freedom while the righteous folks seem to suffer. This is where we must simply rely on the promises of God, knowing that his ways are higher than our ways, and his thoughts are higher than our thoughts:

Isaiah 55:8-9
8 For my thoughts are not your thoughts, neither are your ways my ways, saith the Lord.
9 For as the heavens are higher than the earth, so are my ways higher than your ways, and my thoughts than your thoughts.

Romans 11:33-34
33 O the depth of the riches both of the wisdom and knowledge of God! how unsearchable are his judgments, and his ways past finding out!
34 For who hath known the mind of the Lord? or who hath been his counsellor?

Evil will not always reside in a realm of darkness. As the gospel is preached and salvation comes to regions, the light of Christ and His righteous judgment will expose hidden evil secrets, especially in the economic sector. A general law applies to money which states that it is never destroyed; it just transfers from one hand to another. It's essential to be positioned in places where you will be able to receive the wealth that will fall out of the hands of the wicked. A very interesting verse that took me quite some time to figure out is found in Luke 16:

Luke 16:9
*9 And I say unto you, **Make to yourselves friends of the mammon of unrighteousness; that, when ye fail, they may receive you into everlasting habitations**.*

I finally understood that Jesus was saying that we should make ourselves friends to those that are wealthy and are self-absorbed in their wealth. When their ungodly bubble bursts, we will be there, ready, willing and able to minister to their spiritual needs. This reminds me of when Joseph gained favor with pharaoh and was exalted to a high position in Egypt after he interpreted pharaoh's dream:

Genesis 41:38-45
*38 And Pharaoh said unto his servants, Can we find such a one as this is, **a man in whom the Spirit of God is?***
*39 And Pharaoh said unto Joseph, Forasmuch as God hath shewed thee all this, **there is none so discreet and wise as thou art:***
*40 **Thou shalt be over my house, and according unto thy word shall all my people be ruled:** only in the throne will I be greater than thou.*
*41 **And Pharaoh said unto Joseph, See, I have set thee over all the land of Egypt.***
*42 **And Pharaoh took off his ring from his hand, and put it upon Joseph's hand, and arrayed him in vestures of fine linen, and put a gold chain about his neck;***
*43 **And he made him to ride in the second chariot which he had; and they cried before him, Bow the knee: and he made him ruler over all the land of Egypt.***
*44 **And Pharaoh said unto Joseph, I am Pharaoh, and without thee shall no man lift up his hand or foot in all the land of Egypt.***
*45 And Pharaoh called Joseph's name Zaphnathpaaneah; and **he gave him to wife Asenath the daughter of Potipherah priest of On**. And Joseph went out over all the land of Egypt.*

Here are a few observations from the passage above:

- Being led by the Spirit of God will yield timely wisdom
- Despite one's circumstances (Joseph was in prison), one can be exalted from a place of despair and misfortune to a table full of kings and world leaders in the blink of an eye
- Moving in the gift that God has given you can tenderize the hearts of anyone, even the super-rich, to the point where they will be able to digest the wise words that God has placed in your mouth for them
- Because of timely ministry, the gratitude of the one ministered to will shower the minister with abundant favor and blessings
- Obedience will make one ruler of many

- New relationships can develop because of one's willingness to be there for those that are in power and have influence.

Daniel had a similar situation in his dealings with King Nebuchadnezzar (Daniel 2). Exaltation, favor and blessing were the results of Daniel's interpreting of a dream for the king:

Daniel 2:46-49
46 Then the king Nebuchadnezzar fell upon his face, and worshipped Daniel, and commanded that they should offer an oblation and sweet odours unto him.
*47 The king answered unto Daniel, and said, **Of a truth it is, that your God is a God of gods, and a Lord of kings, and a revealer of secrets, seeing thou couldest reveal this secret.***
*48 Then **the king made Daniel a great man, and gave him many great gifts, and made him ruler over the whole province of Babylon, and chief of the governors over all the wise men of Babylon.***
49 Then Daniel requested of the king, and he set Shadrach, Meshach, and Abednego, over the affairs of the province of Babylon: but Daniel sat in the gate of the king.

Ultimately, everything in the earth belongs to the Lord. Even the possessions of the ungodly and wealthy belong to God, the King of Kings, and Lord of Lords. Just as the proverb that speaks of a good man leaving an inheritance for his children and children's children, so does God leave an inheritance for His children.

Romans 8:17
And if children, then heirs; heirs of God, and joint-heirs with Christ...

All Christians are joint-heirs with Christ. All things are put in subjection under His feet (Hebrews 2:8). 'All things' include everything that is in the earth. To be 'in subjection' is to be under the power and authority of something. To be an 'heir' is to be entitled by law or by the terms of a will to inherit the estate of another.[4] The terms in which we are allotted the position of being a joint-heir with Christ are found in the New Covenant. Being in Christ grants us access to everything that God has in the earth.

So, what does this all mean? It means that the term 'prosperity' isn't a boogey-man term after all. Sure, there is imbalance that we can point to in some churches or ministries that preach about money all the time. And yes, some of the material items that some pastors possess can raise eyebrows – especially if the congregation seems to be in a place of financial hardship. But these things should not detour us from expecting to be blessed and be prosperous. Money is a tool that can unlock many doors of influence and allow the kingdom of God to come into regions that have been untouched. I believe that if we keep this point in perspective, we will have a better understanding of the purpose of being prosperous.

Chapter Eleven:
War and Peace

I am for peace: but when I speak, they are for war.

Psalm 120:7

There is a time for war, and a time for peace. These were the words that were written by Solomon in Ecclesiastes 3:8. The chapter begins with the statement that there is a season for everything, and a time for every purpose under heaven. But what does that actually mean when it comes to war and peace?

Psalm 82:3
3 Defend the poor and fatherless: do justice to the afflicted and needy.

The terms 'war' and 'peace' are used hundreds of times in scripture (in the KJV, war – 220, peace – 400), but for different situations and meanings. Plenty of passages that mention 'war' are dealing with what we know to be physical combat. Throughout the Old Testament, we see story after story about Israel going to battle against nations and people groups. But there are also passages that speaking of the war being waged in the spirit realm and in our own minds (psychological warfare). The same is the case with the word 'peace'. It is used in scripture as a word describing the ceasing of violent confrontation. But it is also used to describe one's mental state and well being.

Historical Justification for Physical War

Today, there is this general understanding of the reasons to go to war. Whether that understanding is right or wrong will hopefully be determined by the time we get to the end of this chapter. For the most part, however, the general consensus in regards to the reasons to go to war is as follows:

- To protect the homeland
- To fight for justice
- To assist those that can't defend themselves

If all of the criteria are met to go to war, it is coined a 'just war'. The 'Just War Theory' is a doctrine of beliefs and standards that was created to determine the ethics of warfare. Throughout history, politicians, theologians, philosophers, and ethicists convened to create the boundaries for what would be perceived as a just war. Augustine of Hippo (354-430) and Thomas Aquinas (1225-1274) were two key Christian figures who were involved with the shaping of Christian just war theory. Augustine believed that it was absolutely possible for a Christian to serve God and his country with honor. He believed that God had given a role to government to exercise justice and judgment accordingly and that Christians within government should feel no hesitation to seek justice, whether it be protecting the defenseless, or punishing the wicked. Augustine firmly believed that it was a sin to sit and watch injustice take place and not do anything about it. Augustine's reservations for going to war were apparent when he stated the following in his work, "The City of God":

"But, say they, the wise man will wage just wars. As if he would not all the rather lament the necessity of just wars, if he remembers that he is a man; for if they were not just he would not wage them, and would therefore be delivered from all wars."[1]

Thomas Aquinas utilized the foundation that Augustine had laid, and expounded upon the criteria necessary for a war to be considered just. Below are three significant points:

1. The war must be for a good and just purpose, and not for selfish interests or as an abuse of power
2. War must be debated and agreed upon by the state
3. Peace must always be the central motive

There are two sets of criteria that comprise the Just War Theory. The first set determines 'jus ad bellum', which means the right to go to war. The second set determines 'jus in bello', which means the correct conduct within war.

Jus Ad Bellum

In determining if there is a right to go to war, the following items must be determined:

- Is there a just reason for war? Is there imminent danger to innocent life?
- Is there gross imbalance in the amount of suffering between two parties?
- Will war be waged by a legitimate authority (a sovereign state)?
- Is there a right intention for war? Material gain or protecting a nation's interest is not considered a right intention for war.
- Will force to be enacted be short and precise?
- Have all other means of conflict resolution been exhausted?
- Will the benefits of war be proportionate to the casualties of war?

Jus In Bello

When war begins, there are guidelines of the Just War Theory that govern how each military is to conduct itself.

- Acts of war should always be directed towards combatants, and not towards non-combatants (this includes surrendering, or injured enemy combatants)
- Casualties of war should not be severely disproportionate to the perceived military advantage of the attacker
- The least force necessary should be used at all times in order to limit excessive damage, destruction and death
- Captured enemy combatants should be treated with dignity, for they are no longer a threat
- Unconventional weaponry is not allowed

You may be wondering what the purpose is of me highlighting 'Just War Theory', and how it relates to the overall theme of this book. My objective is to identify the foundation of the 'ground rules' that were created to determine if going to war is just, and whether or not the church today abides by those ground rules. I will discuss this in a bit more detail later in this chapter. Before I do so, I think it's imperative to take a look at what Jesus says about war and peace. It will also be interesting to take a look at Paul's perspective of war and peace as well.

What Does Jesus Say?

From what we can tell from scripture, Jesus understood that there would be wars throughout the world, especially within his generation. Of course, he makes mention of wars and rumors of wars in His Olivet discourse (Matthew 24:6, Mark 13:7 and Luke 21:9). He also makes mention of war in one of his parables:

Luke 14:31-32
31 Or what king, going to make war against another king, sitteth not down first, and consulteth whether he be able with ten thousand to meet him that cometh against him with twenty thousand?
32 Or else, while the other is yet a great way off, he sendeth an ambassage,

and desireth conditions of peace.

Though the theme of this parable is about counting the cost, and being totally sold out to a cause, Jesus demonstrates a conventional wisdom for engaging in warfare. Nonetheless, He advised His followers to be peacemakers:

Matthew 5:9
*9 **Blessed are the peacemakers**: for they shall be called the children of God.*

When Judas betrayed Jesus with a kiss and the multitude accompanying him seized Jesus, one of the disciples pulled out his sword and cut off the ear of one of the servants of the high priest. Jesus told the disciple to put his sword away because the man that lives by the sword (violence) will more than likely die by the sword (violence). This sounds a lot like the principle of sowing and reaping.

Matthew 26:49-52
49 And forthwith he came to Jesus, and said, Hail, master; and kissed him.
50 And Jesus said unto him, Friend, wherefore art thou come? Then came they, and laid hands on Jesus and took him.
*51 **And, behold, one of them which were with Jesus stretched out his hand, and drew his sword, and struck a servant of the high priest's, and smote off his ear.***
*52 **Then said Jesus unto him, Put up again thy sword into his place: for all they that take the sword shall perish with the sword.***

One of the prophetic descriptions of Jesus given by Isaiah was the term 'Prince of Peace' (Isaiah 9:6). Jesus, for the great majority of His earthly ministry exhibited a lifestyle that was void of violence and physical confrontation. His words carried such weight and authority that when the Pharisees and Sadducees sought to have him apprehended, they were hesitant to do so because of the reaction that would be generated amongst the people. However, this does not mean that Jesus was emotionless, as this truth was plainly demonstrated when

He overturned the tables of the moneychangers in the temple (John 2:13-17). No, this wasn't war, in the conventional sense, but it demonstrates confrontation – a combativeness that at first glance seemed out of character for Jesus and His requesting of His followers to be peaceful. However, at times, to bring peace, there must be a holy indignation that rises up in favor of righteousness and justice. What Jesus saw happening in the temple provoked Him to anger, essentially in defense of the people that were being robbed by the money changers and their unjust weights and measures. Jesus understood the significance of this, as it was addressed in the law:

Leviticus 19:35
Ye shall do no unrighteousness in judgment, in meteyard, in weight, or in measure.

Deuteronomy 25:15
But thou shalt have a perfect and just weight, a perfect and just measure shalt thou have: that thy days may be lengthened in the land which the Lord thy God giveth thee.

Solomon speaks of this in one of his proverbs:

Proverbs 20:10
Divers weights, and divers measures, both of them are alike abomination to the Lord.

Jesus was moved with compassion for the people that were coming from miles away to exchange their form of currency for the required currency to give to the temple as a part of their worship of God. The disciples who saw Jesus react to the injustice remembered a passage of scripture that was being fulfilled before their eyes:

John 2:17
17 And his disciples remembered that it was written, The zeal of thine house hath eaten me up.

Jesus possessed zeal for the house of God – a passion and

desire to not allow wickedness and perversion to exist, and for God's house to not be made a mockery. He would not allow corruption at the hands of the money changers to take advantage of the people. Can the same be said of the church today? Are men and women standing up with passion and zeal for the house of God to not allow corruption and politics to invade and corrode the church from the inside-out?

What Does Paul Say?

Perhaps one of the most famous passages of scripture written by Paul in regards to warfare is found in 2 Corinthians 10:

2 Corinthians 10:3-6
*3 For though we walk in the flesh, **we do not war after the flesh**:*
*4 (For **the weapons of our warfare are not carnal**, but mighty through God to the pulling down of strong holds;)*
5 Casting down imaginations, and every high thing that exalteth itself against the knowledge of God, and bringing into captivity every thought to the obedience of Christ;
6 And having in a readiness to revenge all disobedience, when your obedience is fulfilled.

2 Corinthians 10:3-6 (CEV)
3 We live in this world, but we don't act like its people 4 or fight our battles with the weapons of this world. Instead, we use God's power that can destroy fortresses. We destroy arguments 5 and every bit of pride that keeps anyone from knowing God. We capture people's thoughts and make them obey Christ. 6 And when you completely obey him, we will punish anyone who refuses to obey.

Paul addresses the issue of war from a totally spiritual perspective. Flesh and blood is not our enemy. The real enemy is the demonic spirits that create mental barriers between man and the revelation of God and His will for man's life. The believer's weaponry is not physical materials like guns, bullets, tanks, missiles, jet fighters and war ships. The believer's weapons of choice are prayer, proclamations, decrees and prophesying. The believer commands mountains to be removed. The believer uses his spiritual weapons to shut the mouths of antichrist sentiment and thought, and to establish righteous judgment and justice in the land. There is physical war, but more importantly, the spiritual war for souls exists. The good news is that the spiritual war was won by Jesus as He conquered death, hell and the grave. This victory brings peace and reconciliation between God and man. The gospel of peace is the notice to mankind that a way of being reconciled to the Father has already been made!

Romans 10:15
15 And how shall they preach, except they be sent? as it is written, **How beautiful are the feet of them that preach the gospel of peace, and bring glad tidings of good things!**

Paul speaking to the church at Ephesus about spiritual warfare-

Ephesians 6:10-17
10 Finally, my brethren, be strong in the Lord, and in the power of his might.
11 **Put on the whole armour of God**, *that ye may be able to stand against the wiles of the devil.*
12 For we **wrestle not against flesh and blood, but against principalities, against powers, against the rulers of the darkness of this world, against spiritual wickedness in high places.**
13 Wherefore **take unto you the whole armour of God**, *that ye may be able to withstand in the evil day, and having done all, to stand.*
14 Stand therefore, having your loins girt about with truth, and having on the breastplate of righteousness;
15 And your **feet shod with the preparation of the gospel of peace;**
16 Above all, taking the **shield of faith**, *wherewith ye shall be able to quench all the fiery darts of the wicked.*
17 And take the **helmet of salvation, and the sword of the Spirit**, *which is the word of God:*

In his letter to the twelve tribes that were scattered about the land, James wrote the following in regards to peace:

James 3:17-18
*17 But **the wisdom that is from above is first pure, then peaceable**, gentle, and easy to be intreated, full of mercy and good fruits, without partiality, and without hypocrisy.*
*18 And **the fruit of righteousness is sown in peace of them that make peace**.*

James states that the wisdom of God is peaceable and it always produces good fruit, rather than death and destruction. He goes on to say that God's wisdom is without partiality, meaning that it is not unfairly biased in favor of one thing or person over another – God's wisdom shows no favoritism. Furthermore, James states that God's wisdom is without hypocrisy. Hypocrisy is defined as one claiming to have moral beliefs and standards, and yet, their actions do not reflect those beliefs and are the exact opposite of the morality that was said to be tangible. So, where does the American church stand when it comes to war and peace?

The Western Church and U.S. Foreign Policy

I love America. There is no place that I'd rather be than in the United States. I love the freedom, the liberty, the right and privilege to do what I want to do, become who I want to be, and live how I want to live. However, being a student of the last one hundred years of U.S. foreign policy has left a very bitter taste in my mouth. War after war and conflict after conflict throughout American history has not passed all of the criteria that were set forth to determine whether they were just wars and conflicts. In particular, the following bullet point from the list of 'Jus Ad Bellum' criteria has not been met throughout each conflict that the United States has engaged in:

- Is there a right intention for war? **Material gain or protecting a nation's interest is not considered a right intention for war.**

I deliberately made it a point to speak earlier about the money changers that Jesus drove out of the temple. I believe that the same spirits of greed, lust, control, manipulation, pride and murder which were operating through those money changers are operating through international bankers today - bankers who have historically bankrolled both sides of the majority of conflicts that we have witnessed, and are notorious for doing so. Warfare is used as a money-making machine that only a few families that control the international banking industry benefit from, while our sons and daughters are being used as cannon fodder. These modern-day money changers seek to systematically control every country by means of setting up centralized banking institutions in each nation. The Federal Reserve Bank (a consortium of seven privately owned banks) deliberately creates booms and busts in the U.S. economy by raising and lowering interest rates. Historically, during down economic times, especially in the last 100 years, conflicts are conjured up and propaganda is used to draw American citizens into being in favor of going to war, with it all being cloaked with the false narrative of 'patriotism'. There is a two-fold agenda at play:

1. Remove focus from the economic crisis (depression, recession, economic downturn) in which they created
2. Fund warfare on both sides to make tons of money by lending to countries involved in conflict and charging interest.

More importantly, it is absolutely obvious that over the last 25 years, American conflict has been centered on 'national interests' and material gain. Without going into a lot of detail, the only thing that is propping the U.S. economy up right now is what is known as the petrodollar. Petrodollar is a term that is used to denote the agreement that the U.S. made with Saudi Arabia and other oil producing nations in the Middle East in which states that those oil producing nations will only sell their oil in U.S. dollars (USD) in exchange for U.S. military protection of their oil fields. So, what happens when a nation decides to 'buck the system'? You get Iraq, Libya, and most recently, the demonization and provoking of Iran. What did these nations do?

- Saddam Hussein (who was not a saint, by the way) was going to sell Iraqi oil in Euros, and not the USD
- Muammar al-Gaddafi was going to sell Libyan oil in gold dinar, and not the USD
- Former Iranian President, Mahmoud Ahmadinejad, began to sell Iranian oil on an open market, which means any nation's currency would be acceptable, and not the USD

Since the USD isn't worth toilet paper, due to the out of control 'printing' of money by the Federal Reserve Bank, these three sovereign nations understood the worthlessness of the fiat currency and sought more stable alternatives. The U.S., which is basically controlled by a criminal cabal of bankers, didn't want a monkey-wrench thrown into the great ponzi scheme called the petrodollar. Therefore, false narratives were created, and are being created, to overthrow these leaders from the inside out, and inevitably engage in conflict with them. Case in point would be Iraq and the false information of them having 'weapons of mass destruction' (WMD), which led to the U.S. invasion of Iraq. Today, the U.S. controls the Iraqi oil fields and Iraqi oil is being sold in USD. In Libya, rebel groups who were inundated with Al Qaeda (who we blame for September 11, 2001, by the way) were assisted by American cruise missile fire to destabilize the Gaddafi regime. That eventually led to the capture, and execution of Gaddafi. What many people don't know is that almost simultaneously, a central bank was set up in Libya. Robert Wenzel wrote about the oddity of such a thing in an article for the Economic Policy Journal:

> *"This suggests we have a bit more than a rag tag bunch of rebels running around and that there are some pretty sophisticated influences.*
>
> *I have never before heard of a central bank being created in just a matter of weeks out of a popular uprising.*
>
> *This buttresses the suspicions in my earlier post where I highlighted an odd U.S. Treasury statement that froze Gaddafi's assets but made clear that if "subsidiaries or facilities come under different ownership and control, Treasury may consider authorizing dealings with such entities."*
>
> *This continues to look like a major oil and money play, with the true disaffected rebels being used as puppets and cover, as the oil/money transfer takes place."*[2]

And this brings us to the most recent conflict in Syria. The U.S. has no special interests in Syria, but they do have special interests in Syria's closest ally, Iran. I believe that the current conflict in Syria is being used as a prod to draw Iran into conflict so that an international coalition can conjure up a claim for going to war with Iran. Ultimately, the goal will be to topple the Iranian regime, take control of the oil fields, and sell the Iranian oil in USD as well. There is a caveat to all of this though. Russia and China are not going to sit idly by and allow this to happen. China is one of Iran's biggest customers and any intervention by the U.S. in Iranian affairs will directly affect the Chinese economy.

So, are these just wars? Are they just conflicts? Are they not waged for national interests? The sad thing about this is that many in the western church are ignorant when it comes to geopolitics and foreign policy. Instead of being on the side of truth in all regards, the western church falls right in line with the rest of the American public who are manipulated into supporting unjust wars and hypocritical stances of the U.S.

government. The situation in Syria is eerily similar to what we witnessed in Iraq. The red line or red flag, being chemical weapons (WMD), was the excuse that was used for the invasion of Iraq. Syria is a tad bit different because there is evidence of chemical weapons being used and people dying as a result of it. The problem that is at hand is identifying exactly who was responsible for it. Unbeknownst to most Americans, the narrative that is currently coming from Washington D.C. is half correct, at best. Mainstream media, which is corporate and banker owned, refuse to talk about the Syrian rebels who are seeking to overthrow the current regime with Bashar al-Assad at the helm. No one seems to want to talk about the Syrian rebels, just like in Libya, being inundated with a branch of Al Qaeda, called Al Nusra. This group is funded directly by the Saudi government and there are reports that the rebels were responsible for the chemical weapons attack. Furthermore, the Obama Administration is keeping a tight lip when it comes to Al Nusra's involvement in the attack on Christian villages in Syria.[3] Neither will they say anything about the executions of captured Syrian military members, and worse, the beheading of a Catholic priest.[4]

Where is the western church's outrage in regards to these atrocities? More importantly, where is the church's disdain for being lied to over and over again by government officials just to conjure up support for more wars, and more of our young sons, daughters, brothers, sisters, husbands, wives, uncles and aunts being killed over these lies, and special interests? Essentially, thousands of U.S. military members are dying to make a small amount of people (elites) super-rich. How can we continue to be in support of unconstitutional and unjust warfare and claim to have the Prince of Peace living on the inside of us? Am I against war? No, not necessarily. But I am against unjust wars. Warfare that is waged in the name of protecting oil revenues (the petrodollar) are not worth the blood spilled for it, and it is absolutely unjust. To support a foreign policy that puts national interests above life and real peace is to aid and abet in the terrorism that we accuse others of partaking in.

Chapter Twelve:
The Political Divide

And if a house be divided against itself, that house cannot stand.

Mark 3:25

I truly believe that the world and everything in it is a reflection of the condition of the church. If the church is 'sick', then the world will be sick. If the church is healthy, then the world will be healthy. I am in no way, shape or form insinuating that the corporate body of Christ, the true Israel of God, is 'sick'. The true church is always healthy, vibrant, thriving, impacting and influencing the world from generation to generation. The true Israel of God's light shines so bright that all darkness flees from every crevice and every sector of a society. In the case of the political realm, or government, a healthy, thriving, and impactful church will yield a healthy, thriving and impactful government. Unfortunately, this isn't the case in America.

Political Ideological Imbalance

In America, there are two major political parties (Republican and Democrat) that seem presumably on the opposite ends of the spectrum on a myriad of issues. Regrettably, they both attempt to use biblical principles as the foundational support for the conflicting ideologies. The Republican Party trumpets conservatism and personal responsibility (Individualism). On the other hand, The Democrat Party takes an "I'm my brother's keeper" approach and asserts that we are all responsible for taking care of each other (Collectivism). As you can see, on the surface, these two ideologies seem like 'oil and water' and are absolutely incompatible.

Individualism vs. Collectivism

Republicans for the most part adhere to 'individualism'. There are five general traits that define individualism:

1. It endorses individual aspirations, initiative and success
2. It deems individual rights as most important and seeks to highlight the laws that were created to protect those rights
3. To be effective in society, one must make sure that 'their house is in order' before attempting to be influential in the world
4. Being dependent on others (the state) is seen as modern day slavery and shameful
5. The subscriber of individualism seeks to encourage others to become self-sufficient and independent

Contrarily, Democrats hold fast to 'collectivism'. Five qualities of collectivism are as follows:

1. People are encouraged to actively engage society and do what's best for that society as a whole rather than themselves
2. Rights of the individual are trumped in favor of the rights of families, communities and the collective as a whole
3. In favor of changing laws to tear down individualism and promote selflessness
4. In favor of working as a collective and supporting each other
5. Communal or national interests are more important than individual interests

I don't think two ideological positions can be any more polarizing and opposite than these two. And yet, oddly, both of them can be supported scripturally. However, the question must be asked, who in scripture would those supporting passages be talking about? Something that happens more often than not is the taking of scripture out of historical context and applying it to a time and place that it doesn't make sense in. For example, something that collectivists use as a support for their political ideology is the description of the early church in Acts:

Acts 2:44
*And all that believed were together, and **had all things common**;*

Acts 4:32
*And the multitude of them that believed were **of one heart and of one soul: neither said any of them that ought of the things which he possessed was his own; but they had all things common**.*

This would appear to be a slam dunk and walk-off homerun for the collectivist. It seems as if collectivism is supported by these two passages and the character of the early church. However, there is one thing that the collectivist doesn't stress – it is THE CHURCH that had all things in common, not the nation! The first part of Acts 2:44 is even more important than the latter part – 'all that believed were together'. It is the community of believers in Christ that had all things in common. As mentioned earlier in Part 1, the church was coming under heavy persecution at the hands of the unbelieving Jews and Roman Empire and it was imperative that the Christians were together on one accord in order to prevail. It is absolutely preposterous for Democrats who hold a purely collectivist political ideology to use the Christian concept of "having all things common" as the support for their disdain for individualism.

However, I do not want to just stomp on the collectivist position without addressing some inconsistencies with individualism as well. Though I personally believe in the concept of individualism and self-reliance (politically, from a conservative libertarian constitutionalist perspective), I refuse to follow, dogmatically, the systematic lack of compassion that is prevalent amongst some on the Republican side of the aisle. To not consider the socio-economic pitfalls and 'quicksand' that some folks are birthed into, at no fault of their own, is the epitome of selfishness. Just because a person is living in poverty or are not exhibiting self-reliance doesn't mean that particular individual doesn't have a desire to be self-reliant and independent. This is where I believe the church must step up and lend the help necessary to allow people to get back onto their feet, become self-sufficient, and active in society. Notice I said church, and not the state. I believe that it is not the government's responsibility to do this. It is absolutely criminal, in my honest opinion, to take money from hard working individuals and give it to some people that don't want to work and contribute to society.

2 Thessalonians 3:10
*For even when we were with you, this we commanded you, that **if any would not work, neither should he eat.***

Oxymoronic Political Positions

Something that really baffles me is the schizophrenic viewpoints of each party when it comes to the sanctity of life. What's even more mind-boggling is the split amongst church folks when it comes to this subject matter. Of course, the most popular issue when it comes to discussions about 'life' is abortion. Republicans, for the most part, are starkly opposed to abortions, while Democrats are mostly in favor of abortion. Republicans, or conservatives, see life beginning at conception. It has been medically proven that a heart starts beating approximately 22 days after conception.[1] The purpose of the heart is to pump blood through the body. As we learn from scripture, life is in the blood:

Leviticus 17:14
For it is the life of all flesh; **the blood of it is for the life thereof***: therefore I said unto the children of Israel, Ye shall eat the blood of no manner of flesh: for the life of all flesh is the blood thereof: whosoever eateth it shall be cut off.*

It makes absolutely no sense to me for someone that is a Christian to be in support of abortion. It is the literal stopping of a life, as life is defined by scripture. But at the same time, I have a bone to pick with Christian Republicans and conservatives who are vocal and outspoken about pro-life when it comes to abortion, but are in support of the inhumane death penalty. Christians should be on the side of life in all regards, and not just the abortion issue. God is no respecter of persons, and this includes the unborn as well as the inmate that happens to be on death row. Ultimately, God is the final judge and he repays for transgressions, not man:

Romans 12:19
Dearly beloved, ***avenge not yourselves****, but rather give place unto wrath: for it is written,* ***Vengeance is mine; I will repay, saith the Lord****.*

Who are we to decide when a man should live or die? What gives us the authority to take a baby or adult's life? Do we not believe that God will judge the spilling of blood, whether it is innocent (aborted baby) or not (murderer on death row)? Once again, it brings back to memory Jesus' words for the disciples when one of them drew their sword and chopped off the ear of the chief priest's servant (Matthew 26:51). Jesus told the disciple to put the sword away because those that live by the sword shall die by the sword. And this is something that brings me to another point – militarism. The pro-militarism slant of the Republican, conservative ideology is not congruent with being pro-life. Granted, I must say that the Republican Party of today is not what it was in the early 20th century. It has been hijacked by individuals that seek to change the face of globalism with the barrel of a gun, bombs and covert affairs. These people, coined neo-conservatives, or 'neo-cons', have no remorse for the innocent bloodshed of people in other lands. These are the same people who salivate for profits and natural resources in other sovereign nations and will do whatever it takes to pilfer rape and pillage those nations. So there's an ongoing inner-struggle within the Republican Party in which those that are from the traditional conservative platform (that of not engaging in entangling alliances, as George Washington spoke of) are in a political conflict with the neo-cons for control of the party.[2] The interesting thing about this is that the neo-cons are really cut from the same cloth as the progressives that are the far left – liberals. They are not conservative at all in that they love to spend billions of dollars on the military industrial complex. This is just as bad as the far left spending billions of dollars implementing Keynesian economic policies, which is nothing short of creating money out of thin air to cover national debts. Meanwhile, the American citizenry is stuck with the bill via taxation and inflation.

Ungodly Allegiance

"Choose this day who you will serve." This is the sentiment echoed in Joshua 24:15. American Christians are forced to make a choice between godliness and compromise. In today's political arena, nothing gets done unless there is 'give and take', 'you scratch my back and I'll scratch yours', or money under the table or imbedded in bills that will go into politicians' pockets. Big business, big 'pharma' and the banking industry are just as much on Capitol Hill as any senator or representative from any state. Fascism (the unethical alliance between government powers, business and banking industries) has taken hold of the political process and it has destroyed democracy and the republic. The founding fathers of this nation warned against this. The sad thing about it all is that politicians from both sides of the aisle are having their pockets greased in order to support legislation that will be beneficial to big business and the banking industry, while sticking the citizenry with the bill. Governmental officials with relatives that sit on the boards of companies see to it that those companies are protected from lawsuit and that laws are passed that will financially benefit those companies.

But in regards to the 'big ticket', 'hot button' topics like abortion and homosexual marriage, how the American church responds as a whole is a testament to the status of the church. Will American Christians vote their conscience which should be shaped and molded by biblical principle, or do they fall prey to political pressure from the party that they are affiliated with? And should Christians be aligned with a political party to begin with? Is it feasible for a Christian to agree with items on a party's platform that are not necessarily anti-God, or exemplifying anti-godly principles, but ignore those one or two items that are absolutely anti-God? Should Christians vote for legislation that has many parts, but certain parts of it are not in alignment with the will of God?

I believe that it is time for American Christians to take a long, hard look at their political affiliations and ideology and ask themselves a serious question – Is there any part of that party's political platform that is obviously anti-God, anti-Christian and anti-Kingdom? If the answer is 'yes', then we must reject being tied to dogmatic political ideology and speak truth to power at all times. We should not compromise in any way and yield to ungodly standards, laws, practices and ideology. To do so would be the co-signing to the spiritual deterioration of the land, and the blood will most definitely be on our hands because no matter how we slice it, judgment always begins in the house of God. God is solely concerned with how we, the church, respond to situations and circumstances. To reject the ways of the Lord, even in our political affiliations, says a lot in regards to how we view God's desire to have influence in the political realm from a kingdom-minded perspective.

PART THREE

ROOT CAUSE OF THE INSANE WESTERN CHURCH

Chapter Thirteen:
Biblical Illiteracy

Study and be eager and do your utmost to present yourself to God approved (tested by trial), a workman who has no cause to be ashamed, correctly analyzing and accurately dividing [rightly handling and skillfully teaching] the Word of Truth.

2 Timothy 2:15 (AMP)

I remember when I was young the thing that I hated to do most in school was read. Granted, I was a very good student. I loved school. I loved to learn. Math and science were my favorite subjects. Perhaps that was because there was always one correct answer and there was no wiggle room for other 'interpretations' in math and science. The answers were always straight forward, and absolute. But when it came to reading and comprehension, let me be quite honest here – I hated it because it seemed as if the entire process of reading and comprehending took way too much time and effort! Reading was boring. Unfortunately, my disdain for reading lasted even through my college years! Yes! I'm being transparent here! My study habits at the University of Illinois in the mid-90s were horrible! It was only by the grace of God that I made it out of there alive! Anyone that has gone to college, or is in college now, knows for a fact that those first two years are what I label as "weed out" years. Courses required tons of reading, comprehension and paper writing. Oddly, writing papers didn't bother me at all. But keeping up with the required reading for each class wasn't my forte. Nonetheless, I had to do it, and I learned to… deal with it – not love it, but deal with it at that time!

Today, there are many children, and sadly, many adults that fall into the same 'non-reader' category. They, just like I use to, despise reading and would rather do something else with their time! The cares of life and many media distractions hypnotize people's minds and hook them on garbage and nonsense instead of what really will set them free. Knowledge truly is power. But knowledge cannot come if there is no reading and comprehension. One cannot aspire to be a doctor, lawyer, accountant, engineer or any professional if he or she has not bought into the necessity to read and comprehend. Likewise, one cannot be all that God has called him or her to be if they have not bought into the necessity to read and comprehend scripture.

Comprehension is Critical

Try to tell a two year old to read and comprehend a map while you drive. I hope you have enough gas in your car to drive for about 5-7 years! They don't have the ability to read and comprehend. The sad thing about this is I'm pretty sure that there are plenty of adults that are clueless when looking at a map. The same goes for some adults that attempt to read scripture. Comprehension is defined as the act of understanding what you are reading. Reading comprehension is an intentional, active and interactive process that occurs before, during and after a person reads a particular piece of writing.[1] Comprehension is absolutely essential to life. Just think about all of the things that we have to read on a daily basis so that we remain safe and out of harm's way. Comprehension is fundamental to functional literacy. Unfortunately, many people can read, but many are not capable of fully grasping information because they lack the skills necessary to comprehend what has been read. There are four areas of life that are directly impacted by a lack of comprehension:

1. **Social** – Trouble communicating and relating with

others; will cause timidity, fear, shame and withdrawal from society
2. **Emotional** – Frustration, irritability, depression and trauma ensue with lack of comprehension
3. **Intellectual** – Struggle academically; can't pick up information fast enough in school or on a job
4. **Spiritual** – The soul is mal-nourished; spiritual weakness then leads to physical weakness

The 5 W's of Basic Comprehension

In the church today, especially the American church, there are a lot of what I call 'functioning biblical illiterates'. Functioning alcoholics are folks who have been oppressed by alcoholism for so long that they have learned to adapt and continue to operate seemingly okay in their day-to-day tasks. These people are killing themselves on the inside, but no one seems to notice any difference on the outside. The same is the case with functioning drug abusers. Cocaine abuse is prevalent in the arts and entertainment industries. It has even tackled government officials and executives of big business. But these individuals are able to mask their slave-like addiction to drugs and do what their respective jobs require of them. Shamefully, the same thing is happening in our churches – not necessarily with alcohol and drug abuse, though these things do happen, but more directly in regards to church folks acting and doing the 'church work', preaching and teaching what appears to be what the bible says, but are illiterate when it comes to scripture and its content. Misreading or not comprehending the dosage instructions on a pill bottle could kill someone. Similarly, misreading or not comprehending what scripture is and what it says can result in spiritual stagnation and missing the mark in regards to God's purpose for us in the earth today.

There is what I call the 5 W's of basic comprehension. When reading scripture, and then trying to comprehend or understand what has been read, these 5 W's must be satisfied.

They are as follows:

1. **WHO?** – Who are all of the parties involved? Who is the author? Who is the intended audience?
2. **WHAT?** – What is the overall message? What is the subject matter? What is being said?
3. **WHEN?** – When are the things described taking place? When was it written? When did the intended audience read it? What are the social, political, and economic conditions during that time? (Context question #1)
4. **WHERE?** - Where is the location that it was written? Where is the location that it was first read? (Context question #2)
5. **WHY?** – Why was the text written? What is the purpose for the text?

Lack of Proper Hermeneutics

Biblical Hermeneutics is the study of the general principles of biblical interpretation. For both Jews and Christians throughout their histories, the primary purpose of hermeneutics, and of the exegetical methods employed in interpretation, has been to discover the truths and values of the Bible.[2] To be successful, this process must take into account the cultural, historical, and language barriers that limit our understanding of the original writings. There are no shortcuts to the hard work necessary to accomplish this task.[3] In his book, *"Hermeneutics: Principles and Processes of Biblical Interpretation"*, Henry A. Virkler teaches a five-step process in which one can use in order to adequately interpret scripture. The steps to that process are as follows:

1. **Lexical-Syntactical Analysis** – The examination of the

way words are used; the order, punctuation and tenses of a sentence; Lexicons, concordances and other grammar aides are used to fully understand the meaning of words
2. **Historical and Cultural Analysis** – The knowledge and understanding of the socio-political landscape of the time when the text was written and read; understanding the religious conditions of the time period in which the text was written and its relation to the people during that time
3. **Contextual Analysis** – The examining of a verse or passage within the framework of the chapter, the book or epistle that it is written in, as well as the backdrop of the entire Bible in general
4. **Theological Analysis** – Poor biblical interpretation is often due to the creating of a theology based off of one verse instead of looking at how the subject matter of that verse is spoken of in other books or epistles in the Bible; scripture must be used to interpret scripture; no one verse can be used to come to a conclusion on an issue
5. **Special Literary Analysis** – It is always necessary to understand the genre of scripture. Sometimes a text can have overlapping, or multiple genres. Those genres are-
    - **Narratives** – Scriptural accounts of associated events offered to a reader or listener in a series of written or spoken words to tell a story; sometimes there are narratives within a narrative, or multiple stories within a story. Narratives compose approximately 40 % of the Old Testament and a large part of the New Testament.
    - **Histories** – Scriptural accounts related to past events; history is facilitated by the formation of a 'true discourse of past' through the production of narrative and analysis of past events relating

to the human race.4 In the case of scripture, the history primarily details the past accounts of God's dealings with Israel;
- **Prophecies** – Recorded foretelling of the future of Israel found in both the Old and New Testaments;
- **Apocalyptic Writings** – Scripture that unfolds and unveils things that were previously unknown and are prophetic in nature, depicting a cataclysmic end of the world; also encouraged the people to hold fast in light of what was happening in the world because redemption was near
- **Poetry and Psalms** – Passages of scripture that were written in a notably poetic nature; Psalm, Proverbs, Ecclesiastes, Songs of Solomon, and the Song of Moses found in Deuteronomy 32 are most noteworthy
- **Letters** – Messages addressed to specific groups of people; Paul's epistles were written to various 1st century churches and church leaders

Within the above listed genres of scripture, there are even more specific literary styles or rhetorical strategies that can be found. The recognition and understanding of these different styles is absolutely critical to fully comprehending the texts. The literary styles are as follows:

- **Allegory** - a figurative application of a story or narrative. This is a figurative sentence or discourse in which the principal subject is described by another subject resembling it in its properties and circumstances. Paul's stated allegory in Galatians 4:21 is a classic in the New Testament. We as Isaac are children of promise and of the freewoman. Paul's description of the Christian armor in

Ephesians 6:11-17 is listed in the standard works as an allegory. It is certainly worthy of study in our fight against sin and Satan.[6]

- **Figurative Language** - using words to imply another meaning or to evoke an emotion.[7] Words used with a meaning that is different from the basic meaning and that expresses an idea in an interesting way by using language that usually describes something else : not literal.[8]
- **Metaphor** - a comparison reduced to a single word expressing a similarity without the signs of comparison. The simile says that it is like it; the metaphor says it is it. In Luke 13:31-32, Jesus said of Herod, "Go and say to that fox." If he had said "Go tell that man that is like a fox," it would have been a simile, but Jesus uses the forceful metaphor. "Ye are a temple of God" is a metaphor in 1 Corinthians 3:16. In Matthew 26:26-28 Jesus took a loaf and said "this is my body" and he took a cup and said "this is my blood of the covenant"; these are metaphors.[9]
- **Simile** - a comparison in which anything is likened to another and the comparison is stated by the words "as" or "like". An example is 1Peter 1:2, "All flesh is as grass, and all the glory thereof as the flower of grass." Jesus used a striking simile in describing hypocrites in Matthew 23:27, "Ye are like unto whited sepulchres, which outwardly appear beautiful, but inwardly are full of dead men's bones, and of all uncleanness.[10]
- **Literal** - words that do not stray from their defined meaning; the "normal" meanings of the words; [11] the intended meaning of a text corresponds exactly to the meaning of the individual words.[12]

Hebraic Idiomatic Language

Another linguistic tool that the reader of the bible must keep in mind is the usage of idioms in the text. An idiom is-

- an expression that cannot be understood from the meanings of its separate words but that has a separate meaning of its own
- a form of a language that is spoken in a particular area and that uses some of its own words, grammar, and pronunciations
- a style or form of expression that is characteristic of a particular person, type of art, etc.[13]

For example, there are some idioms in the English language that, when we hear them, we immediately know the meaning of them because we are accustomed to hearing them. Common idioms in America, and their meaning are-

- "It's raining cats and dogs" – It's raining very hard
- "He was sick as a dog" – He was very sick
- "She jumped the gun" – She did something too early
- "He rubbed me the wrong way" – He was annoying
- "That was out of the blue" – That was unexpected

Likewise, there are Hebrew idioms that, if we don't understand them within the context of Hebrew culture, we will totally misunderstand the true meaning of them and the text that they are in. Some Hebrew idioms are as follows:

Matthew 5:17-18
*17 Think not that **I am come to destroy the law, or the prophets: I am not come to destroy, but to fulfil.***
18 For verily I say unto you, Till heaven and earth pass, one jot or one tittle shall in no wise pass from the law, till all be fulfilled.

Marji Hughes, in an article entitled "Hebrew Idioms in Scripture", brings clarity to this passage by saying-

> *"In light of this, we could paraphrase these verses to read, "I have not come to abolish the Torah, but to complete it - to make the meaning full" Yeshua did not come to abolish, but to make full the meaning of what Torah and the ethical demands of the Prophets require. He came to complete our understanding of the Torah and the Prophets so that we can more effectively try to be and do what they instruct us to be and do."* [14]

A few more Hebraic Idioms are as follows (interpretation in parentheses):

Exodus 3:8
And I am come down to deliver them out of the hand of the Egyptians, and to bring them up out of that land unto a good land and a large, unto **a land flowing with milk and honey**... (a land that is fertile)

Job 20:20
Surely **he shall not feel quietness in his belly**... (he shall remain greedy)

Psalm 3:7
Arise, O Lord; save me, O my God: for thou hast smitten all mine enemies upon the cheek bone; thou hast **broken the teeth of the ungodly**. (made the ungodly powerless)

Proverbs 18:20
A man's belly shall be satisfied with the **fruit of his mouth**... (what he says)

Isaiah 60:16
Thou shalt also **suck the milk of the Gentiles**... (receive the wealth of other countries)

Matthew 11:15
He that hath ears to hear, let him hear. (everyone should listen very carefully)

Apocalyptic Language

Perhaps the most misconstrued understanding of scripture is in regards to the various usages of apocalyptic language. As mentioned earlier, apocalyptic writings refer to scripture that unfolds and unveils things that were previously unknown and are prophetic in nature, depicting a cataclysmic end of the world. Within this literary style are words and phrases that have apocalyptic meaning. But when these words, phrases or passages are interpreted literally, it distorts the true meaning and yields an interpretation that does a disservice to the actual text. There are two very significant cases that I want to talk about in the Olivet Discourse (Matthew 24, Mark 13 and Luke 21). For the proper interpretation of these two cases, one must understand how those phrases are utilized elsewhere in scripture – specifically the Old Testament.

Case #1: sun be darkened, moon not give her light, stars fall from heaven, powers of heavens shaken (Matthew 24:29, Mark 13:24-25, Luke 21:25)

When reading these verses, the reader that takes a literalist approach will come to the conclusion that Jesus was speaking about a future constellational cataclysmic event that would denote the literal end of the literal heavens and earth as we know it. However, when we take a look at how these words, terms and phrases are used in the Old Testament, we can get a clearer picture of what Jesus was really trying to convey. David Chilton, author of "Paradise Restored: A Biblical Theology of Dominion", speaks of this in more detail:

> *"At the end of the Tribulation, Jesus said, the universe will collapse: the light of the sun and the moon will be extinguished, the stars will fall, the powers of the heavens will be shaken. The basis for this symbolism is in Genesis 1:14-16, where the sun, moon, and stars ("the powers of the heavens") are spoken of as "signs" which "govern"*

> the world. Later in Scripture, these heavenly lights are used to speak of earthly authorities and governors; and when God threatens to come against them in judgment, the same collapsing-universe terminology is used to describe it."15

Before giving examples of how this type of language is used in passages that denote a coming judgment on a people, I first want to bring your attention to how these similar phrases are used in Genesis – specifically, with one of Joseph's Dream.

Genesis 37:9-11
9 And he dreamed yet another dream, and told it his brethren, and said, Behold, ***I have dreamed a dream more; and, behold, the sun and the moon and the eleven stars made obeisance to me.***
10 And he told it to his father, and to his brethren: and his father rebuked him, and said unto him, ***What is this dream that thou hast dreamed? Shall I and thy mother and thy brethren indeed come to bow down ourselves to thee to the earth?***
11 And his brethren envied him; but his father observed the saying.

So, Joseph had a dream that the sun, moon and stars bowed down to him. It is absolutely apparent that Joseph's father knew exactly what the meaning of that dream was because in his rebuke of Joseph, he asks, probably condescendingly, if he, his mother and brothers were to bow down to Joseph. In other words, Joseph's dream was insinuating that there would come a time in the not too distant future in which Joseph's parents and his brothers would indeed be under the authority of Joseph. This, of course, did occur when Joseph was taken captive by the Egyptians and later was exalted to a position just below pharaoh:

Genesis 41:41-43
41 And ***Pharaoh said unto Joseph, See, I have set thee over all the land of Egypt.***
42 And Pharaoh took off his ring from his hand, and put it upon Joseph's hand, and arrayed him in vestures of fine linen, and put a gold chain about his neck;

43 And he made him to ride in the second chariot which he had; and they cried before him, Bow the knee: and he made him ruler over all the land of Egypt.

Later on in Genesis 43-45, we see the fulfillment of Joseph's dream when his family journeys to Egypt for provision due to the seven years of famine that Joseph had predicted to Pharaoh. His family indeed was subject to Joseph's authority.

Take a look at the following examples of the usage of cosmic images that did not literally take place, but figuratively, and poetically, depicted a judgment that came upon a land or people group:

The fall of Babylon to the Medes-

Isaiah 13:9-10
9 Behold, the day of the Lord cometh, cruel both with wrath and fierce anger, to lay the land desolate: and he shall destroy the sinners thereof out of it.
*10 For **the stars of heaven and the constellations thereof shall not give their light: the sun shall be darkened in his going forth, and the moon shall not cause her light to shine.***

Amos prophesied for Israel, and this concerned the destruction and captivity of 721 B.C. by the Assyrians (see 6:14, and 5:27). The literal sun did not literally go down at noon and darken the earth. These were symbolic terms signifying the desolation and sorrow of the Israelites due to their calamity[16]-

Amos 8:9
*9 And it shall come to pass in that day, saith the Lord God, that **I will cause the sun to go down at noon, and I will darken the earth in the clear day**:*

Ezekiel predicting the destruction of Egypt-

Ezekiel 32:7-8
7 And when I shall put thee out, **I will cover the heaven, and make the stars thereof dark; I will cover the sun with a cloud, and the moon shall not give her light.**
8 All the bright lights of heaven will I make dark over thee, and set darkness upon thy land, saith the Lord God.

Obviously, none of these passages literally took place. The literal sun, moon and stars never literally fell or were darkened. These phrases and terminology depicted one thing, and that was the impending judgment that was to come upon those nations and people groups.

Case #2 – coming in the clouds of heaven (Matthew 24:30, Mark 13:26, Luke 21:27)

David Chilton did another splendid job in pointing out that the phrase 'on clouds' or 'in clouds' was used before in the Old Testament, but never referred to a literally 'surfing on the clouds' by the Lord:

> *"In the first place, all through the Old Testament God was coming "on clouds," in salvation of His people and destruction of His enemies: "He makes the clouds His chariot; He walks upon the wings of the wind" (Ps.104:3). When Isaiah prophesied God's judgment on Egypt, he wrote: "Behold, the LORD is riding on a swift cloud, and is about to come to Egypt; the idols of Egypt will tremble at His presence" (Isa.19:1). The prophet Nahum spoke similarly of God's destruction of Nineveh: "In whirlwind and storm is His way, and clouds are the dust beneath His feet" (Nab. 1:3). God's "coming on the clouds of heaven" is an almost commonplace Scriptural symbol for His presence, judgment, and salvation."* [17]

This past weekend, I heard the praise song "Days of Elijah" not once, but twice on the radio! The chorus of the song is as follows:

> *Behold He comes! Riding on the clouds!*
> *Shining like the sun! At the trumpet call*
> *Lift your voice! It's the year of Jubilee!*
> *And out of Zion's hill salvation comes!*

I love the song, but unfortunately, the context is entirely wrong and it is due to the misapplication of the phrase "coming on the clouds" in the Olivet Discourse. The sentiment of the great majority of Christians in the American church today is that there is coming a day (soon) when Jesus would literally 'crack the sky', come surfing down on a cloud so that He could rule and reign on a physical, literal throne in physical, literal Jerusalem. This is not what Jesus meant! He was using the same literary style of Old Testament prophets to depict a coming judgment upon the generation that He was speaking of, and not some generation 2,000 years in the future.

Exegesis vs. Eisegesis

Some view exegesis and hermeneutics as one and the same, or two terms that are interchangeable. I totally understand that point of view. But I look at exegesis as the interpretive tool used to convey or explain a text to others, while hermeneutics, to me, is the ground work that must be done before exegesis. Proper hermeneutics will yield proper exegesis.

However, what is seen in a lot of western churches and on Christian television today is a heavy dosage of eisegesis. Unlike exegesis (the interpreting of a text utilizing other biblical texts and the parameters that we use with proper hermeneutics), eisegesis is the act of interpreting a text through the lens of one's own presuppositions, agendas or biases. A reader that is slave to eisegesis is reading into the text what isn't there, and heralding that as truth. It is used to prove an already held opinion of a text. This is called 'confirmation bias', which is the tendency of people to favor information that confirms their beliefs or hypotheses.[18] Eisegesis ignores all of the parameters of proper biblical hermeneutics and exegesis and unfortunately creates biblical narratives that simply don't exist. It is the 'adding to the book of prophecy' and the 'taking away from the book of prophecy' in which the Lord forbids in Revelation 22:18-19:

Revelation 22:18-19
*18 For I testify unto every man that heareth the words of the prophecy of this book, **If any man shall add unto these things, God shall add unto him the plagues that are written in this book:***
19 And if any man shall take away from the words of the book of this prophecy, God shall take away his part out of the book of life, and out of the holy city, and from the things which are written in this book.

This is an extremely weighty matter, as evident by the Lord's strong warning against the manipulation of the prophetic words. Of course, this was in regards to Revelation, the letter John wrote to the seven churches in Asia in the first century. But I believe that there is a very important principle that must be heeded here. The proper interpretation of scripture is absolutely imperative because it has lasting ramifications on the overall outlook of the church and its understanding of the role that it plays in the future of humanity and in the earth. Entire interpretive systems have been built on a faulty foundation of poor hermeneutics and poor exegesis (eisegesis), which have had a profoundly negative impact on the American church as a whole. One of those faulty systems of interpretation is 'Dispensationalism'.

Chapter Fourteen:
Dispensationalism

That in the dispensation of the fulness of times he might gather together in one all things in Christ, both which are in heaven, and which are on earth; even in him: In whom also we have obtained an inheritance, being predestinated according to the purpose of him who worketh all things after the counsel of his own will: That we should be to the praise of his glory, who first trusted in Christ.

Ephesians 1:10-12

In Chapter Six, I wrote briefly about the three general eschatological viewpoints in the church today – Futurism, Historicism and Preterism. Each of these views have variations and splintered perspectives. But within Futurism, there is one particular eschatological ideology that has influenced the western church more than any other viewpoint, and that is dispensationalism. John Nelson Darby (1800-82) is considered the founder of dispensationalism. In an effort to address the necessity for the Word of God to be applicable to the modern generation and generations to come, Darby created a system that he thought would bring clarity to God's relationship with man in different ages or epochs. Within the system, Darby came to the conclusion that God deals differently with Israel and the church.

What is Dispensationalism?

The most influential, and yet, the most debilitating theological point of view in the western church today is dispensationalism. Vern S. Poythress, in his book entitled "Understanding Dispensationalists", defines dispensationalism as the following:

> "...a particular view of the parallel-but-separate roles and destinies of Israel and the church. Accompanying this view is a particular hermeneutical stance in which careful distinction is made between what is addressed to Israel and what is addressed to the church. What is addressed to Israel is 'earthly' in character and is to be interpreted 'literally'."[1]

Dispensationalism arrived in the United States via various writings by Darby. In the late 19th and early 20th centuries, prophetic conferences spawned across the country in which allowed dispensationalism to gain traction and influence. In his dissertation, "The Hermeneutics of Dispensationalism", Daniel P. Fuller comments on this phenomenon and the influx of dispensationalism by stating-

> "... America was attracted more by Darby's idea of an any-moment Coming than they were by his foundational concept of the two peoples of God... Darby, by his insistence on the possibility of Christ's coming at any moment, made Christ Himself, totally apart from any event, the great object of Hope. Darby was accepted [in America] because, as is so often the case, those revolting from one extreme took the alternative presented by the other extreme."[2]

The Scofield Reference Bible, in particular, contributed more than any other single work to the spread of dispensationalism in the United States.[3] You could probably go into 50% or more of the Christian homes in America and find a book shelf or Christian book collection that has this reference Bible. Cyrus I. Scofield (1843-1921) picked up the torch of John Darby, ran with it and added to Darby's dispensationalism. There are four distinct points in which delineate Scofield's brand of dispensationalism from any other eschatological position in the early 20th century:

- The belief that the history of the world is divided into epochs, or dispensations
- The belief that there are two peoples of God – Israel and the church
- The belief in a pretribulational rapture
- The belief that the bible is to be interpreted literally

According to Scofield, there are seven dispensations in human history:

1. **The Dispensation of Innocence** (or Freedom), (Gen. 2:8-17,25), prior to Adam's fall,
2. **The Dispensation of Conscience**, (Gen. 3:10-18; Rom. 2:11-15), Adam to Noah,
3. **The Dispensation of Government**, (Gen. 9:6; Rom. 13:1), Noah to Abraham,
4. **The Dispensation of Patriarchal Rule** (or Promise), (Gen. 12:1-3; 22:17-18; Gal. 3:15-19), Abraham to Moses,
5. **The Dispensation of the Mosaic Law**, (Ex. 20:1-26; Gal. 3:19), Moses to Christ,
6. **The Dispensation of Grace**, (Rom 5:20-21; Eph. 3:1-9), the current church age, and
7. **The Dispensation of the Kingdom** (a literal earthly 1,000 year Millennial Kingdom that has yet to come but soon will) (Is. 9:6-7; 11:1-9; Rev. 20:1-6).[4]

Each one of these dispensations is said to represent a different way in which God deals with man, specifically a different testing for man. "These periods are marked off in Scripture by some change in God's method of dealing with mankind, in respect to two questions: of sin, and of man's responsibility," explained C.I. Scofield. "Each of the dispensations may be regarded as a new test of the natural man, and each ends in judgment - marking his utter failure in every dispensation."₅

Dispensationalism teaches God has always had a different plan for natural Israel and the church. Lewis Sperry Chafer, American theologian, founder and first president of Dallas Theological Seminary, was also a prominent supporter and early voice of dispensationalism. He agreed with Scofield's viewpoint of a 'dual-track' program of God in which deals with both Israel and the church separately:

> *"The dispensationalist believes that throughout the ages God is pursuing two distinctive purposes: one related to the earth with earthly people and earthly objectives involved, while the other is related to heaven with heavenly people and heavenly objectives involved."*₆

Dispensationalism sees natural Israel (the modern day nation of Israel – political Israel) as still being the 'apple of God's eye' and not forgotten by God. They view the 'Dispensation of Grace', or the church age, as being a parenthetical age, and not an eternal age. They interpret Romans 11:25 as being evidence for the church age being a temporary age:

Romans 11:25
*For I would not, brethren, that ye should be ignorant of this mystery, lest ye should be wise in your own conceits; that **blindness in part is happened to Israel, until the fulness of the Gentiles be come in**.*

The dispensationalist believes that 'the fulness of the Gentiles be come in' refers to a future point in time when a God ordained set number of non-Jewish folks become believers in Jesus Christ. Consequently, at that very point, the scales will fall off of the eyes of the Jewish people, and they will then accept Jesus as Lord and Savior. To seal this viewpoint, the dispensationalist believes that the entire nation of Israel and all Jews in the world will be saved, according to Romans 11:26:

Romans 11:26
And so all Israel shall be saved*: as it is written, There shall come out of Sion the Deliverer, and shall turn away ungodliness from Jacob:*

Until the fulness of the Gentiles come in, according to dispensationalism, Israel is in a 'holding pattern' as it relates to the sovereign plan of God. This period of inactivity abruptly comes to an end when the 'rapture' of the church takes place. The rapture is the popular term used to describe one perceived view of the Lord's return based on the writings of the Apostle Paul in 1 Thessalonians 4:17. The word "rapture" comes from the Latin *rapere* used by the Vulgate to translate the Greek word *harpazo*, which is rendered by the phrase "caught up" in most English translations.[7] The mainstream view taught within dispensationalism is labeled as 'Pre-Tribulation Rapture'. This is the belief that the rapture will occur sometime prior to the beginning of "Daniel's 70th Week," interpreted as the final seven years of this age. In this view, believers will be translated into immortal bodies in the Rapture before the great persecutions by the Antichrist and seven years of Tribulation. Central passages for this view include 1 Thessalonians 4-5, Revelation 3:10, and all the passages that describe the Tribulation, but lack the word ekklesia in them (e.g., Daniel 9; 12; The Olivet Discourse; and Rev. 4-18.)[8]

Dispensationalists' literal interpretation of scripture binds them to some significant beliefs, aside from those that have been mentioned already. The dispensationalist believes-

- in a future Antichrist and that he will bring 3-1/2 years of peace and 3-1/2 years of persecution
- Antichrist, Satan, the Beast and False Prophet will be literally destroyed at Jesus' second coming
- in the literal destruction of the earth as we know it
- in a literal descending of a 'new heaven' upon a 'new earth' where the saints will live in peace forever as Jesus rules from a literal throne in Jerusalem

Significant Problems with Dispensationalism

Now that the basic tenets of dispensationalism have been covered, I will begin to talk about each one and point out the weaknesses of each point. Below is a list of the problems, and after that, I will discuss each one in detail:

- The belief that the church age is not eternal
- The belief that modern day Israel is God's chosen people
- The belief that there will be a future rapture of the church (Chapter 15 – The Rapture Theory)
- The belief that there will be a future Antichrist, Man of Sin, and Beast (Chapter 16 – 'Antichrist', 'Man of Sin' and the 'Beast')
- The belief in a literal destruction of the world and the creation of a literal new heaven and literal new earth (Chapter 17 – 'New Heaven' and 'New Earth')

The Belief That the Church Age is Not Eternal

I can generally agree with dispensationalism and its delineation of the various epochs, or ages in which God dealt with mankind. My agreement with this point is not anything that is of any significance because the mere belief in dispensations does not distinguish dispensationalism from many other views. Throughout church history there has been a universal understanding of the different ages or dispensations. However, in regards to scripture and the heart of God, there are only two ages that really matter. Paul made reference to these ages on two occasions in his epistles:

Ephesians 1:21
*Far above all principality, and power, and might, and dominion, and every name that is named, **not only in this world, but also in that which is to come:***

1 Timothy 4:8
*For bodily exercise profiteth little: but godliness is profitable unto all things, having **promise of the life that now is, and of that which is to come.***

Most people may think that Paul's usage of the word 'world' in Ephesians 1:21 is referring to the actual earth, and subsequently, would interpret this verse as saying that there would be another 'earth to come'. But when 'world' is defined appropriately, the reader would understand that Paul is referencing that current age, or dispensation in which he and the intended readers were living in. The current age at that time was the age of the Old Covenant. The world or age that was to come was the New Covenant age. This was the great contrast of the 1st century. The tension between the existing Old Covenant system and the inauguration of the New Covenant was the focus of the saints, and was pivotal in the annals of the history of mankind in general.

You will not find any reference in scripture that supports the notion that the church age is a 'parenthetical' age – that is, an age or period of time that is temporal. As a matter of fact, you'll find the exact opposite of this:

Ephesians 3:20-21
20 Now unto him that is able to do exceeding abundantly above all that we ask or think, according to the power that worketh in us,
*21 **Unto him be glory in the church by Christ Jesus throughout all ages, world without end**. Amen.*

Ephesians 3:21 (AMP)
*21 To Him be glory in **the church and in Christ Jesus throughout all generations forever and ever**. Amen (so be it).*

I don't think a rebuttal to the dispensationalist view of a temporal church age could be any clearer. Paul states emphatically that the church age is an eternal age – throughout ALL generations, as the Amplified Bible version puts it.

The belief that modern day Israel is God's chosen people

I believe I did a pretty thorough job of explaining how this is a fallacy in Chapter 7 – The Apple of God's Eye. If necessary, please go back and re-read that chapter. The fact of the matter is that God is absolutely no respecter of persons, just as Paul stated:

Romans 2:11
*For **there is no respect of persons with God.***

Ephesians 6:9
*And, ye masters, do the same things unto them, forbearing threatening: **knowing that your Master also is in heaven; neither is there respect of persons with him.***

Colossians 3:24-25
24 Knowing that of the Lord ye shall receive the reward of the inheritance: for ye serve the Lord Christ.
*25 But he that doeth wrong shall receive for the wrong which he hath done: and **there is no respect of persons.***

Even in James' epistle to the Hebrew Christians that were scattered about, he spoke poignantly about not having respect of persons because it was not the character of God:

James 2:1-5 (CEV)
*1My friends, **if you have faith in our glorious Lord Jesus Christ, you won't treat some people better than others**. 2 Suppose a rich person wearing fancy clothes and a gold ring comes to one of your meetings. And suppose a poor person dressed in worn-out clothes also comes. 3 You must not give the best seat to the one in fancy clothes and tell the one who is poor to stand at the side or sit on the floor. 4 That is the same as saying that some people are better than others, and you would be acting like a crooked judge.*
*5My dear friends, pay attention. God has given a lot of faith to the poor people in this world. **He has also promised them a share in his kingdom that he will give to everyone who loves him.***

God is not concerned with ethnicity or gender. Being in right-standing with God and entry into His kingdom is based on faith, and faith alone. No group of people has a monopoly on the blessings of the inheritance of the kingdom. Furthermore, we must understand who the Israel of God is. The Israel of God is not the modern day political state of Israel. The Israel of God is a spiritual family that is made up of Jews and Gentiles who come together as one in Christ Jesus. That body of believers is the church. Paul speaks of this group of believers as being the Israel of God:

Galatians 6:15-17
*15 For **in Christ Jesus neither circumcision availeth any thing, nor uncircumcision, but a new creature.***
*16 **And as many as walk according to this rule, peace be on them, and mercy, and upon the Israel of God.***
17 From henceforth let no man trouble me: for I bear in my body the marks of the Lord Jesus.

Galatians 6:16-17 (MSG)
*Can't you see the central issue in all this? It is not what you and I do—submit to circumcision, reject circumcision. It is what God is doing, and he is creating something totally new, a free life! **All who walk by this standard are the true Israel of God—his chosen people.** Peace and mercy on them!*

Paul speaking about there not being a difference between Jew and Greek-

Romans 10:12
*For **there is no difference between the Jew and the Greek: for the same Lord over all is rich unto all that call upon him.***

Galatians 3:28
There is neither Jew nor Greek**, there is neither bond nor free, there is neither male nor female: for **ye are all one in Christ Jesus.

Colossians 3:11
Where there is neither Greek nor Jew**, circumcision nor uncircumcision, Barbarian, Scythian, bond nor free: but **Christ is all, and in all.

The dispensationalist looks at Romans 11:25-26 without fully grasping what Paul says about who constitutes Israel, and even who is a Jew, for that matter.

Romans 2:28-29
*28 For **he is not a Jew, which is one outwardly**; neither is that circumcision, which is outward in the flesh:*
*29 But **he is a Jew, which is one inwardly; and circumcision is that of the heart, in the spirit, and not in the letter;** whose praise is not of men, but of God.*

Furthermore, if the chosen people of God were decided by ethnicity, Paul shoots that down with the following:

Romans 9:6-7
*6 Not as though the word of God hath taken none effect. For **they are not all Israel, which are of Israel:***
*7 **Neither, because they are the seed of Abraham, are they all children**: but, In Isaac shall thy seed be called.*

In essence, the belief that the modern day political nation of Israel becoming a state in 1948 is a sign that God has remembered them and a sign that is suppose to trigger some prophetic timeline as it relates to "end times" is absolutely preposterous and biblically unfounded. Citizens of Israel and Jews all around the world must come into the kingdom the same way that every other unbeliever comes in. There is no preferential treatment for Jews, or any people for that matter in regards to the kingdom of God.

Chapter Fifteen:
The Rapture Theory

In a moment, in the twinkling of an eye, at the last trump: for the trumpet shall sound, and the dead shall be raised incorruptible, and we shall be changed.
1 Corinthians 15:52

Perhaps the most fantastical false narrative in dispensationalism is the notion of a future rapture, or 'snatching away' of all Christians before a seven year tribulation period. Their argument stems from a literal interpretation of 1 Thessalonians 4:13-18:

1 Thessalonians 4:13-18
13 But I would not have you to be ignorant, brethren, concerning them which are asleep, that ye sorrow not, even as others which have no hope.
14 For if we believe that Jesus died and rose again, even so them also which sleep in Jesus will God bring with him.
15 For this we say unto you by the word of the Lord, that we which are alive and remain unto the coming of the Lord shall not prevent them which are asleep.
16 For the Lord himself shall descend from heaven with a shout, with the voice of the archangel, and with the trump of God: and the dead in Christ shall rise first:
17 Then we which are alive and remain shall be caught up together with them in the clouds, to meet the Lord in the air: and so shall we ever be with the Lord.
18 Wherefore comfort one another with these words.

The first thing that must be noted is the context of the passage. It is absolutely apparent that Paul is responding to a question by those in Thessalonica regarding what would happen to those that died before them (verse 13). In verse 18,

Paul tells the people to 'comfort each other with these words'. This is more evidence that they were concerned about what would happen to their loved ones at the resurrection of the dead. Therefore, Paul tells the people that they should not fret because it was a surety that the dead in Christ would rise first – before the living saints (verse 16). That is pretty much the crux of the matter.

Now, as to what Paul is referencing and the timing of this event, we must take a few things into consideration. First and foremost, the trigger of such an event is found in verse 16:

1 Thessalonians 4:16
For the Lord himself shall descend from heaven with a shout, with the voice of the archangel, and with the trump of God: and the dead in Christ shall rise first:

Where else in scripture do we see a 'coming of the Lord' and the sound of a trumpet? It's none other than in the Olivet Discourse (Matthew 24).

Matthew 24:30-31
30 And then shall appear the sign of the Son of man in heaven: and then shall all the tribes of the earth mourn, and they shall see the Son of man coming in the clouds of heaven with power and great glory.
*31 **And he shall send his angels with a great sound of a trumpet**, and they shall gather together his elect from the four winds, from one end of heaven to the other.*

If the 'trump of God' in 1 Thessalonians 4:16 is the same as the 'great sound of a trumpet' in Matthew 24:31, then we must determine when this sounding of the trumpet takes place. The context in which the trumpet sound occurs is found in the following verses:

Matthew 24:32-34
32 Now learn a parable of the fig tree; When his branch is yet tender, and putteth forth leaves, ye know that summer is nigh:
33 So likewise ye, when ye shall see all these things, know that it is near, even at the doors.

*34 Verily I say unto you, **This generation shall not pass, till all these things be fulfilled.***

Everything mentioned before verse 34 had to take place before the 'passing of that generation'. But what generation was Jesus referring to? To understand the full meaning of the Olivet Discourse, it is critical to take a look at Matthew 23. In this chapter, Jesus blasts (condemns) the scribes and Pharisees, beginning in verse 13. The most significant verses in this passage are found in verses 31-36:

Matthew 23:31-36
*31 Wherefore ye be witnesses unto yourselves, that **ye are the children of them which killed the prophets.***
*32 **Fill ye up then the measure of your fathers.***
*33 **Ye serpents, ye generation of vipers**, how can ye escape the damnation of hell?*
*34 Wherefore, behold, **I send unto you prophets, and wise men, and scribes: and some of them ye shall kill and crucify; and some of them shall ye scourge in your synagogues, and persecute them from city to city:***
*35 That **upon you may come all the righteous blood shed upon the earth**, from the blood of righteous Abel unto the blood of Zacharias son of Barachias, whom ye slew between the temple and the altar.*
*36 **Verily I say unto you, All these things shall come upon this generation.***

Unbeknownst to most people, Jesus is bringing to remembrance the prophecy of Moses in which he declares that judgment will come upon those that kill the servants of God. Deuteronomy 32 is one of the most fascinating prophetic passages in scripture because it describes in absolute prophetic detail the coming judgment and utter destruction of them that were considered God's own people. It would definitely be beneficial to read the chapter in its entirety, but for the sake of time, I will attempt to just highlight what I consider the most prominent verses in this passage (and hopefully not put the entire chapter in!):

Deuteronomy 32:4-5, 15-26, 28, 31, 35-36, 41-43
4 He is the Rock, his work is perfect: for all his ways are judgment: a God

of truth and without iniquity, just and right is he.
5 **They have corrupted themselves, their spot is not the spot of his children: they are a perverse and crooked generation.**

15 But Jeshurun waxed fat, and kicked: thou art waxen fat, thou art grown thick, thou art covered with fatness; then **he forsook God which made him, and lightly esteemed the Rock of his salvation.**
16 **They provoked him to jealousy with strange gods, with abominations provoked they him to anger.**
17 **They sacrificed unto devils, not to God**; *to gods whom they knew not, to new gods that came newly up, whom your fathers feared not.*
18 Of the Rock that begat thee thou art unmindful, and hast forgotten God that formed thee.
19 And when the Lord saw it, he abhorred them, because of the provoking of his sons, and of his daughters.
20 And he said, **I will hide my face from them,** <u>**I will see what their end shall be: for they are a very froward generation, children in whom is no faith.**</u>
21 They have moved me to jealousy with that which is not God; they have provoked me to anger with their vanities: and **I will move them to jealousy with those which are not a people; I will provoke them to anger with a foolish nation.**
22 For a fire is kindled in mine anger, and shall burn unto the lowest hell, and shall consume the earth with her increase, and set on fire the foundations of the mountains.
23 **I will heap mischiefs upon them**; *I will spend mine arrows upon them.*
24 **They shall be burnt with hunger, and devoured with burning heat, and with bitter destruction: I will also send the teeth of beasts upon them,** *with the poison of serpents of the dust.*
25 **The sword without, and terror within, shall destroy both the young man and the virgin, the suckling also with the man of gray hairs.**
26 I said, **I would scatter them into corners, I would make the remembrance of them to cease from among men:**

28 For they are **a nation void of counsel, neither is there any understanding in them.**
29 O that they were wise, that they understood this, <u>**that they would consider their latter end**</u>*!*

31 For their rock is not as our Rock, **even our enemies themselves being judges.**

35 **To me belongeth vengeance and recompence;** *their foot shall slide in*

*due time: for the day of their calamity is at hand, and the **things that shall come upon them make haste.***
36 For the Lord shall judge his people, and repent himself for his servants, when he seeth that their power is gone, and there is none shut up, or left.

41 If I whet my glittering sword, and mine hand take hold on judgment; I will render vengeance to mine enemies, and will reward them that hate me.
42 I will make mine arrows drunk with blood, and my sword shall devour flesh; and that with the blood of the slain and of the captives, from the beginning of revenges upon the enemy.
*43 **Rejoice, O ye nations, with his people: <u>for he will avenge the blood of his servants</u>, and will render vengeance to his adversaries, and will be merciful unto his land, and to his people.***

You might be saying to yourself right now, "Whoa! I never saw that before!" Just as Jesus did with reciting other Old Testament prophets, He did the same thing with this prophecy that was given by Moses. The generation that Moses foresaw was the same generation that Jesus was reprimanding in Matthew 23, and it was His contemporaneous generation, or the generation that He was living in at that very moment. What is the significance of all this? It creates a timeframe or a context for which the event that Paul spoke of in Thessalonians 4 was to take place.

So, what was this "catching away" suppose to look like? Were dead bodies supposed to literally break out of their tombs and float into the air to meet the Lord, and those that were alive would follow? I do not believe that this is the message that Paul was trying to convey because in doing so, he would discredit himself and the rest of scripture as well. Remember, for scripture to maintain the claim of infallibility, or inerrancy, there cannot be any contradictory passages within that would shoot down a 'rapture theory'. Consequently, we find in Hebrews 9:27 a verse that would seemingly create a problem for rapture supporters:

Hebrews 9:27
*27 And as **it is appointed unto men once to die, but after this the***

judgment:

Due to the linguistic structure and the style of writing, I believe that Hebrews was a letter written by Paul to the Hebrew Christian church in the 1st century. That being the case, the assertion that Paul would say to the Thessalonians that their living bodies would be caught up in the air (1 Thessalonians 4:17), while telling the Hebrews that 'every man must die', would seem absolutely contradictory. I submit to you that Paul was speaking of the dead in Christ rising at the coming of the Lord (which, by the way, was the wrath and judgment that was released upon the Jews for their killing of the apostles and prophets, and culminated with the destruction of the temple in 70 AD), and thereafter, every saint of God that dies immediately ascends to be with the Lord forever. Keep in mind that Paul's sole purpose of this passage was to comfort the hearts of those that had questions about the future of their loved ones that had passed away. Paul comforts them by reassuring them that the dead in Christ had not been forgotten and that they would proceed to meet the Lord before those that were still living.

Another passage that must be taken into consideration when trying to fully understand what Paul is trying to convey is found in Revelation 14:13:

Revelation 14:13
13 And I heard a voice from heaven saying unto me, Write, **Blessed are the dead which die in the Lord from henceforth**: *Yea, saith the Spirit, that they may rest from their labours; and their works do follow them.*

I will talk about this verse in more detail later on, but in regards to the rapture theory which hinges upon a 'catching away' of dead and living saints at the end of time, this passage presents a terrible dilemma. Dispensationalism, the popular end-time view point, teaches that at the end of the world, there is a 'rapture' of the saints, and after this point, there is no more dying, no more tears, etc. However, in John's letter to the seven churches in Asia, he writes that he heard a voice from heaven saying 'blessed are the dead which die in the Lord from now on!' This leads to the conclusion that after this event (the coming of the Lord) there would still be people that are dying! I believe that this is congruent with the sentiment of Paul in 1 Thessalonians 4:17. At the coming of the Lord, the dead in Christ did rise and meet the Lord in the air (heaven). I believe that this rising was spiritual in nature because flesh and blood cannot inherit the kingdom.

1 Corinthians 15:50
*Now this I say, brethren, that **flesh and blood cannot inherit the kingdom of God**; neither doth corruption inherit incorruption.*

Paul later states in his first letter to the Corinthians that they would all be changed in a moment - in the twinkling of an eye (1 Corinthians 15:51-52). But this passage must also pass the litmus test of Hebrews 9:27 which states that every man must die. 1 Corinthians 15:50-54 must be interpreted through the same lens that 1 Thessalonians 4:15-18 is interpreted with because they are addressing the same event. I also submit to you that the 'twinkling of an eye' statement that Paul makes is synonymous with something else that he mentions regarding what happens after physical death:

2 Corinthians 5:6-10
*6 Therefore we are always confident, knowing that, **whilst we are at home in the body, we are absent from the Lord:***
7 (For we walk by faith, not by sight:)
*8 **We are confident, I say, and willing rather to be absent from the body, and to be present with the Lord.***
9 Wherefore we labour, that, whether present or absent, we may be accepted of him.
*10 For **we must all appear before the judgment seat of Christ**; that every one may receive the things done in his body, according to that he hath done, whether it be good or bad.*

In a second letter to the very same people that Paul talked about 'changing in the twinkling of an eye', he writes about what happens after the death of a saint. They are immediately translated into the presence of the Lord (v. 8). Also, in verse 10, he states that they all (and we all) must appear before the judgment seat of Christ. This is verification and validation of what is mentioned in Hebrews 9:27 – 'it is appointed to man once to die, then judgment'. Therefore, I believe that the ideal of there being a future literal 'catching away' of dead and living saints is preposterous, one, and two, it is totally taken out of the context in which Paul was speaking. With the initiation of the 'catching away' being tied to the trump of God, in which is the same as the trumpets that we see in Matthew 24, there is no way that we can assume that the event is speaking of a future point in time.

Chapter Sixteen:
Misinterpreting 'Antichrist', 'Man of Sin' and the 'Beast'

That ye be not soon shaken in mind, or be troubled, neither by spirit, nor by word, nor by letter as from us, as that the day of Christ is at hand.
Let no man deceive you by any means: for that day shall not come, except there come a falling away first, and that man of sin be revealed, the son of perdition;
Who opposeth and exalteth himself above all that is called God, or that is worshipped; so that he as God sitteth in the temple of God, shewing himself that he is God.

2 Thessalonians 2:2-4

Another hallmark of dispensationalism is the belief that there is a coming 'Mr. Diabolical' that is labeled either 'The Antichrist', the 'Man of Sin', or the 'Beast'. Essentially, dispensationalists believe that after the church is 'raptured', this 'Boogey Man' character will be cunning and seductive in orchestrating a peace treaty at the beginning of the seven year tribulation period. They believe that the first 3-1/2 years will be peaceful, but the latter 3-1/2 years will be filled with tribulation, violence, murder, and the forced coercion to take "the mark of the beast". However, when understanding these various terms within the context of scripture, the truth of the matter paints a picture that is absolutely foreign to the false narrative that dispensational futurists are presenting to the masses.

'Antichrist'

It is absolutely dumb-founding to me how the term

'antichrist' has been taken and transformed to denote one future evil, spooky dude, when the only references made to 'antichrist' had nothing to do with one particular individual in the future. The term 'antichrist' appears just four times in John's letters to the saints that were living during his lifetime. Below are the four verses that speak of antichrist(s):

1 John 2:18
*Little children, it is the last time: and as ye have heard that **antichrist** shall come, even now are there many **antichrists**; whereby we know that it is the last time.*

1 John 2:22
*Who is a liar but he that denieth that Jesus is the Christ? He is **antichrist**, that denieth the Father and the Son.*

1 John 4:3
*And every spirit that confesseth not that Jesus Christ is come in the flesh is not of God: and this is that spirit of **antichrist**, whereof ye have heard that it should come; and even now already is it in the world.*

2 John 1:7
*For many deceivers are entered into the world, who confess not that Jesus Christ is come in the flesh. This is a deceiver and an **antichrist**.*

There are a few significant things to note here:

- According to 1 John 2:18, there are 'many antichrists', and not just one Mr. Diabolical
- According to 1 John 2:18, antichrists were prevalent in John's generation, denoting that it was 'the last time' (end of days, latter days, last days, end of the world)
- According to 1 John 2:18, the people were told that antichrists would soon come in their day
- According to 1 John 2:22, antichrist is anyone that denies the Father and the Son
- According to 1 John 4:3, antichrist is a spirit, and not a man
- Again, according to 1 John 4:3, the people were told

that the spirit of antichrist would come in their day, and that it was already prevalent in the world
- According to 2 John 1:7, an antichrist is a deceiver – one that denies that Jesus Christ came in the flesh, and many of these deceivers had already entered into the world at that time

In his eschatological classic book, "The Parousia: The New Testament Doctrine of Our Lord's Second Coming", J. Stuart Russell states the following about antichrist:

> *"It is certainly remarkable, considering the place which this name has filled in theological and ecclesiastical literature, how very small a space it occupies in the New Testament. Except in the epistles of St. John, the name antichrist never occurs in the apostolic writings. But though the name is absent, the thing is not unknown. St. John evidently speaks of 'the antichrist' as an idea familiar to his readers,---a power whose coming was anticipated, and whose presence was an indication that 'the last hour' had come. 'Ye have heard that the antichrist cometh; even now are there many antichrists; whereby we know that it is the last hour.'"*[1]

During the time that John was writing these letters, the early church began experiencing apostasy, or the falling away from the faith. This was the prophetic fulfillment of what Jesus had warned about in Matthew 24:

Matthew 24:4-5, 11, 23-26
4 And Jesus answered and said unto them, **Take heed that no man deceive you.**
5 For **many shall come in my name, saying, I am Christ; and shall deceive many.**

11 And **many false prophets shall rise, and shall deceive many.**

23 Then **if any man shall say unto you, Lo, here is Christ, or there; believe it not.**

*24 For **there shall arise false Christs, and false prophets**, and shall shew great signs and wonders; insomuch that, if it were possible, **they shall deceive the very elect.***
25 Behold, I have told you before.
*26 Wherefore **if they shall say unto you, Behold, he is in the desert; go not forth: behold, he is in the secret chambers; believe it not.***

David Chilton addresses the fact that the apostles were constantly warning against false teachers and false apostles:

> *"...Again and again the apostles found themselves issuing stern warnings against tolerating false teachers and "false apostles" (Rom. 16:17-18; 2 Cor. 11:3-4, 12-15; Phil. 3:18-19; 1 Tim. 1:3-7; 2 Tim. 4:2-5), for these had been the cause of massive departures from the faith, and the extent of apostasy was increasing as the era progressed (1 Tim. 1:19-20, 6:20-21; 2 Tim. 2:16-18; 3:1-9, 13; 4:10, 14-16). One of the last letters of the New Testament, the Book of Hebrews, was written to an entire Christian community on the very brink of wholesale abandonment of Christianity..."*[2]

It was the evidence of these apostates being prevalent and the actual falling away from Christianity by many in the 1st century due to false doctrine, false teaching and false apostles, that signified that it was 'the last time', or 'end of days'. As mentioned before, the 'end of days' refers to the end of the old covenant age. These apostates were antichrists because they denied Christ. They had once believed the gospel of Jesus Christ, but then fell away and began trying to deceive the other saints into falling away as well.

Dispensational futurists must absolutely deny the fact that John, when using the term 'antichrist', was referring to actual individuals in the first century that fell away from the faith. This is the danger of taking scripture and misapplying it to a generation that it was not intended to be speaking of. Today, we have millions of people in the United States that are literally looking for 'THE Antichrist'. Throughout modern history, many world figures have been labeled as being the Antichrist. From Joseph Stalin, to Adolf Hitler, to Mao Zedong, to Mikal Gorbechev, to Saddam Hussein, to Mahmoud Ahmadinejad, to whoever is the Pope of the Roman Catholic Church, to George Bush Jr. and Sr., and to Barack Obama – they have all been labeled at one time or another as THE Antichrist. This nonsense has to stop immediately!

'Man of Sin'

In dispensationalism, the terms 'Antichrist', 'Man of sin' and 'Beast' are often used interchangeably. The dispensationalist sees these terms as referring to the same future Mr. Diabolical that will terrorize the inhabitants of the earth if they were not 'raptured'. However, when keeping scripture in historical context, a much different, much clearer and more concise picture is painted in which identifies what these terms are, and who they are applied to. I just talked about the term 'Antichrist' and how it never refers to a future devilish dude 2000+ years after John's epistles were written. Now, let's take a look at the term 'Man of sin' to bring more clarity to what it actually refers to. The only mention of 'man of sin' is found in 2 Thessalonians:

2 Thessalonians 2:2-10
2 That ye be not soon shaken in mind, or be troubled, neither by spirit, nor by word, nor by letter as from us, as that the day of Christ is at hand.
*3 Let no man deceive you by any means: for that day shall not come, except there come a falling away first, and that **man of sin** be revealed, the son of perdition;*
4 Who opposeth and exalteth himself above all that is called God, or that is worshipped; so that he as God sitteth in the temple of God, shewing himself that he is God.
5 Remember ye not, that, when I was yet with you, I told you these things?
6 And now ye know what withholdeth that he might be revealed in his time.
7 For the mystery of iniquity doth already work: only he who now letteth will let, until he be taken out of the way.
8 And then shall that Wicked be revealed, whom the Lord shall consume with the spirit of his mouth, and shall destroy with the brightness of his

coming:
9 Even him, whose coming is after the working of Satan with all power and signs and lying wonders,
10 And with all deceivableness of unrighteousness in them that perish; because they received not the love of the truth, that they might be saved.

To determine who this 'man of sin' is, we must take into consideration some contextual evidence within the above passage that will give us a time frame in which the 'man of sin' was to exist. First and foremost, it must be noted that Paul is writing about this to the church at Thessalonica for some particular reason. It would make no sense whatsoever for Paul to write about something that was supposed to happen 2000+ years in the future, and send it to that 1st century church. Furthermore, evidently, this was not the first time in which Paul had spoken to them about a coming 'man of sin', as we see is suggested in verse 5 – *'Remember ye not, that, when I was yet with you, I told you these things?'*.

Throughout the passage, Paul gives descriptors in which assists in identifying this 'man of sin'. J. Stuart Russell created a list of those descriptors. The 'man of sin' is-

1. An individual; a man
2. A public person
3. A person holding a high rank of authority
4. A heathen; non-Jewish
5. One that claims divine names and demands worship
6. One that pretends to exercise supernatural powers
7. Characterized by enormous wickedness
8. Distinguished by lawlessness as a ruler
9. Not at the fulness of his power at the time of the writing of the epistle; there was someone that impeded his influence
10. Impeded by a person that the Thessalonians knew; that person would soon be taken out of the way
11. Is doomed to destruction
12. Is the preceding figure to the 'coming of the Lord'[3]

There is only one person in the annals of history that could possibly fit the bill for every descriptor that was given by Paul. That would be none other than Nero, the first persecuting emperor of the saints in the 1st century. Nero was the vilest, most ruthless, repugnant, wicked, and evil man that existed during the time period in which this epistle was written. At that time, Roman emperors were considered to be 'gods' amongst the people and were openly worshiped as such. Statues and coins that bore their images were inscribed with the word 'Divus' (god) on them.[4]

Nero was restrained from having total power and becoming emperor by his still living step-father, Claudius. His equally power-thirsty and corrupt mother, Agrippina, plotted to have Claudius killed so that her son, Nero, could then take the throne. But the wrath of her son eventually turned on her, as well as other members of his family. In "The Life and Epistles of St. Paul", W.J. Conybeare and J.S. Howson states-

> "...Hitherto, his public measures had been guided by sage advisers, and his cruelty had injured his own family rather than the State. But already, at the age of twenty-five, he had murdered his innocent wife and his adopted brother, and had dyed his hands in the blood of his mother... His degrading want of dignity and insatiable appetite for vulgar applause drew tears from the councillors and servants of his house, who could see him slaughter his nearest relatives without remonstrance."[5]

Perhaps most importantly, as it relates to the contradiction that is presented within dispensationalism, is the fact that the man of sin, being Nero in the first century, preceded the coming of the Lord. 2 Thess. 2:8 says that the 'man of sin' (Nero) would be destroyed 'with the brightness of his (The Lord's) coming'. 'Brightness' denotes the dawn, or the beginning of the Lord's coming. Hence, it is at the beginning stages of the Lord's coming that Nero would taste death, according to Paul. This did take place historically. According to Suetonius (Gaius Suetonius Tranquillus) (c. 69 – after 122), a Roman secretary and historian, Nero committed suicide in 68 AD when he had been pronounced a public enemy by the senate and was sentenced to execution.[6] One of the things that signified the beginning stages of the Lord's coming (which, as mentioned earlier, was a judgment and wrath to be released upon the Jews for killing the apostles and prophets, as prophesied by Jesus in Matthew 23) was the gathering of the Roman armies outside of the city gates of Jerusalem, which took place in the year 66 AD:

Luke 21:20-22
*20 And when **ye shall see Jerusalem compassed with armies, then know that the desolation thereof is nigh.***
21 Then let them which are in Judaea flee to the mountains; and let them which are in the midst of it depart out; and let not them that are in the countries enter thereinto.
*22 For **these be the days of vengeance, that all things which are written may be fulfilled.***

Of course, there are figures throughout all of history that fit some of the descriptions of the 'man of sin'. But no other man in history fits the bill as well as Nero does. And the fact that Paul speaks of him in a contemporaneous sense further solidifies the position of Nero being the 'man of sin'. It would make no logical sense for him to speak to the Thessalonians about some evil individual that would have similar traits thousands of years in the future. Paul addressed the issue because it was 'at hand', as he mentions in 2 Thessalonians 2:2:

2 Thessalonians 2:1-2
1 Now we beseech you, brethren, by the coming of our Lord Jesus Christ, and by our gathering together unto him,
*2 That ye be not soon shaken in mind, or be troubled, neither by spirit, nor by word, nor by letter as from us, as that **the day of Christ is at hand.***

'Beast'

We are introduced to this entity called the 'Beast' in Revelation 13. The first verse of this chapter is chalked full of indicators as to who or what the 'beast' is:

Revelation 13:1
And I stood upon the sand of the sea, and saw a beast rise up out of the sea, having seven heads and ten horns, and upon his horns ten crowns, and upon his heads the name of blasphemy.

Recalling a prophecy of Daniel will lead us to more clarity of what the 'beast' really is. We see in Daniel 7 the mentioning of four beasts coming up from the sea that are different than each other (Daniel 7:3). This dream that Daniel had is a parallel interpretation of the dream that king Nebuchadnezzar had in Daniel 2:

Daniel 2 (Great Image)	Daniel 7 (Beasts)	Meaning
Head of Gold	Like a lion	Babylonian Empire
Breast / Arms Silver	Like a bear	Median/Persian Empire
Belly / Thighs Brass	Like a leopard	Grecian Empire
Legs of Iron	Dreadful w/ iron teeth & ten horns	Roman Empire

The different parts of the 'great image' in Daniel 2 and the different beasts in Daniel 7 represent four different kingdoms. The Roman Empire is the kingdom that 'crushed' all other kingdoms and was the prevailing empire at the time of John's writing of Revelation. The word 'sea' in Revelation 13:1 is not to be taken literally, but is a representation of the people of the presiding kingdom. David Chilton, on the word 'sea'-

> "...after the Fall, the picture of the raging deep is used and developed in Scripture as a symbol of the world in chaos through the rebellion of men and nations against God: 'The wicked are like the tossing sea; for it cannot be quiet, and its waters toss up refuse and mud' (Isa. 57:20; cf. 17:12).

> *Thus John is told later that 'the waters which you saw... are peoples and multitudes and nations and tongues' (Rev. 17:15). Out of this chaotic, rebellious mass of humanity emerged Rome, an entire empire founded on the premise of opposition to God."*[7]

So, the 'beast' was undoubtedly the Roman Empire, but it also refers to the Roman Emperor in which the Empire would be a reflection of – and that would be Nero. His character and personality literally resembled that of a savage beast. Nero persecuted the Christians because they would not bow down to his self-proclaimed god-like status (similar with all the Caesars). Outside of the agora (Roman marketplace) stood statues of Nero in which the patrons were required to worship with the burning of incense. The ashes from the incense were then smeared on the forehead or the hand, signifying that they had worshipped the image of the beast, and that allowed the patron to buy and sell in the marketplace. This is what John was referencing in Revelation 13:16-17:

Revelation 13:16-17
*16 And he causeth all, both small and great, rich and poor, free and bond, to **receive a mark in their right hand, or in their foreheads:**
17 And that **no man might buy or sell, save he that had the mark, or the name of the beast**, or the number of his name.*

Even more astonishingly, John gave a critical hint to his first century readers by telling them exactly who the beast was. He identified the beast with the number 666:

Revelation 13:18
*18 Here is wisdom. Let him that hath understanding **count the number of the beast: for it is the number of a man; and his number is Six hundred threescore and six.***

In the Hebrew language, each letter has a numerical value. Hence, the number of anyone's name during that time could be tabulated by adding up the sum of the numbers that represent each letter. Now, why would John give the 'number of a man' to a first century reader if 'that man' would not live until 2000+ years in the future? Why would he tell the reader to 'count the number of the beast' if that beast did not exist in their time, but was something that would exist in the far future? He gave them this number because 'that man' lived during that time. He understood that the one that could decipher who 'that man' was had to be learned and understand Hebrew to be able to interpret it. 'Nero Caesar' (Neron Caesar) in Hebrew is Nron Qsr. It transliterates into Hebrew as נרון קסר. The numerical values of each of these characters are as follows:

Resh (ר)	Samekh (ס)	Qoph (ק)	Nun (נ)	Vav (ו)	Resh (ר)	Nun (נ)	Sum
200	60	100	50	6	200	50	666

Yet, there was another beast, the 'beast of the land' that John made mention of also:

Revelation 13:11
*11 And I beheld **another beast coming up out of the earth**; and he had two horns like a lamb, and he spake as a dragon.*

This 'beast of the land' is the antichrist spirit that dwelt among the unbelieving Jews and was causing saints to fall away from the faith. This 'land beast' is the 'clay' that is found in Daniel's prophecy (Daniel 2). It co-mingled, and co-ruled the people of the land (the Jews / Israel) along side of the stronger element, the 'iron', which represented the Roman Empire:

Daniel 2:33, 41-43
*33 His legs of iron, **his feet part of iron and part of clay**.*

*41 And whereas thou sawest **the feet and toes, part of potters' clay, and part of iron, the kingdom shall be divided; but there shall be in it of the strength of the iron, forasmuch as thou sawest the iron mixed with miry***

clay.
42 And as the toes of the feet were part of iron, and part of clay, so the kingdom shall be partly strong, and partly broken.
43 And whereas thou sawest iron mixed with miry clay, **they shall mingle themselves with the seed of men: but they shall not cleave one to another, even as iron is not mixed with clay.**

The 'beast of the land' is also the whore of Babylon (the woman of Revelation 17), who rode on the beast (Rev. 17:7). Revelation 17:6 says that she was "drunken with the blood of the saints, and with the blood of the martyrs of Jesus." Who else have we heard would have the blood of the saints on their hands? It's none other than the Pharisees and scribes that Jesus was giving the 'woes' to in Matthew 23:

Matthew 23:34-35
34 Wherefore, behold, **I send unto you prophets, and wise men, and scribes: and some of them ye shall kill and crucify; and some of them shall ye scourge in your synagogues,** *and persecute them from city to city:*
35 **That upon you may come all the righteous blood shed upon the earth,** *from the blood of righteous Abel unto the blood of Zacharias son of Barachias, whom ye slew between the temple and the altar.*

I believe that without going into extreme detail of every single piece of evidence which further describes who 'the beast' is, you can already see that there is undisputable evidence that John's mentioning of 'beast', with its multiple applications, absolutely refers to and highlights a first century fulfillment. Unfortunately, what dispensationalism, the popular end-time viewpoint, teaches is that these references do not point to entities in which the first century reader would easily identify. Rather, the information given to them by John really isn't relevant to them because the arrival of these entities would be 2000+ years in the future. Absolutely preposterous! The dispensationalist must unapologetically ignore the fact that Revelation was a letter written to a first century audience about things that were to 'shortly come to pass' (Rev. 1:1) because the 'time was at hand' (Rev. 1:3). Consequently, because the dispensational futurist is looking for a future 'Dr. Evil', his whole viewpoint on other things regarding the kingdom, New Jerusalem, and 'new heavens' and 'new earth' will be severely skewed as well.

Chapter Seventeen:
Misinterpreting 'New Heaven' and 'New Earth'

For as the new heavens and the new earth, which I will make, shall remain before me, saith the Lord, so shall your seed and your name remain.

Isaiah 66:22

    Dispensationalists and mainstream futurists, in general, believe that there is coming a time when the literal heaven and earth will be destroyed by God. Afterwards, according to this viewpoint, God will create a literal new heaven and earth to replace the former heaven and earth. Another interesting component of this viewpoint is the belief that the saints who were caught into the air to meet the Lord (1 Thess. 4:16-18) would literally descend back down with Jesus, the new heaven and new earth. It is at this point where the dispensationalist believes that the saints of God will live forever in the presence of the Lord, with Jesus sitting on a literal, physical throne in a literal, physical place that they believe would be New Jerusalem. Unfortunately, this is another misleading narrative in the dispensational / futurist paradigm because it negates keeping scripture in context and understanding the metaphorical interpretations of 'heaven' and 'earth'.

    There are plenty of examples in the Old Testament where you will find the terms 'heaven' and 'earth' referring not to the earth and sky literally, but as representations of people and places. More specifically, 'heaven' represents theocratic authority, whereas, 'earth' represents the people, place or nation in which is subject to, or under the authority of that theocratic system. This metaphorical referencing is found plenty of times in some of the books of the Old Testament prophets.

Isaiah 1:2
*2 **Hear, O heavens, and give ear, O earth**: for the Lord hath spoken, I have nourished and brought up children, and they have rebelled against me.*

In the verse above, Isaiah is calling two different people to attention. 'Hear O heavens' is the calling to attention of the theocratic leadership (the religious-political authorities within Judah). 'Give ear, O earth' is the summoning of all of the inhabitants of Judah to attention to heed the word of the Lord.

Isaiah 24:1-5
*1 Behold, **the Lord maketh the earth empty, and maketh it waste, and turneth it upside down, and scattereth abroad the inhabitants thereof.***
2 And it shall be, as with the people, so with the priest; as with the servant, so with his master; as with the maid, so with her mistress; as with the buyer, so with the seller; as with the lender, so with the borrower; as with the taker of usury, so with the giver of usury to him.
3 The land shall be utterly emptied, and utterly spoiled: for the Lord hath spoken this word.
*4 **The earth mourneth and fadeth away, the world languisheth and fadeth away**, the haughty people of the earth do languish.*
*5 **The earth also is defiled under the inhabitants thereof**; because they have transgressed the laws, changed the ordinance, broken the everlasting covenant.*

In the prophetic decree above, Isaiah says that the Lord would make the earth empty and 'turn it upside down'. This was a prophecy which foretold the coming attack of the Jewish people at the hand of the Assyrians. It was a warning to all of the inhabitants of the land that because they had forsaken God, transgressed the law, and broken covenant, the wages of their sin would come in the form of an attack of the land by the Assyrians. "The earth" is metaphorically representative of the land and the people of the land.

Isaiah 34:1-8

*1 Come near, ye nations, to hear; and hearken, ye people: let **the earth hear**, and all that is therein; the world, and all things that come forth of it.*
2 For the indignation of the Lord is upon all nations, and his fury upon all their armies: he hath utterly destroyed them, he hath delivered them to the slaughter.
3 Their slain also shall be cast out, and their stink shall come up out of their carcases, and the mountains shall be melted with their blood.
*4 And **all the host of heaven shall be dissolved, and the heavens shall be rolled together as a scroll**: and all their host shall fall down, as the leaf falleth off from the vine, and as a falling fig from the fig tree.*
*5 For **my sword shall be bathed in heaven**: behold, it shall come down upon Idumea, and upon the people of my curse, to judgment.*
6 The sword of the Lord is filled with blood, it is made fat with fatness, and with the blood of lambs and goats, with the fat of the kidneys of rams: for the Lord hath a sacrifice in Bozrah, and a great slaughter in the land of Idumea.
7 And the unicorns shall come down with them, and the bullocks with the bulls; and their land shall be soaked with blood, and their dust made fat with fatness.
*8 For **it is the day of the Lord's vengeance, and the year of recompences for the controversy of Zion.***

Isaiah prophesied, with unbelievable accuracy, the coming destruction upon Edom, which is also called Idumea. It was to be the 'day of the Lord's vengeance' and the 'year of recompenses'. In other words, it was the fully released wrath of God upon a people group by another people group. The phrase 'let the earth hear', found in verse 1, is in reference to the inhabitants of the land. In verse 4, we see the phrases 'host of heaven shall be dissolved' and 'heavens shall be rolled together as a scroll'. When taken literally, this verse makes absolutely no sense, whatsoever. How is it possible for the heavens to dissolve, and for the heavens to be rolled up as a scroll? Furthermore, since this event did take place historically, why aren't the heavens literally destroyed today? It doesn't take a rocket scientist to understand that this verse is to be interpreted metaphorically. The basic meaning of this verse is the utter failure of 'heaven', or the theocratic governing system that prevailed in the land.

Jeremiah 51:25
*25 Behold, I am against thee, O destroying mountain, saith the Lord, **which destroyest all the earth**: and I will stretch out mine hand upon thee, and roll thee down from the rocks, and will make thee a burnt mountain.*

Through the prophet, Jeremiah, God warns the nation of Babylon about what would come upon them for destroying Judah, which is represented by the word 'earth'. The Lord says "which destroyest all the earth", meaning that it was past tense. Now, a literalist would have to answer the question 'Why is the earth still in existence if this word 'earth' referred to the literal earth?" The Babylonians did not destroy 'all the earth' literally. Since that is the case, the reader is forced to look at the passage metaphorically. It is the only way to derive a sensible conclusion.

So, with all of these various examples of how 'heaven' and 'earth' are used in the Old Testament (and there are plenty of more), how are we to interpret how those terms are used in the New Testament? How are we to understand Jesus' own usage of the terms in the Olivet Discourse?

Matthew 24:29-30, 34-35
*29 Immediately after the tribulation of those days shall the sun be darkened, and the moon shall not give her light, and **the stars shall fall from heaven, and the powers of the heavens shall be shaken**:*
30 And then shall appear the sign of the Son of man in heaven: and then shall all the tribes of the earth mourn, and they shall see the Son of man coming in the clouds of heaven with power and great glory.

34 Verily I say unto you, This generation shall not pass, till all these things be fulfilled.
*35 **Heaven and earth shall pass away**, but my words shall not pass away.*

Here, we see the word 'heaven' used in apocalyptic language, which I've previously pointed out that 'sun be darkened' and 'moon not giving light' refers to the catastrophic falling of a government system or authority. It is no different here. Jesus is prophesying the then coming destruction of 'heaven', which metaphorically defines the theocratic system

Misinterpreting 'New Heaven' and 'New Earth' | 207

that governed Judea. The symbol of this theocratic system was the temple in Jerusalem. Everything regarding the religiosity and politics within Judea was centered upon and within the temple complex. Hence, the temple was the symbol of the Mosaic Law, or old covenant.

Unfortunately, what dispensationalism teaches is that there is coming a time when the literal heaven and earth shall pass away, as referenced in Matthew 24:35. This is a tragic misinterpretation of scripture because it totally ignores the Old Testament precedent for the usage of the terms heaven and earth. Jesus was not referring to a literal destruction, or passing away of the literal heavens and earth. He was referring to the passing away of the old covenant, which was historically symbolized by the destruction of Jerusalem in 70 AD. The writer of Hebrews spoke of this old covenant system that was preparing to pass away in the first century. In Hebrews 8, the writer compares and contrasts the old covenant with the new covenant, and then states the following:

Hebrews 8:13
13 In that he saith, ***A new covenant, he hath made the first old. Now that which decayeth and waxeth old is ready to vanish away.***

'That which decayeth and waxeth old' is in reference to the old covenant. The writer says that it is 'ready to vanish away'. This is the same thing that Jesus says in Matthew 24:35. He says that 'heaven and earth' would pass away. There's another verse that perfectly ties 'heaven and earth' to the old covenant:

Matthew 5:18
18 For verily I say unto you, ***Till heaven and earth pass, one jot or one tittle shall in no wise pass from the law,*** *till all be fulfilled.*

In this verse, Jesus insinuates that 'heaven and earth' are directly tied to the fate of the law. When heaven and earth passes, so will the law. As long as the law remains, heaven and earth remains. This is the sentiment of Jesus. Now, for dispensationalists and futurists that believe that heaven and earth have yet to be destroyed, or passed away, they are stuck with the conundrum of also believing that the old covenant law is still intact as well. They would have to believe that the sacrifice of bulls and goats is honored by God. Furthermore, they would have to believe that every 'jot and tittle' of the law is still in effect. And yet, they would have to explain away Hebrews' mentioning of the old covenant being ready to vanish away in his own generation. Can you see the inconsistency with this viewpoint? It totally presents contradictory statements between Jesus' own words, as well as Jesus and the words written to the Hebrew Christians. Consistency is critical and scripture must be seamless. Contradictions and discrepancies would totally relegate scripture to being fallible and untrustworthy. This is what dispensationalism does with many things in scripture, but especially regarding the terms heaven and earth.

Old vs. New

Now that I have shown how 'heaven and earth' is to be defined using Old Testament precedent, I will turn my attention to the phrases 'new heaven' and 'new earth'. Quite frankly, this is even more simple to me and it should be to you, since the old 'heaven and earth' has been defined as representing the old covenant system. See the following simple equation-

IF
OLD COVENANT = HEAVEN AND EARTH,
THEN
NEW COVENANT = NEW HEAVEN AND NEW EARTH

I should just end the chapter right here, but I'll take a closer look and dispel some modern dispensational beliefs about 'new heaven and new earth'. We see the first New Testament reference of 'new heaven and new earth' in Revelation 21:

Misinterpreting 'New Heaven' and 'New Earth' | 209

Revelation 21:1-5
*1 And I saw a **new heaven and a new earth: for the first heaven and the first earth were passed away;** and there was no more sea.*
2 And I John saw the holy city, new Jerusalem, coming down from God out of heaven, prepared as a bride adorned for her husband.
3 And I heard a great voice out of heaven saying, Behold, the tabernacle of God is with men, and he will dwell with them, and they shall be his people, and God himself shall be with them, and be their God.
4 And God shall wipe away all tears from their eyes; and there shall be no more death, neither sorrow, nor crying, neither shall there be any more pain: for the former things are passed away.
5 And he that sat upon the throne said, Behold, I make all things new. And he said unto me, Write: for these words are true and faithful.

In this vision that John has, he says that he saw a new heaven and a new earth because the first heaven and earth had passed away. This is congruent with what Jesus and the writer of Hebrews stated about heaven and earth passing, or vanishing. John says that he saw the holy city, New Jerusalem coming down out of heaven. The writer of Hebrews speaks of this to the Hebrew Christians and tells them that they had already entered into this same place that John saw coming down:

Hebrews 12:22-24
22 But ye are come unto mount Sion, and unto the city of the living God, the heavenly Jerusalem, and to an innumerable company of angels,
*23 **To the general assembly and church of the firstborn, which are written in heaven,** and to God the Judge of all, and to the spirits of just men made perfect,*
*24 **And to Jesus the mediator of the new covenant,** and to the blood of sprinkling, that speaketh better things than that of Abel.*

New heaven and new earth is the new covenant. The new covenant is for new Jerusalem. New Jerusalem is from heaven, and thus, is also called heavenly Jerusalem. Accordingly, heavenly Jerusalem is called 'Mount Zion', 'the city of the living God', 'the general assembly', and 'the church of the firstborn'. Basically, new Jerusalem is the church. New Jerusalem is also the kingdom, in which 1st century saints were already pressing into (Luke 16:16). Of course, Jesus is the mediator of the new covenant, which is the same as saying that Jesus is the head of the church (Eph. 4:15).

An argument against what I'm presenting from the dispensational futurist viewpoint is in regards to the mentioning of God wiping away all tears, and there being no more death, crying and pain in new heavens and new earth. This would definitely present a problem if, and only if this passage (and Revelation in its entirety) was to be interpreted literally. But this is not the case. At the very beginning of Revelation, John lets the 1st century reader (seven churches in Asia) know that the letter would be highly symbolic.

Revelation 1:1
*1 The Revelation of Jesus Christ, which God gave unto him, to shew unto his servants things which must shortly come to pass; and he sent and **signified it** by his angel unto his servant John:*

The Greek transliteration for the word 'signified' is *sēmainō*, which means to give a sign, indicate, or make known. Revelation was a letter that apocalyptically painted a vivid picture of the end of the old covenant age, and the emergence and eternal sustaining of the new covenant age – an age that is endless. So, in regards to how we are to interpret Revelation 21, it must be interpreted covenantly – the demise and destruction of the old covenant; the establishment and eternal reign of the new covenant. That being said, we must look at what John ties 'tears, death, crying and pain' to – the old covenant:

Revelation 21:4
*4 And God shall wipe away all tears from their eyes; and there shall be no more death, neither sorrow, nor crying, neither shall there be any more pain: **for the former things are passed away.***

The tears, death, sorrow, crying and pain have no power, spiritually, because 'all things are made new' in the new covenant (v. 5). Death will not stop us from being in His presence forever. Nor does sorrow, crying, and pain have any effect on our relationship with God through Jesus Christ. This is what Paul meant when he penned-

Romans 8:38-39
*38 For I am persuaded, that **neither death, nor life, nor angels, nor principalities, nor powers, nor things present, nor things to come,***
*39 **Nor height, nor depth, nor any other creature, shall be able to separate us from the love of God, which is in Christ Jesus our Lord.***

Furthermore, to believe that there is coming a time when sin and death would not be in existence during the times of new heaven and new earth would be disagreeing with what Isaiah says about new heaven and new earth:

Isaiah 65:17-20
*17 For, behold, **I create new heavens and a new earth**: and the former shall not be remembered, nor come into mind.*
18 But be ye glad and rejoice for ever in that which I create: for, behold, I create Jerusalem a rejoicing, and her people a joy.
19 And I will rejoice in Jerusalem, and joy in my people: and the voice of weeping shall be no more heard in her, nor the voice of crying.
*20 There shall be no more thence an infant of days, nor an old man that hath not filled his days: **for the child shall die an hundred years old; but the sinner being an hundred years old shall be accursed.***

Did you catch that? In Isaiah's prophetic decree, he mentions, in essence, that there will still be death, and there will still be sinners. This throws another cog in the wheel of dispensationalism in which teaches that in new heavens and new earth, there will be a 'utopian society' with no evil, no sin and no death because they (evil, sin and death), along with the devil, beast and false prophet, will all be thrown into a literal 'lake of fire' (Rev. 20:10). Applying a literal hermeneutic to Revelation is the worst thing that can be done. You cannot interpret these passages literally, or else you end up with an interpretation that is pretty much science-fiction, rather than biblical-historical fact.

Heaven, Earth, and Elements

Dispensationalism takes a totally literal approach in its interpretation of 2 Peter 3. It sees a literal burning up and melting away of heaven and earth, and the creating of a literal new heaven and new earth. The problem with this interpretation is that it negates historical context, audience relevance, the usage of Jewish idiomatic-apocalyptic language, and how certain words and terms are used by other authors in the NT, namely, the apostle Paul.

First, let's take a look at the context. Exactly when are the events in this chapter supposed to take place? Peter gives the reader a clue early in the chapter:

2 Peter 3:1-4
1 This second epistle, beloved, I now write unto you; in both which I stir up your pure minds by way of remembrance:
2 That ye may be mindful of the words which were spoken before by the holy prophets, and of the commandment of us the apostles of the Lord and Saviour:
*3 **Knowing this first, that there shall come in the last days** scoffers, walking after their own lusts,*
4 And saying, Where is the promise of his coming? for since the fathers fell asleep, all things continue as they were from the beginning of the creation.

Peter sets the timeframe in which all of the things mentioned in this chapter were to begin happening – 'in the last days'. But when are the last days? Interestingly, In Acts 2, Peter uses this same phrase when reciting the prophetic decree found in Joel 2, which was in response to the men mocking those that were speaking in tongues:

Acts 2:15-17
15 For these are not drunken, as ye suppose, seeing it is but the third hour of the day.

Misinterpreting 'New Heaven' and 'New Earth' | 213

*16 But **this is that** which was spoken by the prophet Joel;*
*17 And **it shall come to pass in the last days**, saith God, I will pour out of my Spirit upon all flesh: and your sons and your daughters shall prophesy, and your young men shall see visions, and your old men shall dream dreams:*

Peter undoubtedly understood that the times that they lived in were the last days. The question then is, 'The last days of what?' They were the last days of the Old Covenant, theocratic system.

This brings me to the next point of examination – the word 'elements'. What are the elements that are suppose to 'melt with fervent heat', according to Peter? Well, the first thing that must be done is to examine how the term 'elements' is used in scripture. Fortunately for us, Peter gives us a clue as to where to start our research! Peter makes it a point to remind the intended reader that Paul had written to them (the intended readers) in regards to the very same things that Peter was telling them in his epistle!

2 Peter 3:15-16
*15 And account that the longsuffering of our Lord is salvation; **even as our beloved brother Paul also according to the wisdom given unto him hath written unto you;***
*16 **As also in all his epistles, speaking in them of these things**; in which are some things hard to be understood, which they that are unlearned and unstable wrest, as they do also the other scriptures, unto their own destruction.*

So Paul actually spoke about 'elements' in his epistles? Absolutely! To verify that Paul wrote to the same people that Peter is writing to, all we have to do is take a look at the salutation. Who was Peter writing to? We can identify the intended audience in 1 Peter:

1 Peter 1:1
*1 Peter, an apostle of Jesus Christ, **to the strangers scattered throughout Pontus, Galatia, Cappadocia, Asia, and Bithynia,***

What area listed in Peter's salutation do we know that Paul sent a letter, or letters to? It's none other than Galatia. In Paul's letter to the church at Galatia, we find that he sheds some valuable light on the term 'elements':

Galatians 4:3, 9
*3 Even so we, when we were children, were **in bondage under the elements of the world**:*

*9 But now, after that ye have known God, or rather are known of God, **how turn ye again to the weak and beggarly elements, whereunto ye desire again to be in bondage?***

Let's take a look at the Amplified Bible interpretation of these two verses:

3 So we [Jewish Christians] also, when we were minors, were kept like slaves under [the rules of the Hebrew ritual and subject to] the elementary teachings of a system of external observations and regulations.

9 Now, however, that you have come to be acquainted with and understand and know [the true] God, or rather to be understood and known by God, how can you turn back again to the weak and beggarly and worthless elementary things [of all religions before Christ came], whose slaves you once more want to become?

According to Paul, 'the elements' refer to the ritualistic observation of the temple practices. All of the religious, ceremonial acts that were being done before Christ are considered 'weak and beggarly'. Merriam-Webster defines 'beggarly' as contemptibly mean, scant, petty, or paltry; befitting or resembling a beggar; especially: marked by extreme poverty. In essence, Paul was telling the people that falling away back into that old covenant religious system was meaningless and worthless.

So, the question is, how has the popular end-time viewpoint missed the mark in regards to this passage so badly? Why do they believe that 'elements' literally refers to things corresponding to the physical earth? Why do they believe in a

Misinterpreting 'New Heaven' and 'New Earth' | **215**

literal burning up and dissolving of the heavens and earth when there is precedent within scripture using the very same language that did not result in the literal, physical destruction of the heavens and earth? Perhaps it is time to take off the 21st century goggles and put on 1st century "Hebrew eyes" and read the scripture from a 1st century perspective, with the undergirding understanding of Jewish idiomatic language, metaphors, allegory, and apocalyptic language. Only then will we be able to fully understand this passage, and the plethora of passages like it within scripture.

PART FOUR

RESULTS OF CHURCH INSANITY

Chapter Eighteen:
Hope Deferred, Laziness, Apathy and Fear

For God hath not given us the spirit of fear; but of power, and of love, and of a sound mind.

2 Timothy 1:7

You are what you eat. You reap what you sow. As a man thinks, so is he. These are all clichés, or better yet, principles that have biblical foundation. In nature, for every cause, there is an effect. A bowling ball that sits on a bowling lane without any force applied to it will remain still. But once force is applied to the bowling ball, it will then move down the lane towards the target (arrows on the lane or the pins). However, whether or not that bowling ball hits the target is dependent on the direction in which the force is applied to that ball. Knocking down as many pins as possible is of course the main objective, but the success rate of getting a 'strike' on that first roll is dependent upon various factors that determine the aim for the target (approach, release point, ball revolution (rate of spin), initial target (boards or arrows), lane conditions (oily or dry, and how far oil is down the lane) and ball velocity. These are a lot of things to consider! The same can be said for golf and all of its pre-swing prepwork or any sport where a target is set. Likewise, the church has a target. But hitting the target is solely dependent upon the 'pre-shot preparation' and understanding of the conditions in which it is called to 'play in'.

In Part I, I began with identifying the 'pattern of the

church' – the early church. I talked about its overall focus and the characteristics of the 1st century church which enabled it to 'turn the world upside down' and catapult the church to a position of great influence and notoriety – so much so that it drew the disdain of the Roman Empire and its emperors. Of course, we know that every attempt to thwart the growth and expansion of the church in the 1st century was to no avail, and today, we are the fruit or offspring of the sacrifice of the early church. In Part II, I identified the visible and theological differences between the modern western church and that of the early church. I talked about the different paradigms and ideologies in which are creating confusion in the western church today. In Part III, I acknowledged what I believe are the main culprits of what I call 'church insanity'. Biblical illiteracy being the major issue at hand, can lead to a misinterpretation and misapplication of scripture. Dispensationalism, which is a brand of the futurist eschatological viewpoint, is a by-product of biblical illiteracy. In this part, Part IV, I will discuss how dispensationalism, and the futurist paradigm in general, has totally rendered the western church ineffective, fostering an anti-kingdom mindset, and to some degree, it is an abomination and slap in the face of God.

Hope Deferred

Close your eyes for a few seconds (not literally, because you have to read this!). Imagine a person that was in need of a kidney transplant finally finding out that his best friend was a complete match. Imagine that this person's condition is deteriorating every day, but after months and months of worrying, crying, and becoming increasingly discouraged, his sorrow is turning to joy and hope. His countenance changes for the better and he becomes excited by the thought of being healthy and living a long life. Two days before the surgery, he gets a call from the doctor and he is told that there was an error in the results of the test to see if his friend's kidney would be a match. He gets the heartbreaking news that his friend's kidney is not a match. He goes into an even deeper state of depression and sorrow, and begins to lose all hope and faith. This is called hope deferred.

Proverbs 13:12
Hope deferred maketh the heart sick*: but when the desire cometh, it is a tree of life.*

Proverbs 13:12 (CEV)
Not getting what you want can make you feel sick, but a wish that comes true is a life-giving tree.

The futurist paradigm views the majority of prophetic passages in scripture as yet to be fulfilled. As I have proven in previous chapters, the 'big ticket' eschatological items like the coming of the Lord, antichrist, man of sin, beast, and new heavens and new earth are all things that were relevant in the first century, and indeed came to pass at that time. Everything that Jesus prophesied in His Olivet discourse was fulfilled within the time frame in which he said it would be fulfilled in:

Matthew 24:34
Verily I say unto you, ***This generation shall not pass, till ALL THESE THINGS BE FULFILLED.***

"All of what things?" you may ask. All of these things which were mentioned before the above verse in Matthew 24:

1. The destruction of the temple (v. 2)
2. Deception, false christs, false prophets (v. 4-5, 11, 23-26)
3. Wars and rumors of wars (v. 6)
4. Political unrest, famines, pestilences, and earthquakes in different places (v. 7)
5. Persecution, betrayal and hatred (v. 9-10)
6. Gospel being preached in all the world (v. 14)
7. Abomination of desolation (v. 15)

8. Fleeing from Jerusalem (v. 16-21)
9. 'Sun and moon darkened', 'stars falling from heaven', 'heavens shaken' (v. 29)
10. Jesus 'coming on the clouds of heaven' (v. 30)
11. 'Gathering of the elect' (v. 31)

Most of the items in the list above have been addressed earlier in this book. I have shown how they were fulfilled in the first century. Flavius Josephus (37 CE–100 CE), a Roman scholar and historian, recorded what he witnessed in his work entitled *War of the Jews*. In this piece, he describes in unbelievably vivid detail the destruction of Jerusalem that took place in 70 AD. He totally verifies the fulfillment of every word that Jesus uttered regarding the coming destruction of Jerusalem, which was the vengeance and wrath that was poured out on the Jews for the killing of the apostles and prophets. You can read his work online for free, or download it at the following links:

http://www.biblestudytools.com/history/flavius-josephus/war-of-the-jews/

http://www.josephus.org/warje10.zip

The problem at hand is the misapplication of the hope that the first century saints had for the Lord's coming and assigning that hope to a future generation 2000+ years away. The writers of the various New Testament letters were writing to a first century audience, encouraging them to hold on and remain steadfast and unmovable. They comforted the hearts of the saints by telling them that what they had hoped for was right around the corner and soon to come to pass. Paul identifies what the hope of the first century saints was in his defense before Herod Agrippa (10 BC – 44 AD):

Acts 26:6-8
*6 And now I stand and am judged for **the hope of the promise made of God, unto our fathers**:*
7 Unto which promise our twelve tribes, instantly serving God day and night, hope to come. For which hope's sake, king Agrippa, I am accused of the Jews.
*8 Why should it be thought a thing incredible with you, that **God should raise the dead**?*

It was the resurrection of the dead that the early church was looking forward to. It was the reason for the Thessalonians' question regarding the dead in Christ (1 Thess. 4:16-18). Peter also speaks of the resurrection of the dead, which he says would be revealed in the last time:

1 Peter 1:3-5
*3 Blessed be the God and Father of our Lord Jesus Christ, which according to his abundant mercy **hath begotten us again unto a lively hope by the resurrection of Jesus Christ from the dead**,*
4 To an inheritance incorruptible, and undefiled, and that fadeth not away, reserved in heaven for you,
*5 Who are kept by the power of God through faith unto salvation **ready to be revealed in the last time**.*

What is the 'last time'? Its meaning is the same as 'last days', 'end of days', 'latter days' and 'end of the world'. As mentioned before, this 'last time' was the end of the old covenant age. It was the end of the world as they knew it in the first century. Old things would pass away, and all things would become new. This passing away of old things was signified by the destruction of the temple in 70 AD. Recall that the disciples asked Jesus three significant questions regarding the destruction of the temple, in which Jesus decreed in Matthew 24:2. They asked (v. 3)-

1. When would the destruction of the temple take place?
2. What would signify His coming?
3. What would signify the 'end of the world'?

If the resurrection of the dead is tied to the 'end of the world', and the 'end of the world' was signified by the destruction of the temple in 70 AD, then why is the church today looking for a future coming of the Lord and resurrection of the dead? Let me restate that I believe that the resurrection of the dead began at the coming of the Lord in 70 AD (His coming in vengeance and wrath against the unbelieving Jews that murdered the servants of God), and continues today, per Revelation 14:13:

Revelation 14:13
13 And I heard a voice from heaven saying unto me, Write, **Blessed are the dead which die in the Lord from henceforth***: Yea, saith the Spirit, that they may rest from their labours; and their works do follow them.*

Revelation was John's apocalyptic visual of the destruction of Jerusalem. He heard a voice from heaven saying that those that died after that point in time would be blessed. Why? Because absent from body is present with the Lord (2 Corinthians 5:8). This is the reality for Christians today, and forever more. When we die, we are immediately translated into the presence of God forever. There is no apprehension or questioning anymore, as was the case with the Thessalonians. We can rest assured that when we die, we'll be with Him. Christ's parousia (coming) was the event that triggered the resurrection of the dead. We benefit from the reality of this historical event today.

Unfortunately, the western church is in a state of hope deferred because it is looking for something that will never happen due to the fact that the resurrection has already happened, and it continues to happen. End-time false teaching and preaching has contributed to the creation of an ineffective church that is sharing untruths because it has misappropriated the timing of Christ's coming by not understanding what exactly was Christ's coming. Due to the false narrative of futurism (especially dispensationalism), individual worldviews have been shaped and molded negatively. Instead of walking in the victory of Christ and His salvation, the western church has become withdrawn and self-absorbed with a 'beam me up Scottie' attitude and seeks to escape the world, rather than engage the world and the cultures within it. Futurism also falsely views individuals and entire people groups as the biblical enemies of God (specifically, Muslims, Hindus and all unbelievers), but gives the secular nation of Israel a pass because they perceive them to be the 'apple of God's eye' and 'His chosen people'. This ideology has influenced U.S. foreign policy and has regrettably put a stumbling block in front of the progression of the church and His kingdom.

Laziness

Due to the fact that what I'm revealing in this book is rather foreign to most in the western church, it is definitely a hard pill to swallow. Sadly, but expectedly, the initial reaction of some people that hear the fulfilled eschatological position for the first time is anger, rage, resentment, bitterness, hatred and then 'slander of the messenger'. So much for the fruit of the Spirit being evident! But as I have stated, this type of reaction is expected because the information challenges one's paradigms and preconceived notions. Unfortunately, the next step for many that are confronted with the fulfilled position is the exhibiting of what is clinically called *cognitive dissonance.* Cognitive dissonance is the feeling of uncomfortable tension which comes from holding two conflicting thoughts in the mind at the same time.[1] In simple terms, cognitive dissonance can be the filtering of information that conflicts with what you already believe, in an effort to ignore that information and reinforce your beliefs.[2]

The most pitiful thing that a Christian can do is ignore information that may be foreign to them, and not choose to determine whether it is true or not. Today's church in America lacks individuals who have the courage and character to dive in and see if something that is different than what they are accustomed to is valid, or a fallacy. This is an exhibition of laziness and sloth as it pertains to searching the scriptures. A 'fast food' society has impacted the American church to the point where parishioners or American Christians in general, treat church as a 'spiritual fast food joint'. The majority of food from fast food restaurants isn't good for you. It lacks the vitamins, minerals, and nutrients that are necessary, and contains high levels of saturated fat, sugar and salt, which contributes to the deterioration of health in human beings. Fast food can lead to malnutrition, sickness and disease. Likewise, malnourished souls and an improperly fed spirit man can contribute to a dysfunctional Christian, and dysfunctional church. A lot of the stuff that comes from pulpits throughout America is nothing but 'junk food'. Junk food tastes good, and it makes you feel good and satisfied for a moment. But within an hour or so, you're either hungry again, or you're searching for the Pepto-Bismol or Tums! Similarly, there is preaching and teaching in western churches that is leaving people empty, without sustenance, spiritually sick, and ineffective.

The problem of malnutrition in the western church stems from not being taught how to study the bible, and more importantly, the significance of studying the bible. As I mentioned in Chapter Two, traditionally, Jewish rabbis believe that the greatest or highest form of worship is to study God's word. Studying the word of God is the literal interaction with the redemptive plan for humanity. We cannot say that we worship God if we don't know who God is, His character, His personality, and how He views the world. The essence of worship is the pronouncing of what we 'give worth to'. A man that truly is a worshipper of God will place a high precedent on studying His word. Study of the Word of God should always be the most important thing in our lives.

The antithesis of laziness is what we see the Bereans do when confronted with something that was foreign to them.

Acts 17:10-12
10 And the brethren immediately sent away Paul and Silas by night unto Berea: who coming thither went into the synagogue of the Jews.
*11 These were more noble than those in Thessalonica, in that **they received the word with all readiness of mind, and searched the scriptures daily, whether those things were so.***
12 Therefore many of them believed; also of honourable women which were Greeks, and of men, not a few.

The Bereans didn't reject what Paul was sharing with them. They didn't ridicule him, or respond in anger, malice, and resentment. Verse 11 says that they were ready to hear what Paul had to say. But the Bereans didn't take what they were being told as truth, blindly, but commenced to studying and searching the scriptures to see if what Paul was saying was true or not. Luke, the author of Acts, also wrote that the Bereans were more noble than other Jews in the land because they were most likely more educated. A Berean spirit is what is needed in American churches today. When confronted with something that is foreign, Christians should not immediately reject it, but take the time to search the scriptures to see if what is being shared is true or not. To not do so is the epitome of laziness.

Apathy

Status quo is decimating the American church. There is something fundamentally wrong with what is being preached and taught in churches throughout America. A Christian that is lazy in regards to seeking Truth will inevitably be affected in his or her understanding of how the Christian is to engage the world today. Consequently, a church's effectiveness in a region is reflected by its understanding of its role in that region. Unfortunately, due to the pessimistic and fatalistic message that is presented by the futurist / dispensationalist end-time viewpoint, the western church has become inundated with apathy. Apathy is the suppression of emotions (concern, excitement, motivation, passion). Because the futurist paradigm suggests that the world is getting worse and worse, and that we are to wait for Jesus to come to the rescue (again), it promotes an ideology that caters to withdrawing from society and allowing the evil and ungodliness to take place because of preconceived beliefs that this is supposed to happen in what they believe are the 'last days'. Apathy is the absence of interest or concern about the emotional, social, political, spiritual, philosophical and physical well-being of people, communities, the nation and the world as a whole. An apathetic Christian lacks purpose and he doesn't know the meaning of life or his role in the kingdom of God today.

An apathetic Christian is the by-product of an escapism mindset that is drenched in defeatism. Apathetic Christians display insensibility and sluggishness. They lack the compassion that it takes to move them to participate in advancing the kingdom of God in the earth and addressing problems that they see right before their eyes. The apathetic Christian may feel unable to meet various challenges because he or she feels unequipped, or lacking in the skills necessary to bring healing and change. Many times, apathetic Christians don't perceive the challenges, or they feel as if it is worthless to engage societal dilemmas because they believe that it is a waste of time. They are hooked on the belief that they will be 'raptured' out of the earth where they won't have to deal with the problems of the world anymore.

It is absolutely anti-Christ to not be moved with compassion and concern for the things that we see in the world today. For parents to tell their children that they shouldn't be worried about going to college and becoming well educated is a tragedy. In addition, to tell sons and daughters that they should not be thinking about having a family because 'the end is near' is preposterous and shows a lack of biblical understanding. A lot of Christians read newspapers and watch mainstream news, and it feeds their fatalistic appetites and makes them even the more convinced that they are 'living in the last days', or are 'the generation' that Jesus was speaking about in Matthew 24. They become 'shell-shocked' by what they witness. Shell-shock was a condition that many World War I veterans experienced after returning back home from battle. The soldiers became disconnected from reality and social interaction because of the carnage that they witnessed in warfare. The same thing happens today when people look at the news. Our city streets have become battlefields and full of carnage. People look at the news and begin to feel as if there is nothing that can be done about the violence and wickedness in the land. Instead of standing up and becoming a beacon of light in what seems to be a world of darkness, Christians are compelled to withdraw from society, hide in their bunkers with their bags packed and be ready to see Jesus! This is such a sad state of affairs for the western church, and is the exhibition of the spirit of fear, in which we are told, was not given to us by God!

Fear

An inaccurate biblical worldview will lead to trepidation. A worldview that feasts on fear is a hindrance to Christians getting involved in various sectors of society to become the salt and light that we are called to be in the earth. Fear will cause people to withdraw from society. It will cause people to shrink away from their responsibilities, naturally and spiritually. Fear will hinder one from providing for their family. It will prevent one from being a productive citizen, contributing to, and making a change in society. For the Christian, fear will hinder him or her from doing the work of the ministry. The work of the ministry includes-

- Preaching the gospel
- Instilling hope
- Casting out fear by bringing, and being 'light'
- Demonstrating compassion

Another by-product of fear is stagnation. When someone is

living in a state of fear, he tends to become 'frozen' and immobile in life. Stagnation prevents advancement and reaching higher levels of success and influence. The perfect example of stagnation in scripture is the children of Israel wandering in the wilderness for forty years. A stagnated person perpetually wanders around in a circle and accomplishes nothing. A stagnated Christian or a stagnated church is hindered and will not fulfill their God-given and God-ordained purpose and destiny.

People that live in a state of fear often times look for, or expect bad things to happen to them, around them, or in the earth all the time. The preconceived notion that evil is getting worse and worse empowers the belief that bad things are suppose to happen. Peter experienced this when Jesus called him to walk on water towards Jesus:

Matthew 14:28-33
28 And Peter answered him and said, Lord, if it be thou, bid me come unto thee on the water.
*29 And he said, Come. And **when Peter was come down out of the ship, he walked on the water, to go to Jesus.***
*30 **But when he saw the wind boisterous, he was afraid; and beginning to sink, he cried, saying, Lord, save me.***
31 And immediately Jesus stretched forth his hand, and caught him, and said unto him, O thou of little faith, wherefore didst thou doubt?
32 And when they were come into the ship, the wind ceased.

When Peter saw the winds picking up, he lost focus of Jesus, the Man in which the waves and winds are subject to, and turned his focus to something that caused him to become afraid. His fear then invited a spirit of unbelief and it began to make him sink. God is not the author of fear. He did not impute fear into us.

2 Timothy 1:7
*For **God hath not given us the spirit of fear**; but of power, and of love, and of a sound mind.*

In Job 3, we read about Job cursing his day (his life). The interesting thing is that the very thing that Job was afraid of actually came upon him:

Job 3:25-26
*25 For the **thing which I greatly feared is come upon me, and that which I was afraid of is come unto me.***
*26 I was not in safety, neither had I rest, neither was I quiet; yet **trouble came.***

Likewise, today, the American church that has bought into the lie called dispensationalism, and futurism in general, are in fact 'cursing their day' with their pessimism and fear. 'As a man thinks, so is he...' – the words of Solomon found in Proverbs 23:7. The principle of this verse is absolutely applicable today. Evil and ungodliness is prevalent in America and throughout the world today because of what the western church believes about evil and sin. Since the western church is exporting a teaching that insinuates that evil is suppose to increase and sinful behavior is suppose to become more and more prevalent, then that is what will happen. Are you beginning to see the immense danger of the false narrative of dispensationalism? Due to the fact that it rips scripture out of its historical context and misapplies it to a generation of people that scripture was never addressed to, we get a church today that has forfeited its rightful place as being a beacon of light set on a hill. Fear has caused the church to draw back from engaging the culture and becoming the influencers of society. We have allowed evil to creep into every sector of society because we have withdrawn our presence and our voice in those sectors. What the western church suffers from now is not knowing who or what it actually is, and what it is called to be.

Chapter Nineteen:
Identity Crisis

But God, who is rich in mercy, for his great love wherewith he loved us, Even when we were dead in sins, hath quickened us together with Christ, (by grace ye are saved;) And hath raised us up together, and made us sit together in heavenly places in Christ Jesus: That in the ages to come he might shew the exceeding riches of his grace in his kindness toward us through Christ Jesus. For by grace are ye saved through faith; and that not of yourselves: it is the gift of God: Not of works, lest any man should boast. For we are his workmanship, created in Christ Jesus unto good works, which God hath before ordained that we should walk in them.

Ephesians 2:4-10

Undoubtedly, the most painful thing for most African-Americans is the history of slavery that our ancestors encountered in the past. It wasn't necessarily the being sold into slavery that was the worst thing. Nor was it the traversing the Atlantic Ocean in deplorably inhumane conditions. It also wasn't the demeaning vitriol of slave masters, the whippings, the rape of black women, and the horrible living conditions of black slaves – though, all of these things are definitely stains on the fabric of what is suppose to be a Christian nation. But with all of that, in my opinion (I am not speaking for every black American), I believe that the worst result of slavery is the disconnection that was created between myself and who my ancestors are in Africa. In a natural sense, I don't know who I am. I don't know what African nation or tribe I'm from. I don't know who my ancestors are. Every culture, with the exception of the African-American, can for the most part tell you instantaneously what their family origin is (where they are from and when their family came to America). This sense of having an identity crisis has been a mental stumbling block for some black Americans for centuries. Unlike most cultures, there is no foundation for a sense of national pride and heritage. We cannot say that we're proud to be from 'this nation' or 'that nation'. We don't know what it feels like to celebrate the success or progression of a 'homeland'. This may seem trivial to most non-blacks, but it will always be something that black Americans will have in the back of our minds. Not until recently, modern technology and the ability to examine DNA have allowed black Americans to be able to trace our lineage back to African nations and tribes.

Though I may not know (as of now) what my natural lineage is, or where my ancestors are from in Africa, I do know what my spiritual lineage is! However, it is quite apparent that many in the western church today either do not know what their spiritual lineage is, or they choose not to walk in their true spiritual identity.

We Don't Know Who We Are

It is absolutely imperative that the saints of God know who we truly are. The problem is that what is being taught in mainstream Christendom, namely, the western church, conflicts with and overrides who God says we are. So, who are we? First and foremost, we are the church, individually, as well as collectively. We are the temple of the Holy Ghost:

1 Corinthians 6:19
*What? **know ye not that your body is the temple of the Holy Ghost which is in you**, which ye have of God, and ye are not your own?*

We 'house' the presence of God. God 'tabernacles' with us. The Hebrew translation for 'tabernacle' is *'ohel,* which means tent, nomad's tent, and thus symbolic of wilderness life, transience; dwelling, home, habitation; the sacred tent of Jehovah.[1] We are God's sacred temple. We are His dwelling place.

Revelation 21:3
*And I heard a great voice out of heaven saying, Behold, **the tabernacle of God is with men, and he will dwell with them, and they shall be his people, and God himself shall be with them, and be their God.***

God no longer dwells in buildings or temples made with hands:

Acts 17:24
*24 God that made the world and all things therein, seeing that **he is Lord of heaven and earth, dwelleth not in temples made with hands**;*

We are the temple of the Holy Ghost. God dwells within us, and we dwell within Him. This is the answer to part of the prayer that Jesus prayed in John 17:

John 17:20-26
20 Neither pray I for these alone, but for them also which shall believe on me through their word;
21 That they all may be one; as thou, Father, art in me, and I in thee, that they also may be one in us: that the world may believe that thou hast sent me.
22 And the glory which thou gavest me I have given them; that they may be one, even as we are one:
*23 **I in them, and thou in me, that they may be made perfect in one**; and that the world may know that thou hast sent me, and hast loved them, as thou hast loved me.*
*24 Father, **I will that they also, whom thou hast given me, be with me where I am; that they may behold my glory, which thou hast given me**: for thou lovedst me before the foundation of the world.*
25 O righteous Father, the world hath not known thee: but I have known thee, and these have known that thou hast sent me.
26 And I have declared unto them thy name, and will declare it: that the love wherewith thou hast loved me may be in them, and I in them.

The depth of our relationship with the Father and Son is encapsulated in this prayer. Jesus was praying for the disciples in which He was speaking to in John 16. In verse 24, Jesus says that he wants the disciples (and all of them that believe on their word – V. 20 – this includes not only the 1st century saints that believed, but all that believe throughout history) to be with Him where He will be. Where exactly will Jesus be? We find an answer to that in Acts 7. Stephen is speaking to the chief priest about Jesus being present in the days of their fathers and the children of Israel rejecting Him. He also talks about the prophets revealing to the children of Israel who Jesus was, and how Jesus would come, but they ignored the prophets and killed Jesus, the Just One (Acts 7:52). Stephen recites the words of Isaiah (found in Isaiah 66:1):

Acts 7:48-49
*48 Howbeit **the most High dwelleth not in temples made with hands**; as saith the prophet,*
*49 **Heaven is my throne**, and earth is my footstool: what house will ye build me? saith the Lord: or what is the place of my rest?*

Heaven is the throne of Jesus. The earth is His footstool. It is heaven in which Jesus says that He wants us to be with Him in. Interestingly, in Paul's letter to the Ephesians, he states that he that is saved by the grace of God is already seated in heavenly places in Christ Jesus:

Ephesians 2:5-7
5 Even when we were dead in sins, hath quickened us together with Christ, (by grace ye are saved;)
*6 And **hath raised us up together, and made us sit together in heavenly places in Christ Jesus:***
*7 **That in the ages to come he might shew the exceeding riches of his grace in his kindness toward us through Christ Jesus.***

In John 17:24, Jesus says that He wants the disciples (and all saints) to behold His glory. In Ephesians 2:7, Paul says that in the ages to come (in the generations following their contemporaneous generation), Jesus would show the 'exceeding riches of his grace', which is synonymous with the 'glory' that Jesus wanted them, and us, to behold. In Hebrews 12, the text speaks of the first century saints already coming into heavenly Jerusalem:

Hebrews 12:22-24
22 But ye are come unto mount Sion, and unto the city of the living God, the <u>heavenly Jerusalem</u>, and to an innumerable company of angels,
23 To the general assembly and church of the firstborn, which are written in heaven, and to God the Judge of all, and to the spirits of just men made perfect,
24 And to Jesus the mediator of the new covenant, and to the blood of sprinkling, that speaketh better things than that of Abel.

The 'blood of sprinkling' ties us to our spiritual home. Just as people are learning about their ancestry and where they are from today because of DNA analysis, so is the Christian's spiritual home identified because of the blood of Jesus. His blood that was shed was the 'cutting' of the new covenant. I found it rather interesting that DNA is not found in the red blood cells because of the absence of nuclei.$_2$ DNA is found in white blood cells, which are the cells of the immune system which fights for us! The dichotomy of red versus white is found in Isaiah 1:

Isaiah 1:18
18 Come now, and let us reason together, saith the Lord: ***though your sins be as scarlet, they shall be as white as snow; though they be red like crimson, they shall be as wool.***

Red blood cells don't carry the DNA. Isaiah saw our sins as being 'as scarlet' (red-like). White blood cells carry DNA, which is our true physical identity. When we are 'white as snow', we are made righteous in Christ! We carry the spiritual DNA of Jesus Christ! We are in Him, and He is in us! He is our mediator. He 'reasons together' with the Father on our behalf! I find this to be an awesome comparison! White blood cells help our immune system fight against viruses that may try to attack our bodies. When we are cleansed by the blood of Jesus and made white as snow, the Lord fights our battles!

So, we are the tabernacle of God. We are seated in heavenly places in Christ Jesus. But we are also the church. There is no coincidence that the word 'church' is first mentioned after Peter received a revelation of who Jesus is:

Matthew 16:15-19
15 He saith unto them, But whom say ye that I am?
16 And Simon Peter answered and said, **Thou art the Christ, the Son of the living God.**
17 And Jesus answered and said unto him, Blessed art thou, Simon Barjona: for flesh and blood hath not revealed it unto thee, but my Father which is in heaven.
18 And I say also unto thee, That thou art Peter, and <u>**upon this rock I will build my church**</u>*; and the gates of hell shall not prevail against it.*
19 And **I will give unto thee the keys of the kingdom of heaven: and whatsoever thou shalt bind on earth shall be bound in heaven: and whatsoever thou shalt loose on earth shall be loosed in heaven.**

The Father reveals to the heart of man who Jesus is. The church of Jesus Christ is built upon the foundation of Jesus being the Christ, and the Son of the living God. We are the church. The Greek translation for church is *ekklēsia*, which means 'gathering', or 'assembly'. The church is made up of many members, and is also the body of Christ:

Romans 12:5
So **we, being many, are one body in Christ**, *and every one members one of another.*

Another name for the church, or body of Christ, is a major point of contention with dispensational futurists. Whether they like it or not, the church is also the Israel of God:

Galatians 6:15-17
15 For in Christ Jesus neither circumcision availeth any thing, nor uncircumcision, but a new creature.
16 And as many as walk according to this rule, peace be on them, and mercy, and upon the Israel of God.

Galatians 6:16 (AMP)
16 Peace and mercy be upon all who walk by this rule [who discipline themselves and regulate their lives by this principle], even upon the [true] Israel of God!

We are the true Israel of God. We are Mount Zion. We are the city of the living God. We are heavenly Jerusalem. We are the general assembly and the church of the first born. Just as important, we are also the carriers of the kingdom of God. The misconception of the kingdom of God being some place 'up there' in the heavens has assisted in the substandard mindset of Christians today in the western church. We are bound by our own miniscule thinking of ourselves, and thus, the impact of the church in America is miniscule. Our actions do not demonstrate a people in which the kingdom of God resides in. Jesus said that the kingdom of God is unobservable because it resides amongst the believers:

Luke 17:20-21
20 And when he was demanded of the Pharisees, when the kingdom of God should come, he answered them and said, **The kingdom of God cometh not with observation:**
21 Neither shall they say, Lo here! or, lo there! for, behold, **the kingdom of God is within you.**

If the kingdom of God dwells in our midst, or within us, why is the church today drawing back from its rightful place of co-laboring with Christ in heavenly places and judging the affairs of men? The church is to set the standard and agenda for the nations. The church is to be the collective ambassadors of the kingdom of God. We are the representatives of His ways and how He sees things in the earth. We are Christ in the earth. When the world looks at us, we should reflect the glory and majesty of His kingdom.

Our Kingdom Occupation?

Hope deferred, laziness, apathy and fear have facilitated a

church that is absolutely foreign to what we were called and created to be. Instead of assisting in the growth and expansion of the kingdom of God, we have drawn back and become disengaged from the culture. Instead of being 'salt and light', and a peculiar people, we have relegated ourselves to being assimilated to a society and generation that is becoming the more spiritually depraved and malnourished. The terrible thing about this is that the western church not living up to the standard that was set for it by the early church's action is the main problem. The church is always the litmus test for the spiritual temperature or climate of a nation. An engaged church will affect change in a region. An engaged church will not allow wickedness and perversion to take root and fester in a region. God judges His church first. He is always concerned about the well-being of the church.

1 Peter 4:17
*For the time is come **that judgment must begin at the house of God**: and if it first begin at us, what shall the end be of them that obey not the gospel of God?*

How is it possible for a 'sick' church to minister to a sick world? What authority can we possibly stand on if our condition is just as bad as the condition of the world? God always calls His people back into alignment with His will before he does anything in the land:

2 Chronicles 7:14
***If my people, which are called by my name**, shall humble themselves, and pray, and seek my face, and turn from their wicked ways; then will I hear from heaven, and will forgive their sin, and will heal their land.*

God is concerned with the people that are called by His name. We represent Him. He will not allow His name to be tarnished and ridiculed in the world because of a schizophrenic, double-minded, lazy, slothful and non-engaged people that is supposed to be His own! The principles of both 1 Peter 4:17 and 2 Chronicles 7:14 apply perfectly to today's western church. God is judging His church, pruning it, and bringing it back to remembrance of what it is suppose to be in the earth. Those that get with the program will succeed and have great influence in their respective regions. Those that don't want to fall back into alignment with what the church is suppose to be will be cut off. A church that does not bear fruit will be cut down and die. It is useless. Oswald J. Smith (1889-1986), a Canadian pastor, author, and missions statesman, gave the following quote in which hits the nail right on the head:

> *"Any church that is not seriously involved in helping fulfill the Great Commission has forfeited its biblical right to exist."*

A church that is not focused on evangelism and missions is a dead church. It has no usefulness. It is just occupying space. It has no function. It produces no fruit. It is the antithesis of what God has ordained the church to be, from generation to generation. The church is anointed to preach to every people in every age. The church is to reveal the glory and splendor of Jesus and His kingdom throughout the ages, world without end (Ephesians 3:21). The church should always seek to raise up and prepare the next generation of kingdom ambassadors, apostles, prophets, evangelists, pastors, and teachers. The church agenda should be preoccupied with strategically advancing the kingdom of God and growing the church through evangelism. Just as important, the church should always be the greatest influence in a society. We are 'the dog that wags the tail'. We are the head, and not the tail! We are to be the visionaries and the 'pace car' of the nations. We are to be the suppliers of the needs of the nation (the healing leaves – Revelation 22:2). This is the church's call. This is the church's responsibility. We, the church, are a collection of ministers of reconciliation. The mindset of the church should always be to subdue and take dominion (Genesis 1:26-28). This is how we are built individually as well as corporately. We have the DNA of THEE Overcomer inside of us!

1 John 4:4
*Ye are of God, little children, and have overcome them: because **greater is he that is in you, than he that is in the world.***

It's time that the western church begins to walk in that which it already is – a collection of over-comers and conquerors. The church is comprised of individuals who have been given gifts by God. Each person is to utilize their respective gifts within their fields of influence and shine the light of the kingdom within those areas. Whether it is business, arts, entertainment, media, government, religion, or even the family, we are seasoned with distinction and a flare that is 'other-worldly'. Heaven invades earth when we become awakened to the reality of who we are in the earth – representatives of heaven! We are Christ in the earth. We are the body of Christ. It's about time that we start acting like it.

Chapter Twenty:
Unbridled Denominationalism and Witchcraft

All the ways of a man are clean in his own eyes; but the Lord weigheth the spirits.

Proverbs 16:2

As I have written about in the Part I, the early church was a unified entity and was on one accord. The disciples that followed Jesus understood His passionate plea for His followers to be unified and as one. Paul, in his letters to the various churches, warned his brothers and sisters in the faith to stay away from strife, envy and division:

Romans 13:13
*Let us walk honestly, as in the day; not in rioting and drunkenness, not in chambering and wantonness, **not in strife and envying**.*

1 Corinthians 3:3
*For ye are yet carnal: for whereas **there is among you envying, and strife, and divisions**, are ye not carnal, and walk as men?*

2 Corinthians 12:20
*For I fear, lest, when I come, I shall not find you such as I would, and that I shall be found unto you such as ye would not: **lest there be debates, envyings, wraths, strifes, backbitings, whisperings, swellings, tumults**:*

Philippians 2:3
*Let nothing be done through **strife or vainglory**; but in lowliness of mind let each esteem other better than themselves.*

James also wrote about the negative impact of strife and

division:

James 2:14-16
14 But if ye have bitter envying and strife in your hearts, glory not, and lie not against the truth.
15 This wisdom descendeth not from above, but is earthly, sensual, devilish.
*16 For **where envying and strife is, there is confusion and every evil work.***

There would have been no way possible for the early church to remain united and on one accord if envy, strife and division would have festered. Contrarily, what we see today is, in many cases, the exact opposite of what the early church was. Instead of unity, there is division. Instead of harmony, there is strife. Instead of meekness, there is envy and jealousy. Envy, strife and division has its roots in the misunderstanding and misinterpretation of scripture, which then leads to the ignorance of who and what we are to be in the earth – a unified church that the world sees and is attracted to.

Man-Made Belief Systems

Denominationalism, the separating of the church into different groups or sects based on beliefs or theological schools of thought, has been a major hindrance to the growth and influence of the church as a whole. As Jesus stated, a house divided cannot stand. Denominationalism isn't just an American church problem, but a universal church problem. There are hundreds of different Christian denominations in the world. Just type 'list of denominations' in any internet search engine and you will find plenty of information regarding the history of denominationalism. I simply don't have the time to go through all of it.

The splintering of the church began as early as the 5th century and continues to this very day. Throughout church history, whenever there has been a differing theological position, it usually led to the breaking away from a congregation and the creation of another church or congregation. Whether correct or incorrect, man's opinion of scripture and his overall view of God have facilitated the division within the body of Christ. It was never the will of God for his church to be so divided. It definitely wasn't the message that Jesus conveyed to the disciples and it wasn't the message that the apostles conveyed to the first century church.

Spirits of Pride and Arrogance

Much of the driving force behind denominationalism is the spirit of pride. The feeling of 'being right' about something breeds a false exceptionalism in which that person believes that he is more favored and more important than someone else. This fosters an ideology that leads to conceit and arrogance. The spirit of pride hardens the heart to the point where reproof and correction from God and peers in the faith have trouble reaching the heart. This person becomes unteachable and unreachable. He feels that he's the best thing since sliced bread! He becomes so puffed up with pride that he doesn't realize that he has put himself on his own island and has disconnected from the body. The bad thing about it is this spirit of pride and arrogance is then passed down to his followers and they begin to exhibit the same characteristics and personality of the leader.

Competition Driven

A result of a church leader and its congregation becoming filled with the spirit of pride is its continuous seeking to maintain that false narrative of being 'the greatest' or on another level. Just the thought of a church being 'the greatest church in the world' is filled with conceit and arrogance. That ideology stems from unwarranted and unbiblical competition with others in the body of Christ. We are guilty of rating preachers on how well they preach (flesh and emotionalism being driving factors of that evaluation). 'Pastor A' will see

'Pastor B' on the other side of town putting an addition onto their church building and doesn't want to be outdone. So he increases the size of his church building also. Another example of competition in some denominations is the fact that there are 'try-outs' and 'trial sermons' given by individuals that are seeking to become the lead pastor of a church. Really? Try-outs? Is this really the apostolic model that was laid out by the early church? Absolutely not! I've also seen gospel choir competitions that are full of carnality and worldly gestures. Since when does singing for the Lord become a spectator sport and for entertainment purposes only? These things do not bring glory to God, but they are a feeble attempt to exalt one's self or the image of a church by means that have nothing to do with advancing the kingdom and winning souls. We even judge churches based on church membership. Churches compete with each other in regards to membership. The sad thing about it is that the fluctuations in church membership are mostly due to 'church-hopping' and not new converts. Churches are focused on growing membership, but not winning 'un-churched' souls to the kingdom.

Religiosity and Traditionalism

A lot of what goes on today in churches in America is nothing short of what Jesus condemned the unbelieving Jews of – giving more credence to the traditions of men than honoring and obeying the commandments of God:

Mark 7:6-9 (CEB)
6 He replied, "Isaiah really knew what he was talking about when he prophesied about you hypocrites. He wrote,
7 This people honors me with their lips, but their hearts are far away from me. ***Their worship of me is empty since they teach instructions that are human words.***
8 ***You ignore God's commandment while holding on to rules created by humans and handed down to you.****" 9 Jesus continued, "Clearly, you are experts at rejecting God's commandment in order to establish these rules.*

Mark 7:7
*7 Howbeit in vain do they worship me, **teaching for doctrines the commandments of men.***

The unbelieving Jews cared more about making themselves look good and prominent than following the commandments of God. They cared more about their outward appearance of godliness than about what really mattered in the eyes of God. There was so much emphasis placed on the rituals and patterns of the temple worship that the real issues that were plaguing them were never addressed. The religious cloaks hid their inner depravation, as is evident by Jesus' rebuke of them in Matthew 23:

Matthew 23:25-28
*25 Woe unto you, scribes and Pharisees, hypocrites! for **ye make clean the outside of the cup and of the platter, but within they are full of extortion and excess.***
26 Thou blind Pharisee, cleanse first that which is within the cup and platter, that the outside of them may be clean also.
*27 Woe unto you, scribes and Pharisees, hypocrites! for **ye are like unto whited sepulchres, which indeed appear beautiful outward, but are within full of dead men's bones, and of all uncleanness.***
*28 Even so **ye also outwardly appear righteous unto men, but within ye are full of hypocrisy and iniquity.***

The act of being busy with religious duties and ritualistic performances is prevalent in many of our churches today. There is a false facade of cleanliness, holiness, righteousness. Yet, beyond the facade is rotting flesh, corruption, and all sorts of ungodly behavior. Religiosity is like a stage play full of actors and actresses. The non-biblical traditions that are passed down from older generations remain intact with no questioning of why things are done the way they are done. Religiosity, traditionalism and ritualism are directly tied to the spirit of pride. Pride is a stubborn spirit that boasts against any attempts of correction, rebuke and reproof. When a religious spirit is present, it blinds the church leaders, and as a result, the followers are also blinded as well. The end result of this scenario will always be destruction:

Matthew 15:14
Let them alone: ***they be blind leaders of the blind. And if the blind lead the blind, both shall fall into the ditch.***

Witchcraft and Condemnation

Churches that are full of religion and traditionalism are usually breeding grounds for witchcraft. When one thinks of the term 'witchcraft', he usually visualizes someone that is casting a spell and utilizing incantations to evoke evil spirits to break the will of another individual and get them to do what he wants them to do. I'm not necessarily referring to this type of visual. But the sought after end result is the same – an action taken to override another person's free will.

At the core of witchcraft are the acts of intimidation and manipulation. Intimidation comes into play when church leaders are perceived as 'untouchable' and authoritative. The congregation is so in awe of the church leader that they will believe anything that he says, even if it is non-biblical and dangerous. Fear is generated from the pulpit, along with a lot of 'finger-pointing', in that the congregation is always being put down and talked about like they are forever in the wrong and worthless heathens. When the congregation is fearful of the leadership, it then becomes prey to manipulation. Church leadership becomes task-masters and place unreasonable yokes upon the people with 'church-stuff', without consideration of people's own families and daily responsibilities. A works-related message permeates from the pulpit and people are seduced into subconsciously believing that their service to the church is a prerequisite to the maintenance of their salvation. Manipulation is also displayed in the giving of tithes and offerings. Pastors that request a certain dollar amount for an offering and openly bless those that can give it demonstrate partiality and favoritism when it comes to finances. I've also seen churches that will not allow people to join their church if they do not pay tithes to the church. This, in my opinion, is absolutely irresponsible and is totally inconsiderate to a person or family's financial situation and puts a cost on membership with their congregation. I can't remember reading anywhere in scripture that first century Christians were required to pay anything specific to be a part of a church.

Perhaps the most heinous thing that can be done by church leadership is the preventing of church members to think critically and challenge preconceived ideologies and dogma. A major problem with the Roman Catholic Church prior to the Protestant Reformation was the prevailing stance that the 'commoners' were not skilled enough to be able to interpret scripture. So, the reading and interpretation of scripture was left to a relatively small amount of people. It wasn't until the reformation, and then the game-changing invention of the printing press in the 15th century, that the people were able to have copies of the scriptures in their own possession and read for themselves. As the truth of scripture began to spread throughout the masses, light was shined on the practices of the Roman Catholic Church in which demonstrated gross misrepresentation of scripture, theological ignorance and outright lies and deceit.

Today, churches in America are being operated in the same fashion as the Roman Catholic Church in the 14th-16th centuries. Even though bibles are readily available to everyone, church goers are still overly dependent upon whatever the pastor says, and his words are never verified or challenged. Church leaders will even vilify other theological opinions without allowing the people to search the scriptures for themselves. This is a form of mind control and manipulation as well. Scare tactics are sometimes used to discourage those that do search the scriptures, in that they are told that they will fall away from the faith, or they are on the wrong track, falling prey to 'seducing spirits' and 'doctrines of devils'. Of course no one wants to fall prey to those things! But to not allow the people to search the scriptures for themselves and trust that

Holy Spirit will lead them into all truth is the usurping of the objective of Holy Spirit and taking His occupation on their (church leaders') shoulders.

In Matthew 23, Jesus condemned the scribes and Pharisees for preventing the people from enter into the kingdom:

Matthew 23:13
*13 But woe unto you, scribes and Pharisees, hypocrites! for **ye shut up the kingdom of heaven against men: for ye neither go in yourselves, neither suffer ye them that are entering to go in.***

Similarly, Christians are being prevented from entering into greater levels of understanding, regarding who they are and what they are called to be in the earth. Church leadership stifles and hinders the church when people are not allowed, or taught to think for themselves. This is not to say that there is no place for pastoring and teaching. These two administrations are critical functions in any local church. However, being in the faith is not being subjected to a dictatorship. The church is not an authoritarian institution. Unfortunately, the undergirding problem is that many church leaders are promoting biblical illiteracy and don't even know it. A congregation that is biblically illiterate can easily be intimidated, manipulated, controlled, and dominated. A biblically illiterate people will not be equipped to see themselves as being slaves under the yoke of witchcraft. They also will not be able to see where church leadership is wrong, off base, and teaching things that are theologically unsound and ideologically damaging to the body of Christ as a whole. This, without a shadow of a doubt, is a stumbling block to the progression and advancement of the kingdom of God.

Chapter Twenty-One:
Exodus From the Western Church

And afterward Moses and Aaron went in, and told Pharaoh, Thus saith the Lord God of Israel, Let my people go, that they may hold a feast unto me in the wilderness.

Exodus 5:1

The early church in the first century saw thousands and thousands of people added to the church daily (Acts 2:47, 16:5). This was the response to the prayers of the saints, the preached word, and the demonstrated compassion and power of God. The church was strengthened because of the numbers of people that were added to it. This trend has continued nearly 2000 years later on a world-wide scale. Christianity has grown enormously in sub-Saharan Africa and the Asia-Pacific region, where there were relatively few Christians at the beginning of the 20th century. The share of the population that is Christian in sub-Saharan Africa climbed from 9% in 1910 to 63% in 2010, while in the Asia-Pacific region it rose from 3% to 7%.[1] The fastest growth in the number of Christians over the past century has been in sub-Saharan Africa (a roughly 60-fold increase, from fewer than 9 million in 1910 to more than 516 million in 2010) and in the Asia-Pacific region (a roughly 10-fold increase, from about 28 million in 1910 to more than 285 million in 2010).[2]

However, unlike the growth of the church in other continents, the church in the western hemisphere, specifically, the United States and Europe, has come to a virtual standstill. In the year 1910, 93% of all Christians resided in either the

U.S. or Europe. As of 2010, the 'west's' share of the worldwide Christian population is down to 63%. The proportion of Europeans and Americans who are Christian has dropped from 95% in 1910 to 76% in 2010 in Europe as a whole, and from 96% to 86% in the Americas as a whole.[3] The question that must be answered is what is the cause of the precipitous drop in regards to the percentage of Christians in the western hemisphere? Of course, one of the main contributing factors is that the number of new Christian converts is not keeping up with the growing population in the west. In America, church attendance hasn't necessarily dropped, but the number of people that attend church on a regular basis is not keeping pace with the population growth. Well-known church researcher and author Thom Rainer notes that the failure of churches to keep up with the population growth is one of the Church's greatest issues heading into the future. In a 2002 survey of 1,159 U.S. churches, Rainer's research team found that only 6% of the churches were growing — he defines growth as not only increasing in attendance, but also increasing at a pace faster than its community's population growth rate. "Stated inversely, 94% of our churches are losing ground in the communities they serve," he says.[4]

Beyond the fact that the growth of the church in the west is not keeping up with the growth of the population, I believe that there are some other things that are assisting in the suppression and hindrance of the growth of the church. Here is a list of 4 reasons, other than lagging church growth as it relates to population increase, that I believe must be considered:

1. No hunger to preach the gospel

The culture of the American church has changed. The church in America has become 'big business' in some cases. The pure message of the gospel has been suppressed and cast to the side in favor of business strategies and cheap gimmicks to fill seats. Unlike the early church model which was focused on preaching the gospel with boldness and moving in the tangible power of God, American churches today are either too "super-spiritual" and "up in the third heaven", or they are too legalistic and restraining, not allowing Holy Spirit to do what He wants to do. The word-power balance must come back to the church. Church leaders must be raised up to preach and teach with boldness, and then step out on faith and 'walk on water' – believing that God is the same yesterday, today and forever, and that He desires to show Himself strong in our local church bodies, as well as corporately.

Something that Paul candidly mentioned in his letter to the Romans was his desire to not preach in locations that have already received the Word:

Romans 15:20-21
*20 Yea, so have **I strived to preach the gospel, not where Christ was named, lest I should build upon another man's foundation:***
*21 But as it is written, **To whom he was not spoken of, they shall see: and they that have not heard shall understand.***

Part of preaching the gospel is seeking new territories and people to preach to. Church folks don't need to hear the good news more than once! It's the unbeliever, that brother or sister on the streets or in the bars, and the prostitute that needs to hear the gospel. And yet, week after week, we preach the gospel to the same people over and over again. Just think what would happen if we made it a point to preach to someone new every week? What type of impact would that have on the church population? The great thing about America is that it is truly a melting pot that is filled with people from all over the world with different beliefs and ideologies. God has made it easy for the American church to reach out to unbelievers and those from other religions because they no longer live on the other side of the world from us, but they now live next door! Divine appointments are right before us! The gospel must be preached to other people that don't know Jesus. The American church wastes a lot of time by regurgitating over and over the basic precepts of Christian living, and yet, negates those that are hurting right next door or down the street.

2. America "doesn't need God"

In the parable of the seed and the sower, one of the scenarios was the seed being sown among thorns:

Matthew 13:22
22 He also that received seed among the thorns is he that heareth the word; and the care of this world, and the deceitfulness of riches, choke the word, and he becometh unfruitful.

The cares of this world, along with the deceitfulness of riches, can seduce people from the church and cause them to become dependent upon their own knowledge, intellect, understanding, success and financial stability. Not only that, but it could be anything that we turn into an idol by giving that thing more attention than we do the things of God. There are many people that have been blessed with great paying jobs, no debt, and the materialistic things to go with it. They become the living examples of the prodigal son. Their back turns against God and he or she seeks to do what's right in their own eyes. This mentality is what 'chokes the word' out of him or her. Unfortunately, this is where we are at today in America. As a nation, we have turned our backs on God. As the church in America, we have not made known how God feels about the state of the nation and that He always desires a people to raise the standard.

3. Christian families' slowed growth

Something that isn't difficult to see is that today, Christian families, on average, have fallen for the nuclear family model of 'dad, mom, and 2.5 kids'. This wasn't the case in the 19th and early to mid-20th centuries. 2.5 kids was just a warm-up for many families! Try 10-12 kids – and sometimes even 15-18 children in a family! Big families were much more common place and the norm between 50-100 years ago. If the mom and dad were Christian (which was most likely the case), the parents definitely raised the children in the fear of the Lord. What has happened since then? Selfishness. We have been so overly consumed with taking care of ourselves that we see having more than that 2.5 kid amount as being burdensome. Kids will definitely drain your pockets! This is true; I can testify to that. But at the same time, I trust God that He will meet our needs so that we will always be able to sustain however big of a family that God wants us to have. In 1900, the average household size was 4.60. By the year 2002, the household size dropped to 2.58. Christian families are definitely part of the equation, and the drop substantially affects the size and growth of the church as well.

4. People are disgruntled with the church

Another reason why the church in America isn't growing at the rate that it needs to be is because of what the church appears to be like from the exterior. Some folks are simply fed up with the institutionalized church and they decide to 'do church' differently. The rise of the cell group – house church movement has given believers an opportunity to get involved with a smaller intimate group and they feel much more welcome and free to express themselves and open up. The American church has seen its fair share of corruption and scandal. Infidelity in the pulpit, stealing money, and mind-control and manipulation have been common reasons for people to leave the institutionalized church and head to a more intimate group of believers.

Another reason for people being disgruntled with the church is the belief that the church has lost focus on the main issues. Winning souls to the kingdom, seeing people saved, and caring for people is what the gospel is all about. American churches and denominations have become like social clubs that rarely unite and co-labor with one another. This is absolutely shameful and is a reason for the parting of ways by some.

Lastly, another reason why people are leaving the institutional church is due to obvious false doctrine, false teaching, false prophets, and the list can go on and on. As the days and years go by, the popular end-time viewpoint is being dispelled more and more. The people who have been the purveyors of bad teaching are starting to be held accountable for what they are teaching. The understanding of what sound doctrine is has opened the eyes of many to the atrocity that the western church has become.

So, despite the fact that the universal church is growing, the candle that represents the American church is growing dim. Will we sit back and allow our candlestick to be blown out? Or, do we gird up our loins and get back to our spiritual roots, the early church, and begin to model ourselves after those first century saints?

PART FIVE

THE REMEDY

Chapter Twenty-Two:
Sound Doctrine

But speak thou the things which become sound doctrine:

Titus 2:1

Hopefully, throughout the last three parts of this book, I have convinced you that there is a serious dilemma within the American church. The church of today resembles, in no way, shape or form, the church of the first century. Somewhere along the way, the western church has been sidetracked and led astray from that which it was called to be. Our impact and influence not only in America, but throughout the world, has diminished. What we are being taught, the prism in which we read the bible through, and the paradigm in which shapes and molds our interpretation of scripture has crippled the church and caused it to draw back from engaging society.

The only way to diagnose, and then alleviate the situation that the western church is in is to go back to the beginning. "What beginning?" you may ask.

John 1:1-14
1 **In the beginning was the Word**, *and the Word was with God, and the Word was God.*
2 The same was in the beginning with God.
3 All things were made by him; and without him was not any thing made that was made.
4 **In him was life; and the life was the light of men.**
5 And **the light shineth in darkness; and the darkness comprehended it not.**
6 There was a man sent from God, whose name was John.
7 The same came for a witness, to bear witness of the Light, that all men

through him might believe.
8 He was not that Light, but was sent to bear witness of that Light.
9 That was the true Light, which lighteth every man that cometh into the world.
10 He was in the world, and the world was made by him, and the world knew him not.
*11 **He came unto his own, and his own received him not.***
12 But as many as received him, to them gave he power to become the sons of God, even to them that believe on his name:
13 Which were born, not of blood, nor of the will of the flesh, nor of the will of man, but of God.
*14 And **the Word was made flesh, and dwelt among us**, (and we beheld his glory, the glory as of the only begotten of the Father,) full of grace and truth.*

Sound doctrine begins and ends with a proper understanding of Jesus Christ and His objective in the earth. Doctrine is defined as a set of ideas or beliefs that are taught or believed to be true, or a statement of government policy especially in international relations.[1] To be 'sound' is to be free from injury or disease; free from flaw, defect, or decay; solid, firm, stable; free from error, fallacy, or misapprehension; exhibiting or based on thorough knowledge and experience; legally valid; logically valid and having true premises; showing good judgment or sense.[2] In essence, sound doctrine is the flawlessly valid set of beliefs and the statement of governmental policy. In regards to Jesus Christ, what we believe about Him should be flawlessly valid, and it should verify what Isaiah prophesies about Jesus in relation to His governmental position:

Isaiah 9:6-7
*6 For unto us a child is born, unto us a son is given: and **the government shall be upon his shoulder**: and his name shall be called Wonderful, Counsellor, The mighty God, The everlasting Father, The Prince of Peace.*
*7 **Of the increase of his government and peace there shall be no end**, upon the throne of David, and upon his kingdom, to order it, and to establish it with judgment and with justice **from henceforth even for ever**. The zeal of the Lord of hosts will perform this.*

John introduces the reader to Jesus by referring to Jesus as the Word. Not only was He the Word, but he was also the true Light. In verse 5, John says that the light shined in darkness, but the darkness could not comprehend it. John makes a similar claim in verses 10-11 by stating that He (Jesus) was in the world, but the world didn't know him. Perhaps more significantly, He came unto his own, and they didn't receive him. In verse 14, John states that the 'Word was made flesh' and dwelt among them. What is the point that I'm trying to make?

Before answering that question, it is important to know that to have a stable foundation in the truth of scripture, we must have a stable understanding of the focus of scripture. Sound doctrine is predicated on proper hermeneutics and exegesis, which I discuss in detail in Chapter 13 – Biblical Illiteracy. Without proper hermeneutics and exegesis, there will be no sound doctrine. Without sound doctrine, we'll have chaos!

Understanding the Historical Context of Scripture

One of the primary factors in which helps create a proper hermeneutical structure is the understanding of historical context. When reading scripture, two things must be identified by the reader:

1. When were the books or epistles written?
2. What was the socio-political environment during the time of the writing?

In the case of John 1, context is clearly given on multiple occasions within those first 14 verses:

- John 1:5 – "*...darkness comprehended it not*" denotes a past-tense reference. Whoever John is speaking of is not in reference to anyone 'post-John', but in his past or present (contemporaneous).

- John 1:10 – *"He was in the world... the world knew him not"* further hones in on a past tense reference
- John 1:11 – *"He came unto his own, and his own received him not"* delineates a past tense reference, and also identifies a past tense audience – "his own"
- John 1:14 – *"...the Word was made flesh, and dwelt among us..."* also speaks of a past-tense event in which the Word (Jesus) was manifest in the flesh and he dwelt among the people.

Of course, for the most part, we understand the life and ministry of Jesus and the religious-political unrest that he faced in His day, specifically at the hands of the religious folks – the Pharisees, Sadducees and scribes. Jesus was serving notice to the people that a "new thing" was about to happen. The message of the kingdom and the new covenant did not sit well with the 'powers that be', which resulted in theocratic unrest and Jesus' eventual crucifixion. But something that cannot be ignored in John 1 is that Jesus came to His own, and His own didn't receive Him (did not accept that He was the Messiah – the one that the prophets of old spoke of; refer back to Isaiah 9:6-7). Jesus made it utterly clear in His dialog with the Caananite woman that He had come for the house of Israel:

Matthew 15:21-28 (CEV)
21 Jesus left and went to the territory near the cities of Tyre and Sidon.
22 Suddenly a Canaanite woman from there came out shouting, "Lord and Son of David, have pity on me! My daughter is full of demons." 23 Jesus did not say a word. But the woman kept following along and shouting, so his disciples came up and asked him to send her away.
*24 Jesus said, **"I was sent only to the people of Israel! They are like a flock of lost sheep."***
25 The woman came closer. Then she knelt down and begged, "Please help me, Lord!"
26 Jesus replied, "It isn't right to take food away from children and feed it to dogs."
27 "Lord, that's true," the woman said, "but even dogs get the crumbs that fall from their owner's table."

28 Jesus answered, "Dear woman, you really do have a lot of faith, and you will be given what you want." At that moment her daughter was healed.

    The significance of this passage deals specifically with how faith in Jesus produces blessing, favor and healing. It is a foreshadowing of how mankind's relationship with God would be assessed. The just shall live by faith (Habakkuk 2:4, Galatians 3:11, Hebrews 10:38). He that believes in Jesus will be saved (John 3:15-18). But sandwiched in there is the fact that Jesus' ministry at that very moment in time was geared towards the house of Israel. When reading the gospels (Matthew, Mark, Luke and John), it is imperative that we keep this in mind. Jesus' primary focus was the salvation of Israel. When Jesus went into the temple to speak, it wasn't for the sake of "showing off", but it was in effort to get the people to realize who He was by pointing out the descriptors of Himself in the Old Testament prophets' writings. The miracles and healings that were performed by Jesus were to testify, accompany, and be a witness to everything that was written about Him in the books of the prophets.

    Jesus' frustration and sorrow came to a climax with the Pharisees and scribes not comprehending who Jesus was. In John 8:39-47, Jesus tells them that because they sought to kill Him, their father was not God, but the devil. In Luke 19, it is recorded that Jesus began to weep because the people that He was sent to (the house of Israel) rejected Him, and the ramifications for doing so would be severe:

***Luke 19:41-44** (ESV)*
*41 And when **he drew near and saw the city, he wept over it**, 42 saying, "Would that you, even you, had known on this day the things that make for peace! But now they are hidden from your eyes. 43 For the days will come upon you, when your enemies will set up a barricade around you and surround you and hem you in on every side 44 and tear you down to the ground, you and your children within you. And they will not leave one stone upon another in you, because you did not know the time of your visitation."*

This brings us right to the doorstep of the Olivet Discourse (Matthew 24, Mark 13, and Luke 21). Matthew 23 reiterates the sentiments of Luke 19:41-44, and Jesus is recorded as saying the following to the Pharisees and scribes:

Matthew 23:37-39
37 O Jerusalem, Jerusalem, thou that killest the prophets, and stonest them which are sent unto thee, how often would I have gathered thy children together, even as a hen gathereth her chickens under her wings, and ye would not!
38 Behold, your house is left unto you desolate.
39 For I say unto you, Ye shall not see me henceforth, till ye shall say, Blessed is he that cometh in the name of the Lord.

Matthew 23:38 (AMP)
38 **Behold, your house is forsaken and desolate** *(abandoned and left destitute of God's help).*

The people that Jesus was sent to, as we recall what was written in John 1, were the people that rejected Him. Imagine, God forbid, that you have a family member that is suffering from alcohol or drug addiction, and you try everything in your ability to put that individual in the best position to recover and be set free from that addiction. However, they condescendingly reject all of your efforts, and then seek to vilify and condemn you for trying to help them out. How would that make you feel? Now, imagine how Jesus felt at that very moment, but saddled on top of that state of mind was the fact that He knew that He would have to die for the sins of the people!

Before being apprehended, charged and sentenced to death, Jesus said that the very thing that was set aside for the house of Israel would be taken away from them, or made inaccessible to them, and given to another people. In the parable of the householder that planted a vineyard (Matthew 21:33-46), Jesus cleverly 'pigeon-holed' the chief priest and Pharisees into vocalizing their fate. The parable speaks of the householder sending his servants out to receive the fruits of the vineyard from the husbandmen (the tenants that the householder was renting to). The tenants then beat, killed and stoned the servants. More servants were sent out and the same happened. Finally, the householder sent his own son, thinking that the tenants would honor and respect him. But they didn't, and killed him also. See the following dialog between Jesus and the chief priests and Pharisees:

Matthew 21:40-46
40 When the lord therefore of the vineyard cometh, what will he do unto those husbandmen?
41 They say unto him, He will miserably destroy those wicked men, and will let out his vineyard unto other husbandmen, which shall render him the fruits in their seasons.
42 Jesus saith unto them, Did ye never read in the scriptures, The stone which the builders rejected, the same is become the head of the corner: this is the Lord's doing, and it is marvellous in our eyes?
43 Therefore say I unto you, <u>The kingdom of God shall be taken from you, and given to a nation bringing forth the fruits thereof</u>.
44 And whosoever shall fall on this stone shall be broken: but on whomsoever it shall fall, it will grind him to powder.
45 And when the chief priests and Pharisees had heard his parables, they perceived that he spake of them.
46 But when they sought to lay hands on him, they feared the multitude, because they took him for a prophet.

The chief priests and Pharisees foretold their doom. Their fate was confirmed by what came out of their mouth! Their doom and destruction came in the year 70 AD when Jerusalem was destroyed by the Roman armies. It was the final release of the wrath and judgment that was being stored up against them. This was the total vanishing away of the old covenant system, with its iconic symbol, the temple, being destroyed. It was the sign of the Lord's coming (Matthew 24:1-3). The 'Day of the Lord', the 'coming of the Lord', the Lord 'coming on clouds', the 'last day', the 'end of days', the 'final hour', the 'last time', 'the end of the world', and so on, were ALL referring to this very moment in which judgment would come upon those that killed the apostles and prophets. Everything that represented the old covenant 'melted', 'dissolved' and vanish away. Truly, all things became new because covenantally, the only thing left standing was the new covenant.

Audience Relevancy

This gets me right to the 'meat and potatoes' of what needs to be understood in order to have sound doctrine. Jesus' main focus in His earthly ministry was the house of Israel. They rejected Him, and then the kingdom was made accessible to every nation and people group. This is what we see taking place in the book of Acts. After the stoning of Stephen in Acts 7, you begin to see a shift in regards to the gospel being preached outside of Jerusalem. Of course, Paul (formerly Saul, a Jew that persecuted the saints) was a significant pioneer in the carrying of the gospel to different cities outside of Jerusalem and Judea. The New Testament is a composition of the narratives of Jesus (the gospels), a narrative of the apostles and the early church (Acts), and letters that were sent to various churches and church leaders in the first century. This is extremely important to take into consideration because it highlights audience relevancy. When we write letters (including emails, text messages and instant messages), there is always an intended audience or recipient of what we send. The information that we share in that medium is specifically for that recipient's eyes and ears. It is relevant to them and can be time sensitive. That is, the information that we share with whomever we send it to demands a response or action. The same can be said in regards to the letters sent from Paul to various churches.

Audience relevancy takes into consideration two things:

1. Who was the writer, or author of the content?
2. Who was the writer writing to (the intended reader)?

The intended audiences of Paul's letters are easily identifiable because the audience, or intended reader, is defined in the letter's title (Romans, Corinthians, Galatians, Timothy, etc.). James, Peter, John and Jude also wrote letters to first century saints. The intended audience is typically identified within the first few verses of the first division of each letter. For example, Peter's letters were addressed to a variety of cities and regions which are mentioned in 1 Peter 1:1:

1 Peter 1:1
Peter, an apostle of Jesus Christ, **to the strangers scattered throughout Pontus, Galatia, Cappadocia, Asia, and Bithynia,**

After understanding who the intended audience is, it is absolutely imperative that we then begin to read those letters which were addressed to first century saints through the eyes of those first century audiences. We must identify exactly what those letters meant to them during the time period in which they were written. Generally speaking, the letters of the NT were written to instill hope and encouragement into the first century saints who were witnessing the on-going persecution of the saints at the hands of the unbelieving Jews at that time. They literally saw everything that Jesus had predicted in the Olivet Discourse coming to pass right before their eyes. The letters served as a reminder of the promises of God for those that endured the persecution and chastisement until the end. The end, once again, is in regards to the coming destruction of Jerusalem and everything that represented those that persecuted the saints and killed the apostles and prophets.

It makes absolutely no sense whatsoever to read the letters of the NT as if they are directly addressed to us. It's like taking your next door neighbors mail, opening it, and reading it as if everything within it was directly addressed to you. Never mind the fact that opening someone else's mail is a federal offense! It's such a serious charge, correct? Well, the same can be said when we take scripture, and specifically, the letters that were addressed to a first century audience, totally out of their first century context, and apply them to ourselves living 2000+ years after they were written to a specific people. Now, do not get me wrong here. There is plenty of wisdom, principles and insight that can be garnered by reading these NT letters. Even Peter used a historical account to convey a point to his intended readers:

2 Peter 2:4-9
4 For if God spared not the angels that sinned, but cast them down to hell, and delivered them into chains of darkness, to be reserved unto judgment;
5 And spared not the old world, but saved Noah the eighth person, a preacher of righteousness, bringing in the flood upon the world of the ungodly;
6 And turning the cities of Sodom and Gomorrha into ashes condemned them with an overthrow, making them an ensample unto those that after should live ungodly;
7 And delivered just Lot, vexed with the filthy conversation of the wicked:
8 (For that righteous man dwelling among them, in seeing and hearing, vexed his righteous soul from day to day with their unlawful deeds;)
9 The Lord knoweth how to deliver the godly out of temptations, and to reserve the unjust unto the day of judgment to be punished:

Peter drew from this historical event in which a righteous man (Lot) was totally surrounded by evil. His message was that despite what it looked like around them (the intended audience), the Lord would keep them and protect them against the vast amount of ungodliness and persecution. Later in the chapter, Peter tells the reader how terrible it would be for a saint that had tasted of the goodness of the Lord to all of a sudden fall back into the snare of unbelief and the clutches of the old covenant theocratic system:

2 Peter 2:20-22
20 For if after they have escaped the pollutions of the world through the knowledge of the Lord and Saviour Jesus Christ, they are again entangled therein, and overcome, **the latter end is worse with them than the beginning.**
21 For **it had been better for them not to have known the way of righteousness, than, after they have known it, to turn from the holy commandment delivered unto them.**
22 But it is happened unto them according to the true proverb, The dog is turned to his own vomit again; and the sow that was washed to her wallowing in the mire.

This was a historical reality for many saints in the first century. The persecution and pressure that was being applied to the saints at the hands of the unbelieving Judaizers became unbearable and many fell away. The writer of Hebrews also exhorted the saints in Jerusalem to not fall away:

Hebrews 3:12-13
12 Take heed, brethren, lest there be in any of you an evil heart of unbelief, in departing from the living God.
13 But exhort one another daily, while it is called To day; lest any of you be hardened through the deceitfulness of sin.

The general principle of these passages is applicable to us today. We do live in a world that is filled with wickedness, perversion, deceit and all types of evil. This is absolutely undeniable. As the writer of Ecclesiastes stated, there is nothing new under the sun:

Ecclesiastes 1:9-10
9 The thing that hath been, it is that which shall be; and that which is done is that which shall be done: and there is no new thing under the sun.
10 Is there any thing whereof it may be said, See, this is new? it hath been already of old time, which was before us.

From age to age, and from generation to generation, the saints of God will encounter resistance and levels of evil. The new covenant age, the new heaven and earth that we spiritually reside in is not a utopian bubble. The church is the light of the world because we are the representatives of Jesus. Light exposes darkness. That being said, this does not in any way, shape or form give us legal license to misinterpret and misapply scripture by pulling it out of its first century context. The letters are for us, but they were not written to us. The significance of those letters meant so much more to those first century saints. They understood what they were up against, but the apostles understood what Jesus told them and reminded the first century saints that they must endure, hold on, and eagerly wait for their vindication.

Sola Scriptura

It's always useful to have extra-biblical materials and commentaries that can help a reader of the bible create a context in which he or she can rightly be able to interpret and understand scripture. However, one thing must be made clear – no matter what, scripture, in and of itself, is the final authority. Sola Scriptura is the teaching that the Scriptures contain all that is necessary for salvation and proper living before God. Sola Scriptura means that the Scriptures, the Old and New Testaments (excluding the Catholic apocrypha) are the final authority in all that they address (1 Cor. 4:6) and that tradition, even so-called Sacred Tradition, is judged by Scriptures.[3] In the Westminster Confession of Faith of 1646, a widely held confession of standards and principles that is a by-product of the Protestant Reformation, Chapter 1, Section VII speaks candidly to scripture being the final authority:

> *VII. All things in Scripture are not alike plain in themselves, nor alike clear unto all: yet those things which are necessary to be known, believed, and observed for salvation are so clearly propounded, and opened in some place of Scripture or other, that not only the learned, but the unlearned, in a due use of the ordinary means, may attain unto a sufficient understanding of them.*[4]

The validity of the Word of God is at stake if we do not keep all of scripture in its proper historical context. Our Christology (the study of the nature and person of Jesus Christ as recorded in the canonical Gospels and the epistles of the New Testament)[5], Soteriology (the study of the doctrine of salvation), and Eschatology (the study of last things, or end-times) is directly affected by how we read and interpret scripture. If the parameters of historical context and audience relevancy are not applied when we read scripture, we will be susceptible of coming to theological conclusions that are off course, and thus, can distort the meaning of scripture. What did Christ mean to the first century reader? What did salvation mean to the first century reader? What did 'the end of the world' mean to the first century reader? Without this understanding, we fall prey to developing theological systems of belief (paradigms) that have absolutely nothing to do with what is directly conveyed in scripture. We come up with all types of nonsense that impedes the progress of the church from age to age when we don't keep scripture in historical context. The inerrancy and infallibility of scripture lies in the balance with the modern day futurist paradigm because it insinuates that Jesus lied, and that the apostles were building up false hopes for their first century readers based upon what Jesus had told them Himself. A terrible example of 'eschatology gone wrong' is found in a quote by famed Christian writer, C.S. Lewis. He stated the following:

"Say what you like," we shall be told, "the apocalyptic beliefs of the first Christians have been proved to be false. It is clear from the New Testament that they all expected the Second Coming in their own lifetime. And, worse still, they had a reason, and one which you will find very embarrassing. Their Master had told them so. He shared, and indeed created, their delusion. He said in so many words, 'this generation shall not pass till all these things be done.' And he was wrong. He clearly knew no more about the end of the world than anyone else."

"It is certainly the most embarrassing verse in the Bible..."[6]

Lewis's sentiment regarding the coming of the Lord would have to be the same as any other person with a futurist eschatological paradigm. They would have to believe that Jesus was wrong and that the apostles were wrong also. This is the conclusion that is drawn if proper hermeneutics and exegesis is not used. The lack of understanding of the terms "coming on clouds", "coming in His kingdom", "coming of the Lord" and "day of the Lord" yields this type of false assessment that Lewis demonstrates. The most poisonous thing about his conclusion is that it gives fuel to the fire of agnostics, atheists and unbelievers who believe that the bible is a mere fairytale to begin with! This sentiment and false conclusion is a primary culprit in the insanity that is demonstrated within western Christianity today. The mere thought of having a doctrine that is sound is tossed out the window when the foundation and historical context of scripture is ignorantly discredited by non-biblical interpretive paradigms. It's time that we begin to hold church leaders responsible for butchering scripture and teaching things that are never spoken of. The ignorance of the cataclysmic fulfilling of everything Jesus prophesied about in His Olivet Discourse prevents the church from properly understanding what it is to do and be in the earth, from age to age, world without end.

Chapter Twenty-Three:
An Optimistic Church

And I say also unto thee, That thou art Peter, and upon this rock I will build my church; and the gates of hell shall not prevail against it.

Matthew 16:18

Perception will always assist in the formation of our reality. The way that we see or interpret things will facilitate our conclusion of a matter. As a man thinks, so is he (Proverbs 23:7). The way that we think can either propel us towards our destiny, or prevent us from becoming who we are called to be. It is no coincidence that when we read through Paul's letters written to various churches and church leaders, we can see a concerted effort by Paul to address the importance of changing the way that we think. Though Paul was speaking directly to a first century audience, the principle of his message is applicable today.

Romans 12:2
*And be not conformed to this world: but **be ye transformed by the renewing of your mind**, that ye may prove what is that good, and acceptable, and perfect, will of God.*

Ephesians 4:23
*And **be renewed in the spirit of your mind**;*

2 Timothy 1:7
*For God hath not given us the spirit of fear; but of power, and of love, and of a **sound mind**.*

Titus 2:6
*Young men likewise exhort to **be sober minded**.*

Our interpretation of scripture affects our theological positions. When scripture is read out of context, our interpretation becomes skewed and incorrect. An off-based interpretation of scripture will lead us to believe things in our present day that are absolutely not true. An incorrect eschatological lens spawns an outlook of the future that seems bleak and in despair. This is what the futurist eschatological paradigm has done. It has taken scripture out of its proper context and applied it with a literal hermeneutic to a 21st century time frame. This act has perpetuated beliefs about our day and age that are contrary to the kingdom of God being advanced. Instead of walking in the fulness of who we are in Christ Jesus, our thinking has caused us to shrink from our opportunity to be salt and light in our immediate surroundings. Pessimistic mindsets and defeatist attitudes are facilitated because of what we think about our day and age. In the unseen spirit realm, there is a 'law of attraction' at work in which brings to us what is either feared or longed for. In chapter 18 – "Hope Deferred, Laziness, Apathy and Fear", I talked about Peter's sinking into the water because of the fear that created unbelief when he took his eyes off of Jesus and was distracted by the blowing winds (Matthew 14:28-33). I also talked about how the thing that Job feared came upon him (Job 3:25-26). Unbelief will prevent us from walking in the power and authority that has been granted to us.

Do you remember the story in Mark 9 about the demon possessed boy? The disciples were incapable of casting out the demons, and the father of the boy pleaded with Jesus to help. Jesus responded by saying that 'all things were possible for those that believe'. What was the father's response?

Mark 9:24
*24 And straightway the father of the child cried out, and said with tears, **Lord, I believe; <u>help thou mine unbelief</u>**.*

There was a level of unbelief in the father that may have prevented the boy from being healed by the disciples. Though Jesus told the disciples afterward that the boy could only have been healed after time spent fasting and praying, there is precedent of Jesus not being able to do many miracles because of surrounding unbelief (Matthew 13:58). Similarly, there is a level of unbelief in the western church today that is preventing the church from becoming all that it is called to be.

Schizophrenic Mentalities About the Kingdom

Today, if you watch Christian television, or listen to Christian radio stations, you'll here preachers and teachers speak eloquently about the kingdom of God. You'll hear them speak in terms of the kingdom being here, and that we are kingdom people. There is a rallying cry to become involved in letting the kingdom that is within us be displayed in our sphere of influence. The kingdom of God is righteousness, peace and joy in the Holy Ghost (Romans 14:17). Accordingly, a sign of being in the kingdom is the ability to stand firm in the Lord when all hell is breaking out around you and in your midst. All of these things that are shared about the kingdom, I totally agree with.

Unfortunately, the problem that I have with a great majority of the 'mouthpieces' in the western church today is that while they teach and preach a truth about the kingdom of God, it is then under-cut and rendered neutral by not teaching the whole truth about the kingdom! And what is the whole truth about the kingdom? First and foremost, the kingdom is eternal:

Psalm 145:13
*Thy **kingdom is an everlasting kingdom**, and thy dominion endureth throughout all generations.*

Isaiah 9:7
*Of the increase of his government and peace **there shall be no end**, upon the throne of David, and upon his kingdom, to order it, and to establish it*

with judgment and with justice *from henceforth even for ever*. The zeal of the Lord of hosts will perform this.

Daniel 2:44
And in the days of these kings shall **the God of heaven set up a kingdom, which shall never be destroyed**: and the kingdom shall not be left to other people, but it shall break in pieces and consume all these kingdoms, and **it shall stand for ever**.

Daniel 4:3
How great are his signs! and how mighty are his wonders! **his kingdom is an everlasting kingdom, and his dominion is from generation to generation**.

Daniel 7:14, 18, 27
14 And there was given him dominion, and glory, and a kingdom, that all people, nations, and languages, should serve him: **his dominion is an everlasting dominion**, which shall not pass away, and his kingdom that which shall not be destroyed.

18 But **the saints of the most High shall take the kingdom, and possess the kingdom for ever, even for ever and ever**.

27 And the kingdom and dominion, and the greatness of the kingdom under the whole heaven, shall be given to the people of the saints of the most High, **whose kingdom is an everlasting kingdom**, and all dominions shall serve and obey him.

Luke 1:33
And he shall reign over the house of Jacob for ever; and **of his kingdom there shall be no end**.

Revelation 11:15
And the seventh angel sounded; and there were great voices in heaven, saying, The kingdoms of this world are become the kingdoms of our Lord, and of his Christ; and he **shall reign for ever and ever**.

There is consistency in scripture regarding the kingdom age being an eternal age. This cannot be refuted. But the dilemma comes when we begin to teach and preach, whether knowingly, or unknowingly, that the way that things are now will at some point come to a cataclysmic end, and that scripture affirms that

An Optimistic Church | 279

viewpoint. Better yet, what's the point of telling people to be kingdom-minded, subdue and have dominion over territories, regions, industries and places of influence if all of this is going to come to a screeching halt at some point? Why should I tell my daughters to do good in school, go to college and seek to become successful at whatever their hearts desire if I think the 'world is coming to an end'? I've heard this type of 'double-talk' through some of the most prominent ministers in America. There is no need to name drop because it is so common place! They talk about being kingdom people. They talk about ruling and reigning. They talk about being salt and light in our areas of influence. They talk about invading the '7 mountains of society' (Seven Mountain Mandate – Family, Religion, Education, Government, Business, Media and Arts / Entertainment). They talk about restoring America. They talk about bringing revival to America. And yet, everything that they talk about is made insignificant by the back-drop of pessimism in the form of a futurist eschatological paradigm that sees the world as we know it coming to an end. How much more schizophrenic and double-minded can you be?

Furthermore, this message that is being sent over the airwaves and from pulpits across America is totally contradictory to the kingdom age, in which we now live in, being eternal. Daniel revealed that the kingdom of God would be set up in the days of the 'four kings' (Daniel 2:44). The last of the 'four kings' is the Roman Empire. This is when Jesus came to the earth with the gospel of the kingdom. He stated emphatically that the kingdom had come upon them and resided in their midst because of the miracles that He was doing (Matthew 12:28). He also told the Pharisees that the kingdom was already in their midst (Luke 17:20-21). So, the coming of the kingdom and the time of its establishment is pretty well documented. Seeing, or being in the kingdom of God is based on being born again. This is exactly what Jesus told Nicodemus in John 3:

John 3:3
Jesus answered and said unto him, Verily, verily, I say unto thee, **Except a man be born again, he cannot see the kingdom of God.**

When a man is born again, he becomes a part of God's family – the body of Christ – the church, which consists of Jews and Gentiles. So entering into the kingdom of God is synonymous with entering, or becoming a part of the body of Christ. Paul, in his letter to the Ephesians says that the church of Jesus Christ has no end:

Ephesians 3:21
21 Unto him be glory in the church by Christ Jesus throughout all ages, world without end. Amen.

Ephesians 3:21 (AMP)
21 **To Him be glory in the church and in Christ Jesus throughout all generations forever and ever. Amen (so be it).**

So, if the kingdom age is an eternal age, and the church age is an eternal age, then how is it possible for this current age that we live in (an eternal kingdom / church age) to come to an end? Wouldn't a literal 'end of the world' scenario be the literal end of an age that is supposed to be eternal? This is the conundrum that is presented with the futurist paradigm. The ideology of there being a literal end of the world cancels, challenges, and impedes the progression and advancement of the church and kingdom, world (age) without end. This internal struggle of having half-truths taught and preached in our churches has rendered the western church ineffective and has muzzled the voice of the church.

The Truth Serum

Here is the truth, in a nutshell. Jesus is Lord. Jesus reigns from a heavenly throne eternally. The kingdom is not observable by the naked eye, but it is here, in our hearts and in our midst. The kingdom is everlasting. Where Jesus is, the kingdom is. If Jesus is in our hearts, the kingdom is in our hearts. As stated earlier, we are most definitely called to bring Jesus and the kingdom into every sector of society. We are called to bring the light of Jesus into politics, business, media, the music industry and Hollywood. We are to exalt the name of Jesus in our families. The church must step up and not draw back when it comes to the name of Jesus in the culture that we live in today. We cannot take a back seat to the antichrist sentiment in regards to the education system and military industrial complex (warmongering). We must not whimper and become silent when a minority of the population uses media propaganda and manipulation to paint Christians as being intolerant, bigots, or whatever negative connotation that they strive to place upon us.

It is time that we truly understand who we are, and what we are called to do in the space of time that we are allotted on earth. When I say space of time, I am referring to the amount of time that we are living. Life is too short to not become engaged and impactful.

James 4:14
Whereas ye know not what shall be on the morrow. For what is your life? It is even a vapour, that appeareth for a little time, and then vanisheth away.

Citizens of the western church must fall out of agreement with pessimism and negative mindsets and really begin to take on the mind of Christ. We CAN do all things through Christ that strengthens us (Philippians 4:13). ALL THINGS includes turning this nation, and every nation, upside down for the kingdom of God. Wickedness, perversion, deceit, thievery, mind-control and manipulation will all come crumbling down when the church gets a revelation of what it is called to be. We are world shakers! We are change agents with the backing of the most high God. If God be for us, who, in their demonically depraved minds, could be against us (Romans 8:31)?

There is absolutely nothing in this world that will stand against the progression and advancement of the church. The church is built to steamroll all opposition that is put in front of it. The gates of hell shall never prevail against the church (Matthew 16:18)! Every Christian in America must fully understand this fundamental truth. It is then and only then, that we will collectively come out of our place of apathy and seek to engage the culture and display the kingdom that resides on the inside of us.

What Will it Take?

The American church and its doctrine need a serious face lift. Not in the sense of obliterating the basic tenets of the faith which centers on Christ crucified and His resurrection. But the change must come in regards to our outlook of the future, and the way that we express what we feel about the future. It must come from a place of a proper understanding of what took place in the first century and the ramifications of that time period (I'm specifically referencing the coming of the Lord in 70 AD). Our hope is not the same as the hope of the early church. The New Testament letters were solely focused on encouraging the first century saints to endure until the crescendo of the judgment and wrath that was to be poured out upon Jerusalem came. That was it! Because of that event, we can be confident in the fact that Jesus did exactly what He said He was going to do, and when He said He was going to do it! His 'coming on clouds' in 70 AD can be historically verified and it validates and solidifies our claim of Him being King of Kings, Lord of Lords, Savior, Messiah, and the son of God. We are truly blessed because of that event (Revelation 14:13).

So, in essence, our message must be updated so that we no longer think and speak from a defeatist, pessimistic perspective. Fear, doubt and unbelief should not be in a saint's vocabulary and thought process. Our preaching, our teaching, our prophetic declarations, our music, and outlook on life should be laced with optimism and sealed with the fact that the kingdom is eternal. No longer should we hear songs that have lyrics speaking of longing to be taken out of this place, or being 'raptured'. No longer should we hear sermons that magnify all of the negative things that happen around us, but then is encapsulated with the phrase "...but someday soon...", making reference to Jesus returning to make things better. No longer will we sit on our couches as we flip through television channels and be disgusted by the programming and not be moved with zeal and compassion to do something about it. No longer will we allow our sons and daughters to go overseas to die over oil money and not speak out against it. No longer will we be okay with corporate fascism and its raping and pillaging of the American citizenry and not recall how Jesus, Himself, drove the money changers out of the temple because of their unjust weights and measures.

To 'turn the world upside down', just as the first century church did, it will take boldness, determination and the grace of God to move us in power and influence. The wonderful thing about it is that we already have what it takes on the inside of us. All of us are equipped to be world changers. All of us are equipped to shine the light of the kingdom in the realms of darkness. Christ in us is willing, ready and able to advance the kingdom of God like never before and turn the tides of public opinion. We are the healing leaves of the nations (Revelation 22:2). We are the conflict solvent. We are the answer to all of the problems in society, whether locally, nationally, or internationally. We, the body of Christ, the ambassadors of the kingdom of God, have what it takes to truly make this place heaven on earth. Heaven resides on the inside of each and every one of us saints, and where ever we walk, heaven is there. Whenever we minister to another, heaven is there. Where ever we work, heaven is there. This is the mind of Christ. This is the mind of the over-comer. This is the mind of the conqueror. This was the purpose of God for man from the beginning.

Genesis 1:27-28
27 So God created man in his own image, in the image of God created he him; male and female created he them.
28 And God blessed them, and God said unto them, Be fruitful, and multiply, and **replenish the earth, and subdue it: and have dominion over the fish of the sea, and over the fowl of the air, and over every living thing that moveth upon the earth.**

The church is truly victorious. The church is eternal. There is no stopping the advancement of the church. May we all come into agreement with the eternal nature of the kingdom and walk in that which we are called to walk in – representatives of an eternal kingdom that seeks to bring righteousness, peace and joy in the Holy Ghost to all that dwell in the earth– world without end. Amen.

End Notes

Chapter One: Unified and On One Accord

1. Blue Letter Bible - Lexicon :: G1205
http://www.blueletterbible.org/lang/lexicon/lexicon.cfm?Strongs=G1205&t=KJV
2. Free Merriam-Webster Dictionary
http://www.merriam-webster.com/dictionary/follow
3. Ibid.
http://www.merriam-webster.com/dictionary/vocation

Chapter Two: Power Evangelism and Exponential Growth

1. Free Merriam-Webster Dictionary
http://www.merriam-webster.com/dictionary/compassion

Chapter Three: Dueling Paradigms

1. Free Merriam-Webster Dictionary
http://www.merriam-webster.com/dictionary/paradigm
2. Ibid.
http://www.merriam-webster.com/dictionary/sound
3. Ibid.
http://www.merriam-webster.com/dictionary/stable
4. Blue Letter Bible – Lexicon :: G1515
http://www.blueletterbible.org/lang/lexicon/lexicon.cfm?Strongs=G1515&t=KJV
5. Blue Letter Bible – Lexicon :: G4993
http://www.blueletterbible.org/lang/lexicon/lexicon.cfm?Strongs=G4993&t=KJV

Chapter Five: The Kingdom

1. Worldology – Babylonian Empire
http://www.worldology.com/Iraq/babylonian_empire.htm
2. Worldology – Persian Empire
http://www.worldology.com/Iraq/persian_empire.htm
3. Worldology – Greek and Roman Rule of Mesopotamia
http://www.worldology.com/Iraq/greek_roman_rule.htm
4. Blue Letter Bible – Lexicon :: G1448
http://www.blueletterbible.org/lang/lexicon/lexicon.cfm?Strongs=G1448&t=KJV

Chapter Eight: Ascension Gifts, Spiritual Gifts and Cessationalism

1. Blue Letter Bible – Lexicon :: G4851
http://www.blueletterbible.org/lang/lexicon/lexicon.cfm?Strongs=G4851&t=KJV

Chapter Ten: Prosperity and Poverty

1. "What Is A Mantra?"
http://www.meditationden.com/questions/what-is-a-mantra/
2. Free Merriam-Webster Dictionary
http://www.merriam-webster.com/dictionary/prosperity
3. Ibid.
http://www.merriam-webster.com/dictionary/prosperous
4. The Free Dictionary
http://www.thefreedictionary.com/heir

Chapter Eleven: War and Peace

1. Christian Classics Ethereal Library
http://www.ccel.org/ccel/schaff/npnf102.iv.XIX.7.html
2. Economic Policy Journal
http://www.economicpolicyjournal.com/2011/03/libyan-rebels-

form-central-bank.html
3. RT News – "Al-Qaeda-Linked Rebels Attack Christian Village in Syria"
http://rt.com/news/rebels-syria-christian-village-428/
4. Catholic Online – "Syrian Jihadists Behead Catholic Priest
http://www.catholic.org/international/international_story.php?id=51537

Chapter Twelve: The Political Divide

1. Science for Unborn Human Life – "The Unborn Child Develops So Rapidly"
http://www.sfuhl.org/b_unborn_child_develops.htm
2. Lewrockwell.com – "Entangling Alliances"
http://www.lewrockwell.com/2001/09/ron-paul/entangling-alliances/

Chapter Thirteen: Biblical Illiteracy

1. K12Reader: Reading Instruction Resources for Teachers and Parents – "What is Reading Comprehension?"
http://www.k12reader.com/what-is-reading-comprehension/
2. Encyclopedia Britannica: Hermeneutics (Principles of Biblical Interpretation)
http://www.britannica.com/EBchecked/topic/263195/hermeneutics
3. Probe Ministries – Hermeneutics
http://www.probe.org/site/c.fdKEIMNsEoG/b.4226913/k.82B3/Hermeneutics.htm
4. Whitney, W. D. *The Century Dictionary: An Encyclopedic Lexicon of the English Language.* New York: The Century Co, 1889.
5. Free Merriam-Webster Dictionary
http://www.merriam-webster.com/dictionary/allegory
6. Meridith, J. Noel; "Figurative Language in the Bible"
http://www.theexaminer.org/volume8/number5/language.htm

7. "Figurative Language"
http://figurativelanguage.net/
8. Free Merriam-Webster Dictionary
http://www.merriam-webster.com/dictionary/figurative
9. Meridith, J. Noel; "Figurative Language in the Bible"
http://www.theexaminer.org/volume8/number5/language.htm
10. Ibid.
11. Jaszczolt, Katarzyna M..; Turner, Ken (2003-03-01), Meaning Through Language Contrast. Volume 2. John Benjamins Publishing. pp. 141.
12. Harley, Trevor A. (2001), The Psychology of Language: From Data to Theory. Taylor & Francis. pp. 293
13. Free Merriam-Webster Dictionary
http://www.merriam-webster.com/dictionary/idiom
14. Hughes, Marji; "Hebrew Idioms in Scripture"
http://www.foundationsmin.org/studies/idioms.htm
15. Chilton, David; (2007), Paradise Restored: A Biblical Theology of Dominion. Dominion Press. pp. 98
16. "Prophetic Symbols and Apocalyptic Language Of The Bible"
http://richardwaynegarganta.com/propheticsymbols.htm
17. Chilton, David. pp. 102
18. Plous, Scott (1993), The Psychology of Judgment and Decision Making, McGraw-Hill, pp. 233

Chapter Fourteen: Dispensationalism

1. Poythress, Vern S. (1987), Understanding Dispensationalists, Academie Books: Zondervan Publishing House, pp. 9
2. Fuller, Daniel P.; (1957), "The Hermeneutics of Dispensationalism" Th. D. dissertation. Northern Baptist Theological Seminary, Chicago, IL, pp. 92-93
3. Poythress, pp. 19
4. Dispensationalism - Theopedia, an encyclopedia of Biblical Christianity - http://www.theopedia.com/Dispensationalism

5. Ibid.
6. Chafer, Lewis Sperry, Dispensationalism, Dallas: Dallas Seminary Press, 1951.
7. Rapture - Theopedia, an encyclopedia of Biblical Christianity - http://www.theopedia.com/Rapture
8. Ibid.

Chapter Sixteen: Misinterpreting 'Antichrist', 'Man of Sin' and the 'Beast'

1. Russell, J. Stuart, The Parousia: The New Testament Doctrine of Our Lord's Second Coming, Baker Books, 1999 (Republished), pp. 329-330
2. Chilton, David, pp. 108
3. Russell, J. Stuart, pp. 181-182
4. Ibid., 183
5. Conybeare, W.J. and Howson, J.S., The life and epistles of St. Paul (1856), Chap. Xxvii
6. Suetonius, The Lives of Twelve Caesars, Life of Nero, Chap. 49
7. Chilton, David, pp. 177

Chapter Eighteen: Hope Deferred, Laziness, Apathy and Fear

1. Cognitive Dissonance http://changingminds.org/explanations/theories/cognitive_dissonance.htm
2. Cognitive dissonance http://www.sciencedaily.com/articles/c/cognitive_dissonance.htm

Chapter Nineteen: Identity Crisis

1. Blue Letter Bible - Lexicon :: H168
http://www.blueletterbible.org/lang/lexicon/lexicon.cfm?Strongs=H168&t=KJV
2. NOVA Online | Cracking the Code of Life | Journey into DNA - http://www.pbs.org/wgbh/nova/genome/dna_sans.html

Chapter Twenty-One: Exodus From The Western Church

1. "Global Christianity – A Report on the Size and Distribution of the World's Christian Population", December 19, 2011
http://www.pewforum.org/2011/12/19/global-christianity-exec/
2. Ibid.
3. Ibid.
4. "7 Startling Facts: An Up Close Look at Church Attendance in America", Barnes, Rebecca; Lowry, Lindy
http://www.churchleaders.com/pastors/pastor-articles/139575-7-startling-facts-an-up-close-look-at-church-attendance-in-america.html

Chapter Twenty-Two: Sound Doctrine

1. Free Merriam-Webster Dictionary
http://www.merriam-webster.com/dictionary/doctrine
2. Free Merriam-Webster Dictionary
http://www.merriam-webster.com/dictionary/sound
3. Sola Scriptura | What is Sola Scriptura? | Define Sola Scriptura | Christian Apologetics and Research Ministry
http://carm.org/dictionary-sola-scriptura
4. The Westminster Confession of Faith (1646)
http://www.spurgeon.org/~phil/creeds/wcf.htm#chap1
5. "Christology: A Biblical, Historical, and Systematic Study of Jesus", O'Collins, Gerald, 2009 ISBN 0-19-955787-X, p. 1-3
6. The World's Last Night: And Other Essays, Lewis, C.S., p.97

Scripture Index
(Actual passages and references to passages)

OLD TESTAMENT

Genesis
1:14-16	164
1:27-28	282
1:29-31	92
12:2-3	88
32:28	79, 88
37:9-11	165
41:38-45	128
41:41-43	165

Exodus
3:8	163
5:1	249

Leviticus
17:14	149
19:35	136

Numbers
21:6-9	56

Deuteronomy
25:15	136
32:4-5	183
32:9-10	79
32:15-26	184
32:21	83
32:28-29	184
32:31	184
32:35-36	184
32:41-43	185

Joshua
1:8	30
24:15	113

Job
3:25-26	229
20:20	163

Psalm
145:13	275

Proverbs
13:12	219
13:22	125
16:12	241
18:20	163
20:10	136
23:7	54, 229
27:5	51

Ecclesiastes
1:9-10	269
3:8	131
10:19	117, 125

2 Chronicles
7:14	238

Isaiah
1:2	202
1:18	235
7:15	113

Isaiah		*Daniel*	
9:6	135	2:31-45	65
9:6-7	260	2:33	199
9:7	63, 275	2:41-43	199
13:9-10	166	2:44	276
19:1	167	2:46-49	129
24:1-5	202	4:3	276
34:1-8	203	7:3	197
53:5-8	57	7:14, 18, 27	276
53:10-11	93		
53:10-12	58	*Hosea*	
55:8-9	127	2:23	82
56:4	113		
60:16	163	*Amos*	
61:1-2	26	8:9	166
65:17-20	209		
66:22	64, 201	*Nahum*	
		1:3	167
Jeremiah			
1:5	112	*Zechariah*	
51:25	204	13:6	59
Ezekiel		*Malachi*	
32:7-8	167	3:10	91

NEW TESTAMENT

Matthew		*Matthew*	
3:2	63	6:24	121
4:17	67	6:31-34	36, 122
4:19	9	6:33	68
5:3	68	7:11	92
5:9	135	7:15-20	90
5:10	68	8:22	10
5:17-18	162	8:27	33
5:18	205	9:2	124
6:19-20	121	9:9	10
6:22	53	10:7	68

Matthew

10:39	36
11:15	163
12:25	51
12:34	53
13:11	69
13:22	252
13:31-33	69
14:14	38
14:28-33	228
15:21-28	262
15:14	246
15:32	38
16:15-19	236
16:18	273
16:24	10, 120
16:25	36
16:28	74
18:7	79
18:33	69
19:16-24	120
19:21	10
20:34	38
21:10	33
21:31	69
21:40-46	265
21:43	69
23:13	248
23:25-28	245
23:27	161
23:31-36	183
23:34-35	200
23:34-38	94
23:37-39	264
23:38	264
24:2	221
24:3	74
24:4-5	13, 191

Matthew

24:6	134
24:6-7	13
24:9	13
24:11	191
24:14	77
24:21	75
24:21-22	13, 85
24:23-26	191
24:29	164
24:29-30	204
24:30	167
24:30-31	182
24:32-34	182
24:34	75, 219
24:34-35	204
24:42	13
26:26-28	161
26:39	59
26:42	59
26:44	59
26:49-52	135
26:63-64	74
27:46	57

Mark

1:41	38
2:5	124
2:14	10
3:24-25	51
3:25	145
4:41	33
5:19	38
6:34	39
7:6-9	244
7:7	245
8:2	38
8:34	10

Mark
8:35	36		
9:20-27	38		
9:24	274		
10:13-15	69		
10:21	10		
10:23-25	69		
13:5-6	13		
13:7	134		
13:7-8	13		
13:9	13		
13:19	13		
13:24-25	164		
13:26	167		
13:33	13		
15:34	57		

Luke
1:33	69, 276	9:2	68
2:40	30	9:9	33
2:40-52	29	9:23	10
2:47	29	9:24	37
2:49	59	9:27	74
2:52	30	9:59	10
3:7-9	89	9:62	69
4:18-19	26, 98	10:1-9	12
4:32	103	10:17	12
4:36	103	11:13	92
5:21	33	11:17	51
5:27	10	11:20	68, 103
6:20	68	11:34	53
6:38	91	11:49	94
7:12-15	39	12:31	68
7:28	68	13:18-21	69
7:49	33	13:31-32	157
8:10	69	14:31-32	135
8:25	33	16:9	127
9:1-6	11	16:16	67, 207
		17:1	83
		17:20-21	68, 237
		18:16-17	69
		18:22	10
		18:24-25	69
		19:41-44	26
		21:8	13
		21:9	134
		21:9-10	13
		21:12	13
		21:12-15	35
		21:16-17	13
		21:20	75
		21:20-22	196
		21:23	13
		21:25	164
		21:27	167

Luke
21:36	13
22:31-33	50
22:44	58

John
1:1-14	259
1:43	10
2:13-17	136
2:17	136
3:3	278
3:3-5	69
3:5	67
3:14-15	56
3:15-16	113
3:16	93, 111
3:36	111
5:19	52
5:30	59
10:27	10
10:28	111
11:49-53	60
12:26	10
12:34	33
13:35	98
14:6	23
14:8-11	23
14:12	98
14:12-13	23-24
14:26	35
15:5	111
15:16	112
15:19	112
16:6	14
16:7-16	14
17:11	19
17:14-18	20
17:20-23	19-20

John
17:20-21	99
17:20-26	233
17:23	98, 105
18:36	69
19:30	59
21:25	37

Acts
1:3	70
1:4	15
1:6	69
1:8	15
1:14	18
1:15	16
1:26	18
2:5-13	16
2:15-17	210
2:15-21	78
2:16-21	17
2:17	21
2:25-35	18
2:36	18
2:41	18
2:42-47	18-19
2:44	147
2:46-47	20
4:8	34
4:13	34
4:32	147
4:32-35	19
7:48-49	234
17:5-8	41
17:10-12	32, 225
17:11	32
17:24	233
26:6-8	221

Romans

2:11	178
2:28-29	81, 87, 179
3:4	52
8:17	129
8:18	36
8:28-30	112
8:38-39	209
9:1-5	83
9:1-8	81
9:6	87
9:6-7	180
9:25-26	82
9:30-33	82
10:2	84
10:4-11	84
10:9-10	80
10:12	179
10:15	138
10:17	118
10:17-18	77
10:19	84
11:1	84
11:3-4	84
11:5	84
11:17	86
11:20-21	86
11:23-24	87
11:25	174
11:25-26	87, 179
11:26	175
11:29	104, 107
11:33-34	127
12:2	273
12:5	236
12:6	21
13:13	241
12:19	145

Romans

15:20-21	251
16:17-18	192
16:26	77

1 Corinthians

1:10	106
2:3-5	29
2:4	102
3:3	241
3:6-8	115
3:16	161
4:18	106
4:20	103
5:1	106
5:2	106
5:6-7	106
6:1-8	106
6:18	106
6:19	232
7	106
11:18-34	106
12:1-11	99-100
12:4-6	24
6:15-17	236
6:16	237
12:7	24
12:8-10	93
12:25-27	102
12:31	105
13:1	104
13:8-12	94
13:10	94, 105
13:12	107
13:13	104
14:1	21, 105
14:3	22
14:22	21

Scripture Index | 297

1 Corinthians
14:31	21
14:33	52
14:39	21
15:22	60
15:50	187
15:51-52	187
15:52	181
15:55-57	60

2 Corinthians
1:5-7	37
5:6-10	187
5:8	222
7:4	35
9:7	92
10:3-6	133
11:3-4	192
11:12-15	192
12:20	241
13:11	106

Galatians
2:11-21	49
3:15-19	173
3:19	173
3:28	179
4:3	212
4:9	212
4:21	160
6:15-16	85, 179

Ephesians
1:3-5	113
1:9-11	113
1:10-12	171
1:21	176
2:4-10	231

Ephesians
2:5-7	234
2:11-22	80
3:1-9	173
3:11-13	35
3:17	94
3:20-21	85, 177
3:21	104, 107, 177, 278
4:8	25, 91
4:8-16	95-96
4:11	25
4:11-12	107
4:12	97
4:12-16	26
4:15	208
4:23	273
6:9	178
6:10-17	138
6:11-17	161

Philippians
1:20	35
2:3	241
3:18-19	192
4:7	53

Colossians
1:5-6	77
1:23	77
3:11	179
3:24-25	178

1 Thessalonians
1:5	103
4:13-18	181
4:16	182
4:16-18	201, 221
4:17	175, 186, 187

1 Thessalonians		***Hebrews***	
5:9-11	22	3:12-13	269
5:20	21	8:13	205
		9:26	71, 77
2 Thessalonians		9:26-28	54
2:1-2	196-197	9:27	185, 187, 188
2:2-4	189	10:18-19	35
2:2-10	193-194	11:1	101
2:8	195	12:1-2	55
3:10	125, 148	12:22-24	207, 235
1 Timothy		***James***	
1:3-7	192	1:8	2, 47, 49
1:19-20	192	1:17	104
4:8	177	2:1-5	178
5:8	126	2:14-16	242
6:6-10	118	3:17-18	139
6:10	119	4:8	53
6:17	122	4:14	279
6:20-21	192		
		1 Peter	
2 Timothy		1:1	211, 267
1:7	53, 217, 228, 273	1:3-5	221
2:4-5	192	3:8-9	39
2:15	31-32, 155	4:13	37
2:16-18	192	4:17	238
3:1-9	192		
3:13	192	***2 Peter***	
4:10	192	2:4-9	268
4:14-16	192	2:20-22	268
		3:1-4	210
Titus		3:13	64
2:1	259	3:15-16	211
2:6	54, 274	3:16	52
Hebrews			
2:3-4	94	2:2	111
2:8	129	2:5	106

1 John

2:17	109
2:18	77, 190
2:22	190
3:16-17	39-40
4:3	190
4:4	240
4:12	106
4:18	106

2 John

1:7	190, 191

3 John

1:1-2	123

Revelation

1:1	208
1:1-3	75
2:9	86
3:5	114
3:9	86
3:10	175
3:14-19	73
11:15	276
13:1	197
13:11	199
13:16-17	198
13:18	198
14:13	186, 222
17:6, 7	199
19:10	22
21:1	64
21:1-5	207
21:3	233
21:4	208
22:2	90
22:6	76

Revelation

22:18-19	169

www.ingramcontent.com/pod-product-compliance
Lightning Source LLC
Chambersburg PA
CBHW070137100426
42743CB00013B/2739